D1441181

POLITICAL PHILOSOPHY

Gerald C. MacCallum

UNIVERSITY OF WISCONSIN

PRENTICE-HALL, INC., Englewood Cliffs, New Jersey 07632

Library of Congress Cataloging-in-Publication Data

MacCallum, Gerald C., [date]
  Political philosophy

  (Prentice-Hall foundations of philosophy series)
  Bibliography: p.
  1. Political science. I. Title. II. Series.
JA71.M19   1987   320   86-9350
ISBN 0-13-684689-0

Editorial/production supervision: *Edith Riker*
Manufacturing buyer: *Harry P. Baisley*

Foundations of Philosophy Series
Elizabeth Beardsley, Monroe Beardsley, Tom L. Beauchamp, editors

©1987 by Prentice-Hall, Inc.
A Division of Simon & Schuster
Englewood Cliffs, New Jersey 07632

Printed in the United States of America

10 9 8 7 6 5 4 3 2 1

ISBN 0-13-684689-0   01

Prentice-Hall International (UK) Limited, *London*
Prentice-Hall of Australia Pty. Limited, *Sydney*
Prentice-Hall of Canada Inc., *Toronto*
Prentice-Hall Hispanoamericana, S.A., *Mexico*
Prentice-Hall of India Private Limited, *New Delhi*
Prentice-Hall of Japan, Inc., *Tokyo*
Prentice-Hall of Southeast Asia Pte. Ltd., *Singapore*
Editora Prentice-Hall do Brasil, Ltda., *Rio de Janeiro*
Whitehall Books Limited, *Wellington, New Zealand*

PRENTICE-HALL FOUNDATIONS OF PHILOSOPHY SERIES

Virgil Aldrich	PHILOSOPHY OF ART
William Alston	PHILOSOPHY OF LANGUAGE
David Braybrooke	PHILOSOPHY OF SOCIAL SCIENCE
Roderick M. Chisholm	THEORY OF KNOWLEDGE 2E
William Dray	PHILOSOPHY OF HISTORY
C. Dyke	PHILOSOPHY OF ECONOMICS
Joel Feinberg	SOCIAL PHILOSOPHY
William K. Frankena	ETHICS 2E
Martin P. Golding	PHILOSOPHY OF LAW
Carl Hempel	PHILOSOPHY OF NATURAL SCIENCE
John Hick	PHILOSOPHY OF RELIGION 3E
David L. Hull	PHILOSOPHY OF BIOLOGICAL SCIENCE
Gerald C. MacCallum	POLITICAL PHILOSOPHY
Joseph Margolis	PHILOSOPHY OF PSYCHOLOGY
Wesley C. Salmon	LOGIC 3E
Jerome Shaffer	PHILOSOPHY OF MIND
Richard Taylor	METAPHYSICS 3E

Elizabeth Beardsley, Monroe Beardsley,
and Tom L. Beauchamp, editors

To the memory
of my mother and father,
      and of Paulette,
all of them for nurturing the sources
of whatever good is in this book.

Contents

THREE
The State

FOUR
Nations and Nationalism: Ideological Foundations

PART TWO: GOVERNMENT

FIVE
Government in Political Philosophy

Preface

The concern of this book is with political institutions and conduct and with the justificatory concepts prominent there, such as the ideas of the state, the nation, sovereignty, and citizenship. Other ideas will be mentioned only in passing, since they are dealt with more fully in other volumes in this series. For example, this book contains no discussion of several prominent topics in political philosophy, namely, freedom, rights, justice, and equality.

These topics are not peculiar to political philosophy, but are shared fully by social philosophy, and ample introductions to the first three or to portions thereof are found in Feinberg's book in this series (*Social Philosophy*). The fourth, equality, is not dealt with here because I could not develop my ideas on it adequately without also developing them on the other three.* Were Feinberg's book not in this series, the omission of such a discussion here would constitute a serious gap in this work.

The present work nevertheless offers a rich diet of topics in political philosophy. My convictions given the present state of the discipline, as well as my tastes, have led me to believe a panoramic view of the field more useful than a rehearsal of standard views and positions on a more limited range of problems. The traditional topics of political philosophy continue to be important, but the discipline will benefit if students take a wider purview of the subject than has commonly been the case.

The book intentionally leaves room for contributions by instructors and students. For example, I have left to instructors any necessary elucidation of who the famous figures in the history of the subject (such as Plato and others)

*Some of my views on freedom are developed in "Negative and Positive Freedom," *Philosophical Review*, LXXVI (1967), pp. 312–334.

are and of some of the more well-known ideas mentioned (for instance, contrary, contradictory). Instructors and students thus should enrich their study of this book by other activities, including class discussion. The treatment of many topics depends on this. No considerable improvement over alert and intelligent discussion may be expected by simply resorting to reports of typical treatments of these issues in the literature. Instructors should be selective in the topics they discuss.

The book also contains much that is new. In earlier drafts I mentioned this, but it soon became tedious, and I was told it appeared condescending. So I dropped mention of it in the hope that readers would not suppose that mention of anything here meant that it was commonly found elsewhere in the literature.

Acknowledgments

My thanks go to five former teachers: the late Professors Frank Frazier Potter and Lloyd Fisher, Professors Dwight Waldo, Joseph Tussman, and H. L. A. Hart. At various times each of these persons was an excellent and lasting model of what I was trying to become. My thanks also to my colleagues over the years at the University of Wisconsin at Madison. They gave me the support one hopes for from colleagues. Special thanks to Professor William Hay, who has had an inexhaustible capacity to freshen and illuminate my philosophical perspective. Thanks also to my good friends Professors Marcus G. Singer and Rex Martin for their steady and appreciated support. And thanks to the University of Wisconsin—Madison (the College of Arts and Sciences and the Department of Philosophy) for valuable equipment and services. Thanks also to Charles R. Kelly, M.D., whose skill, wisdom, and patience contributed greatly to my having the time and capacity to do this work. Thanks to Alan Lubert and Professor Norman Bowie for help in clarification. Thanks to the editors of this series, Professors Elizabeth and Monroe Beardsley, for getting me started down the road toward this book and for encouragement along the way, and to Professor Tom Beauchamp, who joined them. The project required more patience and persistence than anyone could have imagined beforehand.

The principal investor of both patience and persistence, and much talent besides, has been my wife, Professor Susan Feagin. People who know us both will speculate that her help made all the difference. It did, in many ways. Without her substantial work, this would have remained an incomplete set of sketches and drafts.

Introduction

As was suggested in comparing it to other books in this series, this book is an introduction to philosophical thinking about the fundamental institutions of political life—the state, government, and citizenship—as well as satellite ideas such as authority, legitimacy, sovereignty, and representation. Because theoretical reflection on these matters has both a past and presumably a future, this book will introduce some bases for understanding the past and participating in the future. Both political life and philosophy have developed within a long tradition of intellectual interchanges. We thus must regard them as something to be uncovered or discovered rather than something to be invented. Of course, one may wish to revise and refocus the interests of others, but in order to do this one needs to understand the focusing effects of previous discussions.

The direction of this book was established by asking what interests can be served or frustrated by the institutions and conduct on which we concentrate. Our effort will thus be to see why such conduct is useful, and what would justify efforts to construct and continue these institutions. Rather than offering carefully guarded and worked-out characterizations of these phenomena, I shall attempt to expose how the need for them arises out of the practical concerns of human life. The challenge is to show how having certain practical, everyday concerns leads to the issues occupying the attention of political philosophers.

WHAT IS THE POLITICAL?

Our first philosophizing is about the nature of our general fields of study, something not at all unusual for philosophers. What is political philosophy? Initially this question separates neatly into two further questions—what is political? and what is philosophy? Neither has a simple answer adequate to our relatively sophisticated and serious purposes. But here, as in philosophy generally, it is important not to sweep that aside. Answers may be helpful though not neatly packaged, but unhelpful if conciseness and simplicity are purchased at the price of suppressing the ways they don't quite fit facts or our purposes. Awareness of the shortcomings of simple answers preserves our capacity to correct and render them more adequate.

The political, as with surprisingly many other concepts, should be known by the contrasts it keeps: its scope fluctuates with changes in the concepts with which it is regularly and variously contrasted. For example, the concept of reason is regularly and variously contrasted with faith, experience, and intuition, each of which gives *reason* a different thrust. If this shifting thrust is not monitored, discussions of reason, its role and implications, will likely go awry. Likewise, the natural is contrasted with an assortment of other phenomena, such as the supernatural, abnormal, artificial, and the forced. Recognizing these contrasts is important in trying to understand resorts to the idea of nature in political philosophy. Both the philosophical tradition of making such resorts, and commentaries on this tradition, have been beleaguered by failure to monitor such shifts.

The political is contrasted in turn with the economic, cultural, legal, and administrative. Although this should not be thought a complete list of contrasting terms, it will do to illustrate the point. Each of these four contrasts has been massively challenged, though still widely used. An extreme position on the first is exhibited by one Marxist writer on the state, Franz Oppenheimer, who contrasts the political and the economic as different means of bringing about the privileges and dominating positions he believes characteristic of states. Political means bring them about through the "unrequited appropriation of the labor of others"; economic means bring them about through the equivalent exchange of one person's labor for the labor of others. The political is therefore contrasted with the realm of equivalent exchange (the fair, and likely often also the voluntary and the cooperative) and is identified as the realm of unrequited appropriation (surely the realm of exploitation). If unrequited appropriation is thus to be made a central feature of the political, a plausible though nasty setting is given for the coercive backing commonly said to be characteristic of the political. Coercive backing may not be necessary in operating a system of unrequited appropriation (the system might operate through manipulation, and so on), but its usefulness would not be unexpected.

A more neutral setting for an understanding of the common role of coercive backing in the political is offered by a different contrast, this one suggested by Alfred Cobban, who characterizes types of nationalism as either political or cultural. Political nationalism embraces nations as organizations with "directive and dominative force," whereas cultural nationalism refers to nations as communal homes of languages, literatures, and customs. Common views of human nature also underwrite the usefulness of coercive backing in connection with this understanding of the political, since it concerns directive and dominative force, though its operation doesn't seem quite so nasty per se.

A distinction between political and legal questions is made within the tradition of American constitutional law. It is, of course, a characterization of the political emerging from American experience, and to be used cautiously, at best, elsewhere. Justices disqualify themselves from dealing with political questions on the grounds that these questions are properly dealt with by representative—that is, political—assemblies. Legal questions are rather to be dealt with by the judicial authorities in terms of whatever rules, principles, standards, and concepts are characteristic of the law of the legal system of which the justices are a part. This distinction identifies the political as that on which the people properly speak (not something either coercive or dominative—indeed, it is difficult on this account to understand how it could be), whereas the legal is that on which (nonrepresentative) judicial agents of the body politic are qualified to pronounce by virtue of their knowledge and expertise.

Lastly, political matters are often contrasted with administrative matters. The former may be seen as concerned with arrival at policy, and the latter as concerned with execution of policy.

Should you retain any doubts that philosophers can endlessly complicate apparently simple issues, it should also be noticed that the political is used to refer to three quite different kinds of things: (1) what is being regulated, (2) the source of the regulation, and (3) the means of regulation. The foregoing contrast between the political and economic gives a clear example of the last of these. Von Clauswicz's famous remark about war ("War is the continuation of politics by other means") gives another. And the common contrast between politics and terror gives a third.* The other contrasts given here are somewhat equivocal on this matter, however, and some sorting out of whether we have the source, means, or the activity regulated can, like shifting contrasts with the other phenomena, cast different light on the nature of the political.

No effort is made here to determine which of the former contrasts is most fitting, if any, but to suggest the effects of the varying contrasts upon discussion of the political. Further, there are two ways of characterizing the political not clearly suggested by any of the preceding, but that are especially prominent in later discussion. They are: (1) the political is concerned with regulation that is organized territorially, not over nomads, and over territories and populations of certain minimum and maximum sizes; and (2) political regulation has a claim to unique universality of scope within the geographical areas in which it is claimed (see Chapter One for further discussion of both).

WHAT IS PHILOSOPHY?

Concerning philosophy one could again make some moves in a contrast game. Some contrasting ideas are science, theology, and ideology. Dangers of unnoticed shifts among them are possible, and one may find it rewarding to explore the resulting fluctuations in one's understanding of philosophy.

*However, see E. V. Walter's book *Terror and Resistance* for a challenge to that contrast.

Reason-giving also is important to philosophy. Philosophers care as much as anyone about giving correct evaluations of institutions and conduct (among other things), but claims to correctness abound, and can only be properly adjudicated when the reasons given for various evaluations are considered. Indeed, it is occasionally said, with the overemphasis mistakenly thought owing to important truths, that philosophers are more interested in the reasons given for a position than in the position itself.

The nature of political philosophy in particular can be illuminated by noting its relationship to actual political practice. One may suppose philosophers are merely workers who clear out the underbrush of conceptual tangles in thinking about political life, or, taking a quite different view, that they are spokes-persons for this or that particular ideology. Positions on this issue have ranged about as widely as anyone can imagine. Josef Pieper, a neo-Thomist, says that ethical philosophy (in which he includes political philosophy) is a matter of theoretical interest untouched by intention to alter things. On the other side of the spectrum, Marxists have promoted the notion that the object of philosophy is not to understand the world, but to change it.

In this regard, years ago, in a job interview, I was asked the following question, "Between the two world wars, I was interested in political philosophy, but then the Nazis came along and changed it all. What do you think of that?" The questioner apparently expected political philosophy to make some difference in the world, and was disappointed when it did not seem to do so. I, on the other hand, thought of political philosophy as the keeper of certain highly important human aspirations and ideals, and though I would have been pleased if it were to have made a difference, I did not expect it to do so. My views have not remained unaltered since, but I still think there is something of value in what they were.

It is often enough claimed that political scientists deal with the realities—what *is* the case—and that political philosophers deal with what *ought* to be the case. This difference has also been characterized as a difference between an empirical and a normative approach. Roland Pennock, on the other hand, has discarded these distinctions and suggested the more nearly correct one, that the difference is that between the "justificatory" (including only the ethical part of what was meant by the equivocal term *normative*) and the "operational" (seeking to explain, and ideally to predict, the operation of political institutions). This distinction seems to fit the facts of the disciplines much better. Nevertheless, political philosophers do not accept uncritically any political scientist's view of what operationally is, any more than political scientists abstain from justificatory remarks about what ought to be. Philosophers do not busy themselves testing hypotheses about the actualities at any particular place or time, but refer to what are thought to be securely known facts about political life. Their concern with matters seemingly so trite is to show the bearing of these facts on our political problems, prospects, and aspirations. With aspirations in particular, for example, it is important to assess not only coherence, but also workability. Thus it is important for philosophers to be explicit about the presence of controversy where controversy exists, and to be ready to acknowledge the possibility that there should be controversy, even though there isn't at present. The important thing is what bearing the alleged facts has on our understanding of the problems and aspirations of political life.

In the discussion that follows, we shall attend principally to how to justify and legitimate efforts to construct or continue political institutions and conduct of various sorts. We are commonly told, for example, that people will benefit by certain institutions or conduct, or that justice will thereby prevail, or that the institutions or conduct have been authorized. What gives these appeals weight? Are they coherent? Attempts at justification often also involve appeals to rules, maxims, habits, practices, roles, offices, functions, purposes, and issues of conformity and obedience. Appeals to such things will be considered here. They are made in the course of explaining why one judges institutions or policies to be desirable, how they do or will operate, and the similarities and differences between them and what we presently have.

ONE

The Idea of Political Community

Political communities are aggregations of human beings unified at least in part by being governed by the same government. Such a characterization, however, is only a provisional beginning to the discussion of political communities. Not every political philosopher understands political community in just this way. This characterization, however, with elucidation, amplification, and occasional modification, will occupy us fully.

In choosing the idea of political community as the fundamental organizing idea of this first part, I have tried to provide an idea of wider scope than that of the state, or roughly equivalent ideas made fundamental in many books on political philosophy. The idea of the state is examined later. It is an important idea, but far too limited, both historically and in several other ways, to serve well as an organizing idea for discussions in political philosophy. As we shall see, there is a spurious historical unity in lumping together city-states, feudal-states, and nation-states as though they were all instances of basically the same phenomenon. Political communities differ vastly from one another in ways insufficiently attended to when only states are considered, and it is important for political philosophers to be fully aware of the existing ranges of variation in internal structure and relationships to other communities found in various political communities.

Political philosophers focus on states as paradigm political communities, but there are also counties, provinces, colonies, protectorates, trustee territories, federated states, federations, and confederations. In addition, there are empires, economic communities, treaty organizations, leagues, and alliances. And, if we go back a bit in history, say to seventeenth- and eighteenth-century Germany, there are duchies, grand duchies, principates, electorates, and hometowns. This is only a sampling of the diversity. Political philosophers would be courting parochial narrowness of perspective to choose the state as their fundamental organizing idea, even if they intended it to have a far wider import than its normal contrasting with the foregoing ideas would indicate. It is better to avoid the dangers of relying on the idea of the state and instead to seek a wider organizing idea—for instance, the political community.

CHARACTERIZATION OF POLITICAL COMMUNITY

Without firm understanding of the minimum qualifying conditions of political community, concrete discussion of either the historical origins or the evaluation of political community is likely to be impossible. We will see that our understanding is unlikely to be as firm as we might wish. But given our understanding of the main features of political community, we may conclude that there is nothing *necessary* to humankind about it. Humans can probably live together in the absence of government; their affairs may be, and for many once were, organized thoroughly along lineage or tribal lines; and their affairs *could* conceivably be conducted at some level by force without any effort to mobilize opinion through concepts of legitimacy. There are, however, open and interesting questions concerning the costs as well as benefits of doing without political community. The debate lies here: how well are human beings likely to do without the accoutrements of political community?

A number of features count toward something's being a political community, and not every recognized political community will have all these features. Further, some things not universally agreed to be political communities will have some of these features, and the features themselves will not have sharp boundaries.

In the first place, not every aggregation of human beings is a society, nor is every society a political community. For an aggregation of human beings to constitute a society there must be a certain degree, though just how much is not perfectly clear, of (1) mutual responsiveness, (2) mutuality of interests, and (3) persistence or longevity to each of these two mutualities. There must also be (a) a government, (b) which lays successful claim to governance, (c) over a geographical territory of some minimum size, and (d) over a population of some minimum size (within that territory). The idea of government is thus complex, and central to our characterization of political community. Part II of this book is devoted to it. For the present, we may say that a government (i) regularly issues regulations and directives to which conformity is generally obtained, (ii) claims, unless formally subordinate to another government, priority in obedience to the regulations and directives issued by it, whatever the context or subject matter (the cash value of this being that the government claims the right always to penalize nonconformity to its regulations and directives), (iii) commonly provides coercive backing to the regulations and directives in question, and (iv) claims legitimacy.

Consider each of the features. Dealing first with those characterizing society, one can perhaps imagine, though only just barely, human beings so insensitive to one another that they could not or would not interact with one another though living in some contiguity to each other. Creatures so unresponsive might be more like zombies than human beings, though societies of humans doubtless have varied significantly in the extent to which their members interact. Imagining them not to interact at all can lead us to realize that the contiguity of humans to one another would not alone be sufficient to constitute a society. Likewise, if they had and could recognize no mutual interests, they would not be capable even occasionally of that coordinated behavior giving an aggregation of human beings sufficient unity to count as a society. Lastly, if the mutualities of responsiveness and interests were so transitory as to be insufficient to provide noticeable continuities, the resulting phenomena might be interesting to study, although such aggregations of creatures might be counted crowds or mobs but not societies.

Dealing next with the features of political communities, and putting aside for the moment (until Part II) anything beyond appeals to intuitive understandings of what governments are; first, if there were no governments laying successful claim to governance, the society would simply not have the mode of unity characteristic of political community. It might have a unity, but its unity might instead be that of a tribe or clan, with which political communities are commonly contrasted and from which they are commonly considered to have grown. As we shall discover in Part II, the gradual departure of societies from modes of organization solely along lineage lines may have played an important role in the development and visibility of some ideas central to our current notions of the political, such as authority and legitimacy, rules and regulations.

The second feature of political communities, that the governments of the communities lay claim over geographical territories, is a feature not much remarked upon in the literature of political philosophy.* One must be somewhat speculative in probing its rationale. Though the territoriality of political regulation or coordination has been an assumed feature of that form of life through most of the history of the idea, the literature has so far left us largely to our own devices to understand why.

The territoriality of political regulation has, in the first place, been identified with the idea that political governance is not over nomads. But nomadic life is not in itself inconsistent with territoriality. Nomads may have some important forms of dominance over a given territory even as they wander through it. But if some important forms of political phenomena are present in such wandering groups, nevertheless the fully developed forms of political life exist more clearly in nonnomadic cultures. As a matter of history, nomadic groups have been mostly organized along tribal or lineage lines. We have already remarked that such development is generally contrasted with political development, and we shall come to understand why this should be so.

Other reasons why fully developed forms of political life seem not to have developed in nomadic cultures have to do, perhaps, with moving from dependence upon foraging to dependence upon cultivation, and moving from personal property in chattels to personal property in land as well. This latter is a move from the only form of personal property clearly possible in nomadic

---

*Until recently—in a discussion principally along quite different lines from that which follows; for instance, Charles Beitz.

existence to an additional form more clearly possible among settled peoples. This, presumably, is in addition to the increased reliance upon rules and regulations in societies not organized along exclusively tribal or lineage lines, again a matter to be explained later. Foraging, in contrast to cultivation, requires little or no investment of time and patience, and in some circumstances little or no social stability. Some considerable patience, stability, and the like are needed if the time between sowing and reaping is to eventuate in harvesting. Likewise, personal property in land requires far greater social stability for its appeal than does personal property in chattels alone.

But the greatest light is thrown upon the territoriality feature of political community by the fact that the political claim to governance is not only over a certain territory but also normally over all the human beings within that territory. The claim may differ with respect to citizens, aliens, and perhaps other classes of noncitizen persons permanently or temporarily within the geographical limits of the territory (something to be discussed at length in Part III). But there will be some claim to governance over each and every person in the territory. Furthermore, the political government normally claims priority among all the other governance-wielding influences over everyone within the territory (more on this in Part II). How are we to understand what lies behind this claim?

Human beings are creatures having geographical locations; and, indeed, their geographical locations turn out to be of very great importance to them both individually and collectively. Humans are creatures occasionally having need of one another's physical presence, and likewise are creatures occasionally severely threatened by one another's physical presence.* These two important facts of human life play central roles in understanding the political.

Because of these facts, attempts to organize important matters in human affairs along lines ignoring geographical location—such as kinship (under modern conditions of the dispersal of kin) or religious affiliation (where religious affiliation is not determined politically, but rather in accord with conscience, or something of the sort) or hair color or physical size—would require at least enormous ingenuity, if they would be practicable at all. This is presuming, of course, that these personal attributes have geographically nonuniform distribution, and thus some humans in propinquity to one another would be subject to one regime, whereas others with whom they were in propinquity would be subject to various other regimes. Of course, this occurs already in border situations in modern political communities, but there is no reason to suppose here that we will get only or even very often the neat geographical borderlines common in modern political life.

In short, the physicality of human beings plays a central role in the importance of territoriality, propinquity, and stability to political life. This, in turn, is connected with the idea (to be discussed more fully in Part II) that political governance claims priority in obedience to the regulations and directives it issues. Given the importance of the physical, and thus the geographical, in human life, and given further the assumption that human beings are distrib-

*These two ideas, together with the exposition that follows in this chapter, constitute in large part an understanding of Hobbe's *Leviathan* offered by H.L.A. Hart in his *The Concept of Law*.

uted on the face of the earth nonuniformly or at least noncentralizably with respect to kinship ties and those other features just mentioned, maybe whatever governance has priority *must* be geographically organized. If not, then our present ingenuity might not be up to organizing in an untroubling and clear way. Some persons may think this position assumes narrower limits upon the potentiality in political life of cooperation, agreement, and mutual understanding than are needed. This issue will be discussed in Chapter Five.

The territorial aspects of political community can be viewed from two perspectives. First there is the claim political communities make to dominion over all humans within certain territories. Claims to dominion have certain similar aspects for every human in the territory. For example, compliance of everyone may be demanded to criminal laws concerning theft and violence. But laws concerning political participation, taxation, and military service may be applied differentially to citizens and noncitizens, or visitors and permanent residents. Second, we may note how it is determined to which government individual humans owe support and compliance. Compliance is not always owed only to the government within whose domains one resides. Generally people owe compliance to at least some of that government's rules and regulations, but when they are aliens or visitors they will commonly owe support and compliance also to some of the rules and regulations of another government. What to do when there are conflicts between rules and regulations of governments can become a complicated matter with respect to the dictates of both prudence and political morality. This chapter will view it primarily from the first perspective.*

The next feature of political communities offered earlier, that the geographical territories and populations within those territories over whom governance is to be claimed be of a minimum size, excludes from consideration groups of humans or territories too small or dependent to develop for themselves anything approximating a normal array of political institutions. The considerations leading to the making of this stipulation will emerge from discussions later in this chapter and in Part II. For the present, two prominent examples from the history of political philosophy will provide important parts of the considerations involved.

Concerning lower and upper limits on the sizes of populations and territories of political communities, Aristotle said they should be large enough so that the system of dependencies would be sufficient to supply the needs of a genuinely human life, and not too large to be heard by a given speaker at a given time. (This will be elucidated shortly).

The use of the word *genuinely* alerts us to the likelihood that the needs in question serve humanity on a very particular view of what human life is all about, a view probably not shared by every commentator. We have no special interest here in what Aristotle believed a genuinely human life to require, though he did have elaborately developed views on the subject. Exposure of views on the subject cannot, however, be avoided here; look for them especially as this chapter proceeds, and also later. Whether carefully worked out

---

*The second perspective will be considered somewhat in Part III, where the grounds persons may have for accepting or rejecting the claims to dominion over them made by political communities will be considered.

or virtually unconsciously presumed, views on what is sufficient to supply the needs of a genuinely human life suffuse political philosophy. Consider, for example, what you and your friends might conclude required in the way of social, material, and technological capacities to lead what you or they would regard as full and satisfying *human* lives. (The emphasis on "human" may be thought troublesome. It threatens to introduce so much that is likely to be debatable or even tricky. But it can remind you of the scope and importance of what you are doing.)

Concerning Aristotle's stipulation that the society not be too large in population to be heard by a single speaker at a given time, one may plausibly assume that Aristotle has in mind what is needed to provide a certain unity required in well-functioning political communities. Aristotle's way of putting it makes it dependent on the technological state of communication at the time about which we are speaking, the operation of certain conclusions about the audial acuity of listeners to speakers, and conclusions also about the powers of the speakers themselves with respect to their volume and clarity of enunciation. These dependencies are worth remarking because exposure of them reveals clearly, in a manner to be duplicated again and again in this book, how deeply embedded and hence how influential assumptions about technological capacities as well as about the capacities of human beings are in political philosophy.

Aristotle also thought external trade important to political community. The concerns underlying this position had to do with what, in his view, would be needed to answer to the fullness of human life. But this position also arose from consideration of the environmental conditions in the Greek societies with which he was familiar, which depended on external trade for a reasonably full range of human needs. For example, they had chronic shortages of such things as grains, which could be remedied by external trade. This consideration was particularly obvious in Aristotle's Greece. Persons living in more abundantly provided environments would have had less reason to think, and thus might not have thought, of such a thing. Thus, assumptions about environments too get embedded in political philosophy.

Hobbes also was a clear commentator on the size of political community. He said that the size of the commonwealth (the political community—considering the size of the population as well as of the territory) ruled must be large enough to support government efforts to afford the population some chance of protection against marauders, whether marauding individuals or marauding social groups of various sorts.

In sum, as these two examples from the history of political philosophy show, stipulations concerning the sizes of political community receive support from consideration of such things as sufficiency in the supply of what i s needed for human life, adequacy of the capacity for coordination in the activities of the members of the society, and security against marauders. Though disagreements in conclusions are surely possible, it remains true that these are the main considerations relevant to the matter.

So much for exposing some of the significance of the stipulated features of society and political community. We still might ask, why select objects having most or all of these characteristics for special study, as in political philosophy?

In the first place, the idea of political community, as so far sketched, identifies conditions present in the lives of an overwhelming majority of human beings through much of recorded history. Secondly, with respect both to what is *of* interest to most human beings in recent history and what is widely thought to be *in* their interests, these conditions have been importantly present even without consideration of any but the most obvious consequences. Thirdly, social scientists generally believe that attention to the structures and operations of such communities will yield information having explanatory and predictive value concerning what happens, and when and where it happens. Lastly, others, among them political philosophers, believe that study of these phenomena can reveal and also provide occasion to think about the moral relevance and evaluation of similar conditions currently almost universally present in human life (the concern of this book).

Thus, though there is nothing inevitable about focusing on this cluster of phenomena, there appear to be good reasons for doing so. Further, we by now have a long and well-entrenched history of doing so, a history vastly though controversially influential upon our perceptions of the moral and prudential situations in which we find ourselves, or very likely might find ourselves. Political philosophy embodies an important part of that history.

EVALUATION OF POLITICAL COMMUNITY

Apart from questions of legitimacy to be discussed in a chapter of their own, evaluation of political communities rests on investigation of the good or harm they do. Theological and other cosmic concerns may be expressed by identifying what constitutes the good or harm done, and we would be unwise to ignore these concerns insofar as we wish to understand the histories of our cultures and detect residues of these histories still embedded in them. But we will focus at present on the good or harm done by political community to prosaic human interests.

In talking about all humankind we must take account of an immense range of environments, climates, resources, temperaments, and cultural histories. Different commentators, differently situated both temporally and geographically, have assessed these matters differently.

We are also dealing with possibilities, not with certainties. These are complicated by differences in degree of likelihood or probability, something most often imprecisely expressed. There are also differences in assessment of how much security we require, desire, or at least have in mind, and what states of cultural and technological development we should expect, and so on. The best we can do in the face of the many sources of likely divergence and misunderstanding is to try to reach an accommodation. What are the grounds we and others have for the views put forward, and what are the possibilities of rational agreement?

If we set out to ask how political communities can serve human interests, we must be clear about what we are doing. We are not asking how they *do* serve human interests; nor are we asking why they were in fact organized. The former question should be asked only in the company of political sociologists; the latter only in the company of political historians.

The salient fact about humans and their circumstances of which *we* might first take note is that they find themselves from the start in one another's company, and this company constitutes both an opportunity and a threat. It constitutes an opportunity because people have needs and desires that can be fulfilled through or with the help of one another. It constitutes a threat because they are vulnerable to one another's attack, because they on occasion need or desire the same scarce goods, or because they are capable of getting irritated, angry, or impatient with one another.

Some opportunities may be utilized and some threats forestalled by measures short of forming a political community. As we have said, aggregates that are not yet political communities have occasionally exhibited decent longevity, and, to some degree at least, mutuality of interests and responsiveness. Depending on the temperament of these people, the scarcity of goods, and the extent of the mutualities present, they may carry the people quite far. Perhaps it is because they are not carried so far as the people wish that their societies have often taken on the additional characteristics that make them political communities. This, however, is only speculative. Perhaps instead there is no such desire but merely a proclivity or a set of susceptibilities leading in this direction.

We need not attend immediately to how collectively and culturally we got here and the role of other people in *that* (though attention to these matters will be important in our later discussion). We can start with where each of us now is and with the condition in which we now find ourselves (and thus do a little simple political sociology, as political philosophers ofen do). How can political communities serve us? What should we now strive for? Much of political philosophy can be illuminated when viewed as stemming from these questions.

The fact that the presence of other people can constitute both an opportunity and a danger to each of us is traceable to certain elemental and undisputed truths about human beings. In pursuing the ramifications of this fact for political philosophy, we might reasonably ask ourselves how we could organize our affairs so as to maximize the opportunities and minimize the dangers presented to each of us by the presence of creatures who may on occasion cooperate with or assist us, and who may on other occasions compete with and, in fact, injure or even kill us.

Reflection on the opportunities and dangers will be influenced by considerably more controversial assumptions and hypotheses than those with which we started about generally shared capacities and susceptibilities of human beings—for example, how regularly and in what directions they can be influenced, persuaded, satisfied, aroused, and so forth. Claims about the fundamental facts of human nature have figured importantly in political philosophy both in determination of what the opportunities and dangers are to political community, and in speculation about how to take maximal advantage of the former and minimize the latter.*

---

*We should again note that no suggestion is intended that members of the societies or political communities have, have had, or ever will have serving the interests appealed to in evaluating the communities as their reasons for forming such communities. They may have had such things in mind or may not have; nothing will depend here on whether they did.

ORIGIN AND EVALUATION

The judgment is common that the origin of a thing (person, institution, or community) should not have anything to do with the evaluation of it. The "mistake" in thinking it does is called the Genetic Fallacy. With political communities, however, the situation is not so simple. It is precisely to the origins of political communities that one is sent to discover their legitimacy, a complex judgment to which Chapter Seven will be devoted.

Philosophers are not, as philosophers, trained to investigate the origins of political communities. Their discussions, however, sometimes appear to embody claims about these origins, and credible accounts of origins do appear relevant to evaluation of political community in general. This appearance of relevance is based upon several sources, some of which provide good grounds for the claim and some of which do not. A large part of the appearance of relevance is based on the importance of governments and evaluating their legitimacy.

But the appearance of relevance is also based in part on the way accounts of the origins of political communities suggest functions and purposes these communities may have.* Talk about functions and purposes calls attention to the need to think carefully about an important historical fact. By common agreement among scholars, overwhelmingly many political communities originate in conquest.

This view contains a suggestion and a couple of types of potential confusion. The suggestion is that conquerors and their descendants probably were self-interested, intelligent, effective, and persistent enough to see to it that the conquest served their interests. Service to some human needs and interests is commonly thought a justifying value of political communities, and such service could be counted in the community's favor. But does the community serve the interests of a larger portion of the population than merely the conquerors and their descendants? If this were thought feasible, even at a cost of some reduction of service to the conquerors and their descendants, but was not done, then the community might be thought unacceptable because it could provide this greater service but didn't. This raises questions about the optimality of the distribution of benefits within communities much discussed by economists and some philosophers. That a community provides some service to some people is something to be said on its behalf, but most persons would be unwilling to accept it without comparison to feasible or likely alternatives.

Thus, confusing questions concerning the evaluation of political institutions find settings in complex nests of assumptions concerning the feasibility or likelihood of various alternatives. This, of course, is true of evaluations of communities generally, and not just those originating in conquest. But it is in

---

*Functions are here understood to be unintended benefits, and purposes intended benefits. Unintended benefits are those actually brought about, while intended benefits may or may not be; thus, claims about the latter should ordinarily be supported by evidence that participants would recognize them to be *benefits*.

the latter type of case where assumptions have been complicated by shifts in historical perspective from the present to the past.

Further complications are introduced by the fact that people will be found to affirm or deny value to serving various interests—for example, of the masses or some particular elite. The situation is exacerbated by the fact that conflict is endemic between certain classes of persons in societies; for instance, these same masses and elites. Thus it is often thought that *if* the interests of some elite are being served, then the interests of the masses are *not* being served. As suggested earlier, the fact that various elites or their ancestors may have had a hand in the origins of the political communities (by conquest and the like) supports presumptions that the interests of these elites are served. Such accumulating assumptions and inferences can definitely cause confusion.

Another type of confusion is present. Conquest is generally by force of arms or other intimidation. But for a political community actually to form and operate as such, there must be eventual acceptance of many things by the subject population. Apart from the importance of beliefs about legitimacy of rule for obtaining obedience (discussed in Chapters Seven and Twelve), there are limits on the use of intimidation to obtain the widespread conformities characteristic of political communities. Serious investigation of this matter would require careful thought about exactly which conformities were required, the technologies available for enforcement and detection of nonconformity, and the reliability of intimidation as a motivating device (a matter requiring not only study of human nature but also discrimination of the strength of the beliefs and the importance attached to the beliefs of the persons involved concerning the matters on which conformity was required).

Even without such investigation, however, most of us believe that we can recognize that there are limits to the use of intimidation to obtain conformity. This leads some commentators to assert that all rule whatever, including rule through conquest, is based on acceptance of the rulers by the ruled. This is a source of confusion, since if one is not careful to distinguish between acceptance that is the product of intimidation through conquest and acceptance otherwise resulting from prudential or moral considerations, one may come to think of all political communities as founded on consent (of some sort or other). This in turn lends plausibility also to various claims about whose interests those communities serve or are intended to serve. The resulting accounts of the purposes and functions of communities may be quite unrealistic. Thus, aside from legitimacy, attempts to connect accounts of origins to evaluation of political communities are full of pitfalls, but may have a point.

ORIGIN: A NOTE ON CITIES

Cities are political communities. What may not be so obvious is that they are archetypal political communities. The words *political* and *politics, civic* and *civil,* via the Greek and Latin languages from which they are drawn, witness this truth. The progenitors of most political philosophy in the cultural tradition of

western Europe, Plato and Aristotle, spoke and thought of the *polis,* the principal political community of their time and place. Out of regard for the similarity between the important features of their political communities and features of the modern nation-state, we currently call their topic the *city-state.*

The origins of cities are controversial. It is commonly believed that they
originated as military camps or as sites of religious observances (the latter
would be misleading if it were not remembered that there was then no distinct
line such as now exists between the sacred and the secular). For our purposes,
the distinctive feature of cities was that they were gatherings of people not
organized exclusively along tribal or lineage lines. Their advent thus marks
the beginnings of something new in the organization of human affairs, something now accepted as a centrally important feature of political community
and something leading, as we shall see, to issues about legitimacy and authority of rule with which political philosophy so largely occupies itself.

ORIGIN: A NOTE ON NATURE AND CONVENTION

A persistent line of inquiry into the origin of government and political community has been commonly identified with the heading "nature and convention." Did government and political society originate in one or the other? One
may also ask a prior question: why care? What issues of interest or importance
hinge on whether these phenomena originate in nature or in convention?

Without attempting here to identify everything of importance, we may pick
out two ultimate interests. First, there is a religious interest. If these phenomena have a natural origin and nature has a divine origin, then they may be
ordained by God; on the other hand, if the phenomena originate in human
artifice, and humans are considered to have free will, then the phenomena
were not ordained by God and may be thus judged differently. Rulers, for
example, might not have anything of the divine about them. There is nothing
inevitable about these conclusions; they may merely provide presumptions to
be developed or overcome by further argument. Second, there is an interest
in whether government and political community are profoundly congenial to
human nature or are at least somewhat "contingent" artifices. If the former,
there may be something especially fitting about them; if the latter, they might
possibly be considered dispensable.

It seems clear, however, that government and political community are human artifices. If, as suggested in the introduction, artifice is to be contrasted
with nature, then the two are not natural. But if the natural is understood to
be the normal, ordinary, usual, or regular, to be contrasted with the extraordinary, unusual, and abnormal, then human artifices so widespread as government and political community might also be natural and reveal something
very profound and deep about human nature. The word *nature* and its cognates have the capacity, as we have remarked in the introduction, to shift in
just this way.

This is, perhaps, a major source of the continuance of debate about
whether things so obviously artifices (that is, products of human activity) as
government and political community are products of nature or of convention.

Perhaps things so normal and usual have an almost inextinguishable claim to being "natural." The contrast between nature and convention persists, perhaps, only because conventions are thought to be at least somewhat arbitrary or contingent. But this view of them will be difficult to maintain in the face of explicit awareness that the conventions in question are also normal, ordinary, usual, and regular among human beings. If they are, it will seem to many persons that they are also natural to humankind. So, in any case, the issues supposedly introduced by the contrast we have been considering need considerable further clarification.

Of course, not all human beings adopt the same styles of political community and government. The styles, then, are not natural either in the sense of not being the products of artifice or in the sense of being usual, normal, and so forth. But here also there are no justifiable grounds, at least in the modern world, for the endless continuation of the debate. In eras when thinkers were relatively ignorant of how widespread and persistent variations in styles of government and political community were, they may have been readier to regard variations from some preferred model as aberrations to be explained away consistently while continuing to regard the preferred model as natural. Some thinkers may regard such a strategy as promising, but as our knowledge of diversities in human practices increases, the strategy must appear less promising. There is still, however, no knock-down argument against it, and debate continues.

Discussion of nature versus convention is also conducted regarding many things besides government and political community, for instance, institutions such as marriage and family, and the division of labor along sexual lines. It is also found in discussions of human aspirations or ideals such as particular conceptions of justice and equality. The issues and alternatives traversed thus far will be equally important to expose in these other areas.

The other contrasts with "nature" introduced earlier have played some role in the discussion of nature versus convention. Though space is not available here to delineate these relationships, an exhaustive discussion of the issue should provide it.

TWO

Human Nature, Mutual Reliance, and Ideals

HUMAN NATURE AND POLITICAL COMMUNITY

Does political community "fit" human nature? We noted in evaluating the former that the presence of other humans presents us with opportunities and threats. It does so because we are creatures having needs, desires (the distinction between these will be discussed later in this chapter), and vulnerabilities that we cannot, all by ourselves, always fulfill or avoid, or fulfill or avoid reliably and effortlessly. We will now examine the situation more fully (though especially the final chapter will examine it yet further).

To take only the clearest cases of opportunities, we happen to be creatures dependent upon food and water for our continued existence. These things are sometimes in short or unreliable supply, or difficult of access. We also, however, happen to be creatures who commonly, for whatever reasons, desire the company and companionship of others, and thus all that that requires and perhaps much to which it may lead. The assistance and cooperation of others may therefore become essential conditions of our efforts to further our well-being.

Similarly, fragile creatures that we are, we are vulnerable to injury. We can be cut, bruised, and mangled relatively easily by one another. And we are, at least presently and surely through most of our known histories, creatures having limited interest in one another's welfare. Under pressure of scarcity of what we want and frustration about getting it, as well as perhaps for other reasons, we sometimes behave nastily toward one another. So long as these two facts are so—our vulnerability to injury by others and our limited interest in one another's welfare—each of us constitutes a potential danger to the others against which it would be prudent to guard oneself.

When we ask how to make the best of the human situation as thus depicted, we trigger more intensive and more controversial consideration of the basic facts about human nature; for example, what human beings are like both from the standpoint of their capacities to stand toward one another as benefactor and beneficiary and also as malfeasor and victim, and what they (and thus we) are like as candidates for, or raw materials of, certain forms of social organization.

To see the scope of this, ask yourself how *you* would organize human affairs so as to maximize the benefits and minimize the dangers of the presence of other human beings. A daydreamy answer of many persons is: "I would organize them so that everyone would do what I wish." Why doesn't this answer, which is momentarily so attractive, survive critical and practical scrutiny? One could criticize it high-mindedly for its selfishness. But criticism of it doesn't depend on that. What if you are and remain, though not yet totally in fantasyland, determinedly low-minded?

Even if, and especially if, low-minded, you would be interested in whether the proposal is practical and whether you would in the end be pleased with the result of getting your wishes uniformly obeyed. You might ask first how you could get other people uniformly to do what you wish. You would be led thereby to consider what resources of power and influence you do in fact possess. This would require some realistic thinking about yourself. But what can count as a resource depends upon not only what you are like but what other people are like, and in particular to what sorts of techniques and devices of influence and control they are susceptible.

If they were as unsensing as rocks or as uncomprehending as newts, speeches to them would not work. If they were as desireless as Indian sages, temptation would not work. If they were proud, fearless, and self-centered, coercion would not work. And so on. Your interest in practicality would force you forward into consideration of further and interestingly disputed claims about human nature, what it is and can become.

You are pushed yet further if you pursue an interest in whether, if everyone else did what you wish, you would in the end be pleased with the result. Of course, the suggestion that you might not like the result may produce surprise. You may ask why in the world you would *not* like it. It sounds wonderful! But it sounds wonderful only because something important is being assumed: either (a) that everything you wish to have other people do will be something you will be pleased to have done once it is done or (b) that though getting what you wish in this regard may not always leave you more pleased than you would have been without it, nevertheless it is the way to maximize your satisfaction.

Probing these assumptions leads to investigation of some of the darker recesses of human nature generally as well as to consideration of the likely distribution among human beings of *knowledge* about what you and they will be pleased to have once gotten. The importance of at least the latter topic to political philosophy and to practical politics has long been understood. In political philosophy it appears as early as Plato's insistence that power, if it is to benefit its possessors, must be combined with knowledge. In practical politics it appears in our long-standing awareness that one of the perennial debates in politics is about who are the experts whose knowledge we need to bring to bear upon political decisions, and that one of the perennial problems in politics is how to utilize experts without being dominated by them.

Some aspects of this general problem will receive further attention shortly. For the present, we recognize that an important part of the knowledge we seek is knowledge of ourselves, both individually and collectively, and of what will bring us lasting satisfaction once we get it. This again brings us to consider human nature, for our satisfactions depend upon the sorts of things that we are now and have a potential for becoming.

In sum, reflection upon a simple fact about the human situation—that none of us is alone—and the asking of an eminently practical question about that fact—how can we make the best of it?—can catapult us into deep concern for the fundamentals and potentials of human nature. Two historically important but apparently quite different political philosophies, those of Plato and Hobbes, may be understood to differ in large part because they address themselves to different aspects of the matters we have just been discussing.

Plato's *Republic* may be reasonably seen as (but not only as) an exploration of the opportunities presented to us by our contiguity to one another. He does not ignore the dangers inherent in that contiguity, and the consequent need to protect ourselves against these dangers, but the features that have made this work of his distinctive in the history of *political* philosophy are attributable to the focus he gives to the question of opportunities.

A crucial part of that focus is exposed when Plato has Socrates say early in the book, "No man is self-sufficing: each has needs." These two claims, standing alone, can be understood in several ways, but the subsequent development of the idea favors the following: human beings have needs for food, protection from external enemies, and the like. They cannot fill those needs efficiently or reliably, or engage in activities for which they have the greatest talent or taste, without some division of responsibilities, so that a system of "mutual reliance" results. Without just yet dwelling on the idea of systematic mutual reliance, or the principle from whose application it can result, we can note that the idea and principle provide a setting for considering how reliance upon other humans can increase the efficiency and reliability with which we satisfy our needs and desires.*

Hobbes's *Leviathan,* on the other hand, may reasonably be understood as (but again not only as) an exploration of one need or desire in particular, our

---

*Does starting, as Plato does, with "*each* [person] has needs . . ." (emphasis added) introduce an individualist bias into the discussion of the political community? (See the *Republic*, Book II, 369 *b*.) This allegation might seem surprising because the starting place is that of Plato in the *Republic,* and he is there certainly not commonly thought to have an individualist bias. Perhaps, however, the bias introduced by this remark is remediable, and the allegation invites us to scrutinize the quote in question more closely. The question invites us to consider various kinds, orders, and settings of human needs, and to ask about the extent to which humans can or could, cannot or could not, fulfill them by virtue of their own individual efforts. In the interests of a full picture of the scope of the problem, one might also urge the consideration of sophisticated as well as primitive needs. We are thus encouraged to take fully formed humans as reference points and to neglect asking how such creatures could come to exist. No attention is given, at this stage at least, to the possibility that some of the needs cited could not be present in creatures whose personal histories included little or no social contact with similar creatures. Thus no attention is given to the possibility that social relations can contribute, and may even

need or desire to protect ourselves against one another. He thus focuses on the threats presented by our contiguity. His view of human nature and the human situation emphasizes the importance of security to humans in the satisfaction of a need for protection, both characterizing and evaluating political communities as serving (but not only as serving) that need.

NEEDS AND DESIRES

From our present perspective on Plato, admittedly a narrow one, and Hobbes, needs and desires are fundamental. Philosophers generally have paid considerable attention to the ideas of needs and desires and to the differences between them. This is not surprising, as claims to the fulfillment of needs are thought to carry a special urgency, and claims to the fulfillment of desires are thought at least to demand the attention of any liberal conception of the fundamental aims of life.*

Besides this, there are some interesting differences between needs and desires. Clearly, we may have needs of which we are unaware, as for example a need for surgery or dental care. Desires of which we are unaware are not, however, supposed so common, and claims that we have them require careful argument. This asymmetry has led philosophers to conclude that there should be differences in the evidence required to show the presence of each.

Needs and desires are related, but there is no simple correlation between them. Something is said to be needed because it is thought that something else is or ought to be desired. The thing or state said to be needed is thus believed necessary for the attainment of the thing or state that it is believed is or should be desired. There are philosophers who separate need and desire more radically than this, but it is unwise to do so because we would be less likely then to have reminders that stipulate what the things claimed to be needed are needed *for*.

Claims about needs are too often based upon questionable suppositions about what is or ought to be desired to permit these suppositions to slip by unnoticed. Indeed, differing claims about needs can sometimes be easily reconciled when these suppositions are exposed, and in any case their exposure helps us to focus what most requires investigating and debating.

In order to avoid pursuit of the wrong quarry, it is important to ask, "What are the things or states said to be needed for?" rather than "What is there a need for?" The latter question is likely to evoke an answer identifying the things or states said to be needed, rather than the suppositions upon which the claim of need is based.

Consider what emerges when the former question is asked and answered.

---

be essential, to not only the satisfaction of a wide range of human needs, but also to the possibility of the needs themselves. To consider the role social relations play in the satisfaction of human needs without at the same time considering the role social relations play as a condition for the existence of such needs is indeed to operate with an individualist bias (see the remark in the first paragraph of this chapter).

*These aspects of needs and desires are considered by Joel Feinberg in his companion volume in this series, *Social Philosophy*.

Generally, the answer will readily take the form of "in order to . . . ," where the blank is filled with an expression identifying either something it is believed is or ought to be desired, or something else allegedly needed (about which the question may be repeated in turn). In evaluating the answers, we should note that not every desire is said to give rise to a need, such as desires a person ought not to have, or that are relatively unimportant or transitory. It must rather normally be, or be closely connected to, something relatively important or long-lasting.

A person is said to desire something when he or she (1) strives for it, (2) looks forward to getting it with pleasurable anticipation, or (3) is pleased to have gotten it. The clearest cases are where all three conditions are fulfilled. Difficulties, doubts, and contentions occur when only one or two of the conditions are filled.

No special difficulties are created by the absence of the first unless it is understood that striving for the thing in question is necessary to have a reasonable chance of getting it. Absence of the second condition alone is likely to provide cases where, for example, commentators contrast the pursuit of duty with the pursuit of pleasure. Cases where the third condition alone is present could be where persons claim that we may have unrecognized desires.

A person's desires are generally expected to be considerably more extensive than that person's needs. Perhaps that is because a person's needs are generally given so much more weight than that person's desires. Further, the conditions under which a person needs something are immensely more variable than the conditions under which a person desires something. This is suggested by the brief consideration that follows of a list of needs supposed to be especially important to political philosophy.

Whether one faults anyone's, including Plato's, particular list of needs and/or desires the fulfillment of which is supposed to be among the possible benefits of political community is less important to us at the start than is a clear picture of the role such claims play in political philosophy. Claims about needs and desires are in this latter context worrisome to many because we understand that they are so often products of habituation and acculturation. One thing worth trying to do, therefore, is to cut away the needs and desires most palpably the products of such influences, and concentrate on what remains, if anything.

Commonly recognized remainders are food, drink, oxygen, and, less clearly, clothing and shelter. The status of the latter is less clear than of the others because, in many environments, it is not perfectly clear that needs for them are not just the products of habituation or acculturation. Still, examination of the others on the list will be instructive.

Food, drink, and oxygen are needed in at least some quantities in order to keep alive.* How much of each and of what kind are certainly more open to

*In the note on individualism, we did not observe *that* certain needs or wants that get satisfied—such as for food, drink, oxygen—may be invariable and others—such as for sex—are not. Whether invariable in their existence or not, however, *how* they are satisfied, as influenced by the society, a segment thereof, or even the individual, may vary—for instance, food, drink, or sex, but not, let us say, oxygen. The urge to satisfy these needs may serve as motives, and the trouble with individualism is sometimes supposed to be that it attributes the

variation than the demands of various cultures would suggest. But even if one sets out merely to keep existing persons alive, reflection on the human condition will show that this must be achieved in one environment by measures quite different from another. The presence of game or fish, fertile land, water, adequate growing seasons, and external enemies is variable. And the technologies by means of which the supplies of needed goods and services are provided are available some places and times but not others. Some conditions will thus confront us with a need for cooperation with other persons; some will not. In toto, however, it does appear that very little of the world's population has ever lived in anything like the probably largely mythical South Sea island paradise where, for example, all the needed supplies are at hand merely for reaching and taking.

Concluding from what has so far been said, confirmation of the presence or absence of a need or desire in a given situation may involve an interplay of appeals to social norms as well as to psychological, anatomical, and ecological facts (and a certain latitude of choice concerning the temporal spans and parameters of possibility). There will as well be points at which a "needed" X can only be presented as a way of providing Y, and not as the *only* possible way of providing Y, though the subsequent steps may be presented as the only possible ways. Thus there will be an interplay of claims such as (a) if you want this, you must have that (with "must" backed by claims about physiology, anatomy, ecology, and limitations derived from consideration of social norms—this last being troublesome), and (b) if you want this, then you might also want that, because getting that is a way (though not the only way) of getting or making it more likely that you will get this. There will be nothing crushingly final about the order of the argument; it will be more like a line of plausibilities.

SYSTEMATIC MUTUAL RELIANCE

Try to imagine what it would be like in circumstances not outrageously favorable to be able regularly to grow, gather, or fabricate on your own everything you need for food, clothing, shelter, and defense. Even in entirely favorable circumstances the task would be overwhelming, and in less favorable circumstances would not leave time for much else. Furthermore, you might often enough have to do with much less than you now feel is necessary. Even if circumstances remain reasonably favorable, what about the common desire not to spend any larger portion of one's efforts on the fulfillment of those needs than is absolutely necessary? We may, in short, believe that coordination with others could save us effort in fulfilling those needs.

We will surely discover other needs besides the obvious ones so far mentioned that need filling. Effort must be available to fill these needs. Its availability might depend at least in part upon what is left over after the needs so far

---

source of all human motives to the individual. As a closer look shows, however, the truth is more complicated than that. In the end, we can have a very complicated motivational mix. It is not surprising that many of the commentators on both sides who try to cut through the complications provide us with simplistic accounts.

mentioned have been filled. Thus, the savings in effort resulting from coordination may be considered urgent. We should remember that the common desire is not merely to live but to live *well*. We would be wise, therefore, to consider carefully what enlargements or narrowings of our vision of what is necessary result from regarding that fact.

We might then find it easier to understand the common divisions of opinion between political philosophers concerning whether and how much coordination, extensively and intensively, of the activities of humans will help. Our political cultures have pursued the coordination ideal more or less vigorously, though not with undivided opinion on the wisdom and desirability of doing so.

The coordination that sustains "reliance" (see the following discussion) upon other persons to provide goods or services, or assistance in providing them, that one would otherwise have to try to provide for oneself or do without will be called *Systematic Mutual Reliance* (SMR). For SMR to be advantageous would require that the system of coordination itself be reliable and not require more effort to operate than it saves. These conditions may be difficult to meet, and their fulfillment should not be assumed. We shall explore them below, and thereby illuminate much about which political philosophers debate.

The reliance is described as *systematic* because we are interested in more than merely short-term coordination for single tasks. The coordinations are labeled *mutual reliance* intending to suggest the concerns that could motivate the coordinations in question, the likely benefits, liabilities, opportunities, and dangers of the coordinations commonly attempted, and to provide an illuminating setting for introduction of the rules, regulations, and order-giving characteristics of political communities.*

The major challenge is to explore the conditions under which SMR would be reasonable. For, if not reasonable, such coordination is unlikely to occur unless it is massively forced or propagandized.** Philosophers have no special competence to say whether two conditions needed for the full cases of reliance to be present are so: (1) full and conscious awareness that certain specifiable

---

*No suggestion is intended here or elsewhere that the benefits and liabilities, and so on, suggested by the setting in question are the only conceivable ones. Nor is any suggestion intended that the motivation suggested by the setting does in fact motivate very many of the coordinations we find in political communities, though it may very well do so.

**This brings sharply to our attention the fact that political and social arrangements having the appearance and effect of SMR may be neither voluntary nor reasonable, and *reliance* may be an unfortunate word. Given the importance of force and propaganda in political life, we might think it wise to widen the scope of our investigation to where its effects have been produced by coercion or manipulation. We would then be talking about how the system functions rather than about the purposes of the persons participating. The purpose of some of the participants might be to avoid the punishment that would be nearly inevitable if they failed to do as they were told. If those doing the telling had in mind a coordinated system of production and services, the result might be much the same as if the participants were to rely upon one anothers' activities. But a request for the conditions under which systematic reliance of people upon one another would be reasonable would distort all that.

Nevertheless, failure to make the request would be a mistake. In seeing the machinery of coordination as possibly merely a result of coercion or manipulation, we might fail to see how

tasks need doing that one is not doing and possibly cannot do oneself, and (2) deliberately leaving them undone and "relying" on other persons to do them. The awareness and/or deliberateness about what is happening may often be absent, or at least not fully and clearly present.

Here, we might try first distinguishing between what people would do or think about the matter when they are enculturated as we are and also what they would do or think when they are not. We might try, in seeking answers that would be true of all humankind, to bypass the effects upon us of our acculturation. Such ambition has led some thinkers to try to imagine what people would do or think if *all* acculturation were cut away. But, as Dewey says about environmental influences generally, there is no point in imagining how people would behave without them because their presence is a condition of any life whatever. We might likewise say about acculturation that, as the presence of *some* is so universal a condition of anything we would recognize as human life, there is no point in trying to imagine how humans would behave without it.

Attempts to engage in such "thought experiments" will merely involve one self-deception or another. We are not helpless in trying to reduce the influence of our own acculturation on our answers, but we should be cautious about the conclusions we are able to draw out of our reflections, and not claim universality for them. The only procedures available to us are perilous, and their usefulness depends upon the extent of our care and imaginativeness. A good place to begin, as Hobbes believed, is to look within ourselves and ask how, after stripping off the effects of our recognizable personal and cultural peculiarities, we might come to rely in the required way upon others.

Take the matter personally. Seeing your own reactions in this "stripped-down" way, when would *you* rely upon others? Perhaps the question should be restricted to reliance in matters highly important to you; for at least some of the matters on which reliance will be desired will surely be of that sort, and that is where your thinking is likely to be most clearheaded. In highly important matters, you will doubtless not be willing to rely upon others and thus leave things undone unless (1) you are so desperate that, knowing yourself unable to carry out successfully alone the activities concerned, you leave those activities undone and hope for the best, or (2) you have good reason to believe that the people on whom you hope to rely will in fact do what you are hoping for them to do. Cases of the first sort may be few in human history. As with a person falling out a window who knows there is no chance of flying nevertheless may flap his or her arms on the way down, people may make efforts, including solitary ones, even when they have every good reason to believe that these efforts will not succeed.

---

deeply it is embedded in the idea of systematic reliance of people upon one another. The latter perception will, however, be promoted by the request for the conditions under which systematic reliance will be reasonable. Furthermore, even if massive force or propaganda were utilized to obtain the coordination in question, they in turn would require, given most technologies of force, manipulation, and propaganda, widespread systematic reliance. So, the question would remain how systematic reliance is made to seem reasonable or dutiful or whatever to enough persons to get started.

People do occasionally give up, but this phenomenon is far from universal in cases of the sort under discussion. In consequence, cases of the first sort are often telescoped into cases of the second sort, with the only clear effect being a lowering of standards as to what is to count as a "good reason" for believing that people on whom one wishes to rely will in fact do what one wishes. Desperation commonly has this effect.

We may therefore expect some unstableness of focus on what is to count as the "good reason" we seek. Furthermore, we should note that some potential "reliers" are likely to have optimistic natures and some not. Does one reaction more than the other reveal a more profound understanding of human nature and the human situation? This question focuses nicely some major divisions among political philosophers.

In order to focus things, suppose, for the present, that we were to describe the systematic reliance needed as *cooperation*. Are human beings by nature promiscuous cooperators, limited cooperators, or not cooperators at all? Perhaps systems of rewards and punishments must be imposed upon persons to obtain their cooperation, so that, as Bentham said, each person in pursuit of his or her own good will be pursuing the good of all. But in that case sufficient cooperation will be needed somewhere else to give a possibility of the effective imposition of the sanctions in question.

SMR is not a framework for understanding all human associations underlying political community; otherwise it could be found deficient on two counts. (1) Much human association is not of the means-ends type, but the attraction is in the *activity* rather than any product of that activity; for example, much so-called "socializing." SMR sees political community as a goal-directed enterprise, but it very well may have originated in or been sustained by various pleasures and gratifications found in joint, coordinated activities for their own sakes. The interplay between pleasures in the products of various activities and the pleasures in the activities themselves is so pervasive in human life generally that it is doubtless to be found also in connection with political community. (2) The involvement of other persons is often essential rather than contingent. Consider the contrast between joining together to roll a log down to a river and joining together with others to enjoy the pleasure and profit of discussing something with them.

Thus, SMR would provide an extremely deficient framework for discussion if it were understood to provide an account either of why humans do or why they might reasonably form associations. Instead, it provides merely an opportune framework for understanding that portion of the rationale for human association underpinning the bulk of the development of modern political philosophy.

In addition, SMR, as so far developed, does not inescapably lead to nor is it inescapably led to by political community. We will discuss this matter further in a while. For the present, the idea that political community is not led to inescapably by SMR finds support in the fact that such reliance may appear in the lineage or tribal associations with which political associations are commonly contrasted. Though not an inescapable result of such reliance, political community is certainly an understandable result, as the following discussion tries to make clear. Concerning whether SMR is an inescapable result of political community, I shall leave that question to you to answer after you have had an opportunity to read the whole of the account presented in this book.

The subdivision of SMR given the most attention is, when intensified in certain ways, commonly called *division of labor,* because it is then based upon an apportionment and specialization of labor. The systematic reliance about which we are talking does not require but permits the separation and specialization of functions characteristic of the sociologists' use of *division of labor.*

Plato, who relies heavily on division of labor, saw it as enabling some further things. The fact that it permits and encourages specialization enables people to develop higher degrees of skill at tasks than they would otherwise be able to, and, if individual tasks are chosen with a view either to aptitude or tastes (how much do these overlap?), then these people may become very good at, or very happy or fulfilled with, what they do.

Intensified and highly structured coordination may thus benefit them in different ways. There is no necessary connection between the benefits of such intensive coordination and the benefits of political community, though political communities often (but not necessarily) make extensive use of such structuring of labor.

No effort is made here to establish Plato's view on this subject. Discussion of it is merely a useful way to introduce divergent understandings of the potential contribution made to human welfare by intensified coordination. Thorough exploration of that contribution potential is necessary if we are to conduct a serious evaluation of an aspiration that seems to play an important role in the appreciation of political community.

Plato's principal interest in the division of labor may very well have been in the possibility it provides for selecting and training each person for the job for which that person is best fitted. Further thought behind this depends upon how the crucial phrase "the job for which one is best fitted" is understood.

One understanding is: of all those from among whom we may select to do this job, this person is best fitted. But another understanding is: of all the jobs this person might be assigned, this job is the one for which the individual is best fitted. The first understanding puts emphasis upon utilizing the talents, aptitudes, and training of the available persons in the most efficient way. The second puts emphasis upon the way job assignments suit the particular talents and tastes of individuals. The first understanding views things from the standpoint of the needs of society, the second from the standpoint of the interests and talents of each individual person.

So far as I know, this difference has not been noted, but it is significant in that the different understandings produce different ideas of how intensified coordination contributes to human welfare. Enforcement of the first would contribute directly and certainly to the welfare of individuals through increased efficiency, skill, and reliability in the provision of needed goods and services for the whole society and therefore, unless tyranny intervened, for its members generally. Other contributions would be indirect, for example, if the task at which persons were better than anyone else were also the task they performed better than any other task, liked best, and the one at which they would be the most "fulfilled." But these further results would be contingent and could not be depended upon.

Enforcement of the second understanding would contribute to human welfare by precisely a reversal of these direct and contingent results. Just as enforcement of the first might dragoon persons into jobs the society needed but that gave them little personal satisfaction, so the second might attend so much to the needs of personal fulfillment that the needs of members of society generally would be slighted. Only if there is a coincidence of result in the enforcement of these two quite different understandings should one remain untroubled by the divergence between them.

SMR AND SCALE

The question for coordinators is not only when to cooperate, but what to do when cooperating. What to do will sometimes, but surely not always, be obvious. Differences in opinion about how to do it will also appear. The differences between highly general goals and the intermediate steps to be taken can themselves appear as differences concerning what is to be done. The likelihood of differences will be increased with enlargements of the scale of the various dependencies and reliances underwritten by the coordination as well as the other ways in which the persons involved are related to one another. If only close friends, close blood relatives, or even persons of exactly the same cultural heritages are involved, even if there are very many of them, one may suppose that there will be a greater reservoir of mutual understanding and even goodwill than might otherwise be the case. When persons are involved in the same scheme of coordination, who have known one another or known of one another's existence, are not related, and have little acculturation in common, little mutual understanding and even little goodwill can be reasonably depended upon.

We long ago have moved in many important matters to very large coordination schemes involving persons not otherwise closely related. It would be reasonable to expect differences of opinion about what is to be done and how to do it. To many social critics this obvious truth motivates advice that we all try to return to less ambitious projects and more primitive circumstances. For the cessation of reliance on mutual understanding alone, and the like, appears to carry with it, if coordination is to proceed, replacement with reliance on rules, regulations, and order-giving. Such marks of authority and power are unattractive to those critics, and they prefer that we avoid them, an attitude scrutinized carefully in this book, as these latter are characteristic features of political life.

Much hard and comprehensive thinking is needed for adequate consideration of whether we *can* move back to an earlier condition, and, if so, at what cost. Claims are common and plausible that nothing on the scale of modern human enterprises would be at all possible without rules, regulations, and order-giving. Even, however, if the claims were to be admitted, the desirability of the marks of government would not be definitely settled, because, while there clearly have been benefits resulting from these large enterprises, there also have been liabilities.

We must also consider that people may differ with one another on what ought to be counted as benefits and liabilities; and they are even more likely to differ on the weight accorded to each of the benefits and liabilities perceived. For example, most people value security. Hobbes, as is well known, valued security above the value placed on it by most persons. The high value he placed on it, as well as the likelihood of threats to it that he perceived in the common human situation, were of central importance in his political philosophy. The present scale of our enterprises has brought us abundant technological resources and complex organizations of markets, which, in turn, have brought us multitudes of goods and services that many persons are inclined to count as benefits. But it has also perhaps brought us to serious liabilities. The liabilities have been connected by many thinkers with the scale of enterprises—a scale so massive that abandonment of reliance upon mutual understanding for the needed coordination might be required. Perhaps we could usefully imagine further advances in technology or in education rendering that abandonment unnecessary.

Until that time, we should perhaps consider ourselves stuck with the need to consider what may be required to manage the rules, regulations, and order-giving apparently required by our exceedingly large systems of mutual dependence.

Try, then, to specify what "directive" functions will be needed to preserve systematic mutual dependencies in the absence of a capacity to rely upon mutual understanding and even perhaps mutual goodwill. An apparatus will be needed to determine what is to be done and how to do it, to communicate the results of these determinations to the persons who are to perform the tasks in question, and, most likely, to observe whether these tasks are done sufficiently well and in timely fashion, and to take steps to remedy the situation if they are not. The remedy may involve persuasion, coercion, reward, or something else. Your consideration of these ordinary options provides an occasion to consider carefully what remedies, in your view of human nature, would be most effective.

Nothing has yet been said about how the needed determinations are to be made, and in what style they are to be communicated to the persons performing the tasks in question. But enough has been said to suggest the general character of the foundations, according to common belief, of the supposed need for administering the coordination of modern human affairs. As we have seen, this need is not unalterable and is dependent throughout upon suppositions concerning human conditions, human desires, and so on, that might be otherwise. The name of the game is to consider the cost of altering these supposed conditions and what must *then* be supposed. These inquiries will expose important roots of political life in human nature and the human situation.

IDEALS AND UTOPIAS

Thinking about the costs and benefits, broadly speaking, of systematic mutual reliances, one may find that its impact on our ideals is mixed. Its crucial feature in this regard is that it makes persons dependent upon one another.

These dependencies, especially when other persons cannot be relied on, are not always blessings, but even apart from that we may justifiably have mixed feelings about them.

First, dependencies provide building stones for the warm feelings of cooperativeness and friendliness believed characteristic of *gemeinschaft* societies (intimate, traditional, informal, as contrasted with *gesellschaft* societies, which have impersonal or contractual relationships among members). Second, they create opportunities for specialization and thus development of talents and interests far beyond what would otherwise be possible. Third, they may consequently also bring about improvements in the quality of products and services and the reliability and efficiency of their provision.

On the other hand, while specialization is thought to provide important opportunities for self-development and excellence, it is also thought to narrow human beings, their capacities, and to render self-reliance unlikely if not impossible. We admire independence, associating it with strength, freedom, and breadth of development. We admire self-reliant persons with "all-round" talents and capacities.

The trouble is not merely with mutual self-reliance and the dependencies it creates. We cannot have it both ways. We cannot simultaneously uphold ideals of self-development involving finely-tuned development of one's special capacities and also uphold an ideal of all-round development of one's talents and capacities. Nor can we uphold *gemeinschaft* ideals in connection with the development of societies and at the same time uphold personal ideals of self-reliance and independence.

This reveals something important about attempts to develop improved and possibly even ideal societies. We are able to uphold conflicting ideals and not always realize that they conflict with one another. It is not surprising, then, that efforts both to improve societies and to render them ideal have gone astray. Such efforts have been singularly unimpressive to many students precisely because one cannot cater to both sets of ideals, and, in catering to one, are thought at best controversial because they do not cater to the other.

The task of the political philosopher at this point is not terribly clear. The philosopher may be inspired by the idea that these sets of ideals are not irremediably in conflict, or may concentrate instead upon determining which set of ideals we really want most and then jettisoning the other, or may simply accept the fact that we want both to be upheld and try to find some "balance" for our efforts to uphold both of them.*

Though doing so has several times gone in and out of fashion, political philosophers have often concerned themselves with depicting utopias. These utopias have often been depicted satirically, and only in order to condemn them, but we are interested presently in the straightforward depictions of them on which satires depend.

---

*Conflicts among ideals often present problems to political and social philosophers. A book published some time ago, Robert S. Lynd's *Knowledge for What?* contains abundant material for thought about conflicts among ideals in our culture. Concerning how to manage the conflicts, consider Brian Barry's *Political Argument,* which contains the suggestion that we use the economist's tool—Indifference Curves—as a means to manage rationally cases requiring that we "balance" ideals.

Plato, in the *Republic* (which is known as an early utopia), pointed out that even if that ideal society had no chance of being actualized, it would nevertheless provide a model to which reformers could look to check the relevance and direction of their efforts at reform. But in a later work, *The Laws*, Plato (and Aristotle is known for saying this also) suggested that things might not be so simple. What would be ideal when conditions were as favorable as possible might be quite different from what would be ideal if conditions were not so favorable. Even as early as the *Statesman* (an earlier work than *The Laws* but later than the *Republic*), Plato recognized that reasonable recommendations in nonideal circumstances might be quite different from recommendations in ideal ones. If, for example, the rulers of a community had extremely high qualifications of intellect and character, a form of government could be proposed that would be unsafe and counterproductive if the character or intellect of the rulers were not so fine.

This raises a major evaluative problem about what is so ideal about ideal societies. Without even considering efforts to *create* such societies, one could observe that efforts to *depict* them have produced disappointing results. Surely there are differing reasons for this.

For one thing, people may find different goals attractive or unattractive. But people may also make different estimates of what is possible and what is not. The complex implications of the latter point have not always been recognized. Depictors of utopias have done their work constrained by their own beliefs about (1) what can be reasonably imagined alterable about human natures and environments, and (2) what technological resources would be available to manage and/or produce the alterations. What are the effects of these beliefs on utopia depictions?

In depicting what would be best, it is a matter for careful judgment just how favorable (and in what particulars) one may imagine circumstances to be. Unless one is going to take the view Plato took in the *Republic* and apparently later abandoned, one doesn't wish to stray too far from the conditions within which practical efforts to improve societies must work. Also, the characters, environments, and histories of various people create either opportunities for or limitations on efforts at reform. Aristotle believed this firmly. He thought people and communities differently located might require different treatments.

Underlying Aristotle's analysis are various assumptions about what alterations in circumstances can reasonably be imagined. Almost every utopian treats some things as fixed and others as alterable, supposing the former if only because we are talking about ideal societies of *humans* in *this* world. Furthermore, depictors may expect that where they draw the line between the alterable and the fixed will let them in for the charge either that they are "unrealistic," on the one hand, or that they "lack vision," on the other.

But what may we consider fixed about human nature and environment? John Dewey warns us that many unattractive features of plans for utopian reform have been mistakenly labeled "inevitable" results of "inescapable" features of human nature or the human situation. So-called instincts for property and war are Dewey's examples of the first.

Claims about what is inevitable should be made cautiously, but we would be foolish to conclude that they ought never to be made. Claims about "permanent" features of human nature and environment are currently unpopular, but some unattractive features of utopias may reflect features of human nature or the human situation that for all practical purposes may be considered inevitable. They would therefore constitute important "permanent" characteristics of political communities, and an account that ignored them would be thereby defective. What would need to be justified, then, is not these features, but their presence in the account. They are in that account because without them it would be defective because unrealistic.

Suppose, to carry the matter further and in a somewhat different direction, our knowledge of the world and our technological capacities to change it are more or less increasing, so that the line between what is fixed and what is alterable about human natures and environments will be correctly drawn differently at different times in history. Therefore, it may be important to notice when the ideal society was put forward. The time may make a difference not only in where the line between fixed and alterable is drawn, but also in conceptions of possible solutions, resolutions, and how to avoid various problems.

Fairness in criticism of depictors of utopias therefore requires two distinct considerations: (1) would the states of knowledge and technology of the depictors' times reasonably lead them to draw the line between the alterable and the fixed about human beings and their environments differently from now? and (2) given the changes in question, would the resources of knowledge and technology that depictors could reasonably imagine available to members of the utopia be significantly different in any particularly important way from now?

We should be prepared, but not too ready, to suppose that there have been advances in our knowledge significant to judging the depictions by sophisticated philosophers such as Plato of what societies would be ideal. For example, "we" probably know considerably more about genetic theory than anyone in Plato's time. Plato was, however, highly interested in the potential of selective breeding, and quite familiar with it in connection with horses. Should we now suppose in light of "our" improved knowledge that Plato needs to be "corrected" in any significant respect?

Again, given the striking advances in the technology of agricultural production, weaponry, weapon delivery, and defense systems, one might think it important to examine carefully Plato's apparent assumptions concerning the importance of division of labor to reliable and timely provision of agricultural and defense needs. It was apparently common in Plato's time for external enemies to attack at times of sowing or harvesting, thus creating a dilemma for those under attack: should they rush to defend their borders or perform the needed agricultural activities? We may not be utterly clear about whether our technological advances have rendered such questions less important than they once were, but the issue seems worth considering and would produce further insight into the problems to be faced in evaluating ideal societies.

We have as yet given no attention to changes that might be made in persons, who are raw materials out of which reconstructed societies are to be built. Many reformers depict societies whose members are improved, sometimes vastly improved, over what we are. Indeed, the reformers are often occupied, as was Plato, with programs of education and even genetic manipulation to improve us. This raises important questions about not only the goals and feasibility of the society, but also about the right of anyone to "reform" persons in the ways proposed.

When we share the goals it may be difficult to keep the importance of this last point in mind. We may be willing to condone it, calling it *education*. But when we do not share the goals we may be inclined to call it *propagandizing*. The right of reformers to "educate" seems much less a point of contention than their right to "propagandize."

The rights of reformers to attempt to alter dispositions, temperaments, or the "nature" of humans may raise exceedingly complex issues, but the apparent complexity may be much reduced if we recognize that the fundamental question we should ask ourselves, as John Dewey correctly said, is not *whether* persons are going to be infuenced by their environment, but *how* (both the model and the technique of achieving the model, or achieving an approximation thereof) they are going to be influenced. Therefore we need not face the question of whether anyone has a right to influence persons *at all*. We need merely to raise the question of whether anyone has a right to influence them *in the particular way proposed*. This makes our task of evaluation somewhat easier, and more sensible.

One's right to do what is proposed depends not only on the acceptability of the goal but also on the way and by whom it is to be effected. Here questions about the justifiability of what is proposed turn into questions about the legitimacy of what is to be done. It is important for us to see now how the issue arises in the present context.

The acceptability of a utopian vision might be thought increased by the degree to which that vision could coexist in the same society with others. Many differences in utopian visions are known to result from differences among persons' tastes, interests, and beliefs. If we believe that these latter differences should be permitted and maybe even fostered, we may think it an important characteristic of any utopian vision that it be compatible with other utopian visions.

But whether tastes, and the like, can be reconciled depends at least upon what these differences are. Some utopian visions could send persons in sharply different directions demanding nevertheless from each great tolerance of other aspirations and life styles, but other visions could send persons in less sharply differing directions though demanding that everyone conform to the directions set. The former visions might more easily coexist than the latter, though other features of them might change this picture.

Indeed, whether toleration of other visions is a desirable characteristic of a utopia will depend upon what one's own utopian vision is and upon one's beliefs about other utopian visions. If one believes that living in the other "utopias" would condemn persons to eternal damnation, remediable injustice, or avoidable degraded and unhappy existences, one will hardly have a very strong or enthusiastic belief that they should be tolerated.

Certain degrees of flexibility on various matters may be stipulated features of particular utopias, but complaints are nevertheless made that the utopias are too rigid. However, Plato pointed out if a society is perfect, then any change *of* it (though not necessarily any change *in* it) must be for the worse. One might reasonably expect, therefore, at least some basic features of the society to be fixed and rigid.

But there is another interesting source of complaint about the rigidity of utopias. Utopias are efforts to answer supremely well to human interests in taking advantage of opportunities provided by the contiguity of humans and avoiding the threats presented by that same contiguity. The opportunities and threats are identified by reference to the needs and desires, temperaments and proclivities of human beings. The working assumption of many writers has been that a clear and univocal account of these is possible. But this working assumption may very well be false, a fundamentally important fact about attempts at utopia-building more fully recognized by novelists than by philosophers. Human natures, individually considered, are often the scene of contending, if not warring, proclivities and desires. When this has been recognized by planners of ideal societies, it has generally been regarded as at least an inconvenience if not an obstacle to their efforts at social planning.

A happy and well-formed person, a good citizen of an ideal community, would have harmonious proclivities and desires. In the view of the planners, this result could be accomplished through programs of education or law. Extinguished or controlled proclivities and desires would be identified as undesirable, immoral, antisocial, self-frustrating, and so on. But lives in which these disharmonies have been eliminated seem relatively meager and impoverished. In the view of many people, no life can answer to the richness promised in human nature if these disharmonies are suppressed. That persons might have some elements of their inharmonious natures suppressed is considered "rigid" and dreadful by some, and necessary to a decent and happy life by others.

Adding fuel to the fire of this particular controversy is an empirical question concerning the possibility of either extinguishing or controlling unwanted proclivities. This empirical question may be added to the valuational issues embedded in the controversy. On the whole, utopia-builders have accepted the internal harmonizing of individual human nature as something both possible and desirable. On the other hand, persons thinking such harmonizing either impossible, undesirable, or both have not been much attracted to utopian visions.

There is one further thing about responsible criticisms of utopias. If, after exercising your best judgment on the preceding questions, there is still a feature of the utopia you are considering that you do not like and that you believe could be removed, your problem is to show that it *can* be removed without producing in its stead something as bad or worse. That is, it is not enough to say merely, "I don't like that," but you must also argue that this undesirable feature is avoidable at a reasonable cost. Imposition of this requirement upon responsible criticism of utopias is a consequence too often overlooked, especially since utopian visions generally do not purport to offer people "pie in the sky," but instead to offer us a vision of the best that can be made of the human condition.

THREE

The State

Political philosophers inquire into and dispute about what the essential or defining features of states are, and so on. They also distinguish between what states are and what they ought to be, and inquire into and dispute about the latter, and about what states ought to aim at, given what they are and what they ought to be.

Before presenting skeptical arguments about the irreproachable value of this concentration on the state, this chapter will consider it straightforwardly. For example, what gives these philosophers assurance that they are thinking and talking about the same thing? When some political philosophers say that states are nothing but collections of individuals organized in certain ways, and others say that states are organic unities different from and more than the sum of the individual persons who are their members or citizens, what gives us (and them) assurance that they are talking about the same thing and thus (perhaps) disagreeing with one another? The answer is that they and we believe (justifiably) that they do or can agree with one another in at least some cases on what are and are not states. Without the prospect of such agreement, we might as well assume that, despite appearances, there is no common focus to their claims, that they may simply be talking about different things, and thus that there may be no disagreement between them.

We now shall survey briefly some principal claims philosophers have made about states. Our discussion recognizes the centrality of the five following questions: (1) Which things are states? (2) What features determine whether or not something is a state? (3) What legitimates or justifies efforts to bring states into being or to continue their existence? (4) What ought states to aim at achieving? (5) What are the best ways for states to be structured or organized?

There is some strain in using these questions to organize our discussion strictly. This is largely because political philosophers in the past have not, to my knowledge, used them to organize their discussions, and we cannot always be clear about whether they were attempting to answer one or another of these questions. The questions will be used here, however, to try to understand what these philosophers have said.

WHICH THINGS ARE STATES?

By and large, political philosophers have not differed much on which things are states and which things are not. The reason for this is clear. The question of which things are states has been settled through modern international usage, independently of the work of political philosophers, by what other states recognize or fail to recognize as states.

There is nothing viciously circular about this. It is as though a number of families were to organize a social register, put themselves on it, and from that prominence decide among themselves which other families were to be on it. If the initial families had power and influence, they, as well as other families, might come to attach importance to whether or not a family was on the social register. Given this history of the matter, we might subsequently find serious arguments and discussions about which families in the communities were *worthy* of being on the social register. The criteria of social-register-worthiness would have to be such as to account for most of the families already on the register and for most of the families subsequently admitted to it.

Given that there are some things everyone recognizes as states, what further is to be recognized as a state is settled by what the agreed-upon states themselves further recognize as a state. Political philosophers have by and large been guided by whatever this practice has produced, and it does not exclude the possibility of controversial cases.

Agreed-upon states may fail to act perfectly in concert, and there may be interesting disagreements about which things ought or ought not to be recognized as states; for example, the barbary pirates, large nomadic tribes not under the domain of an already recognized state, the European Economic Community (give or take a few further "small" developments), the nation members of the EEC (give or take the same developments).

Differences in these controversial cases are derivative rather than fundamental. Disputants do not start with differing views about which things are states, but rather arrive at them because of differing reflections on agreed-upon cases. The basic class of agreed-upon cases grows as a direct result of agreed-upon states recognizing other things as states (see Haskell Fain, "The Idea of the State"). No one who fails to understand the dynamics of that recognition, why it occurs or fails to occur, can reasonably hope to offer a sound account of what counts toward something's being a state, what the nature of states is, and what the essence of being a state is—an account that will at least accommodate a gradually growing list of things that are states.

An account that fails in such accommodation may not be utterly useless or lacking in interest, but it may—unless its point is recast—increasingly seem to lack contact with the real world. The challenge to political philosophers is either to find, from the viewpoint of their characteristic concerns, an account of the nature of states that encompasses and underwrites the pattern of international recognition and explores the dynamics and rationale of such recognition, or to risk losing contact with the world of practical affairs.

THE NATURE OF THE STATE

Political philosophers have written voluminously about the nature and essence of the state, and about what counts toward something's being a state. These are among the major topics in the discipline. Differences in treatments of them account for the distinctive features of some of the main schools or traditions in the history of the field. Hobbesians and Hegelians divide importantly on these issues, giving us, respectively, varieties of individualist and organicist "theories" of the state. Marxists and anarchists each offer yet other views of the essential features of states, though views sympathetic to each other at some points. And pluralists may offer yet different views in the course of their attempts to articulate the place of states among other institutions of social and economic life.

George Sabine notes that the modern use of the term *state* to mean more or less the body politic first appeared in Italy (from the Italian *stato*) in the sixteenth century, probably because of Machiavelli. The term, as already indicated, can be considered a technical one of international law, or, in accordance with the usage of some political scientists, as signifying any politically autonomous community whatever. It has, however, a certain historical peculiarity, and we will presently try to identify that.

We will find the rationale for the predominant views of the characteristics of states in an effort to distinguish states from (1) principalities, duchies, and grand duchies, and other petty territories too small to receive the full dignity of the designation *state;* (2) empires, these being too large to fit comfortably under the designation; (3) tribes and clans organized along blood lines; (4) communities personally ruled (the statement "l'état, c'est moi" makes sense only because we all recognize that the king was not pretending that he did without an assisting government); and (5) estates or corporate societies in which the society is regulated exclusively through traditional or intermediary institutions, not, as with modern states, directly by the state.

It is precisely here, in connection with these five contrasts, that we will find the sources of the temporal and cultural partialities attaching to *state*. It is not that none of them attaches to the alternative terms that have been prominent in political philosophy, but that all five together have not previously attached to any of the terms.

(1) *How small can states be?* If the free city of Dantzig, the city-states (*poleis*) of ancient Greece, and the hometowns (*Kleinstadten*) of seventeenth- and eighteenth-century Germany were all designated states without qualification,

it would merely indicate that the term *state* was being overextended. Widespread unease would probably be produced by such unqualified designation. What considerations would underlie this probable unease?

Apart from the working of contingent considerations of political history, there are the following three related theoretical considerations. (a) The word *state* supplies a certain dignity and standing on the international scene. Political communities of this small size do not, especially at present, seem to many people to be worthy of the dignity or standing presumptively bestowed by the term. (b) Such political communities are in the modern world pygmies among giants relative to the other political communities more comfortably called *states*. Given modern armament and defense systems, their sovereigns are consequently notably far from having that capacity emphasized by Hobbes as necessary for the existence of a commonwealth: that the sovereign have the power to protect the citizens of the commonwealth from external enemies. It is true, of course, that the rulers of small political communities currently freely called *states* also lack that capacity. But the conditions we are discussing are not necessarily sufficient for denial of the title *state;* they may merely give some reason to deny the title. (c) Such small communities notably lack the capacity to provide from within their borders the goods and services needed for their members to have a capacity to live well. Of course, as we have noted earlier, Aristotle believed that even the city-states of ancient Greece needed external trade in order to have the self-sufficiency he thought necessary to political community. Many large modern states depend heavily upon importation of needed goods for their survival. The impact of the dependence upon our issue hinges upon how widespread and how heavy it is. As with many issues in intellectual life, one should expect no firm boundaries concerning how much is enough, though there will be clear cases of enough or not enough.

(2) *How large can states be?* Some writers—Willoughby, for example—believe that states must form societies and not be mere aggregations of humans—a conclusion that we also would expect to accept if we regard states as political communities. This suggests a rationale for the distinction between states and empires.

Empires are paradigmatically though not exclusively political, and are most broadly characterized as extensive enterprises operating under a unified authority. They may be extensive geographically or demographically, so that their subjection to a unified political authority is unlikely to be accompanied by any other unity, for example, of language, literature, lengthy common history, or political culture. Lacking very many of the latter unities, and perhaps not having any of them at all, the empire as a whole may be difficult to see as *a* society.

It will very likely encompass several distinguishable societies, and perhaps some or all of them will be states, including the central, organizing, and superior political authority of the empire—as in the case of Great Britain in the British empire of the late nineteenth century. The absent unities may owe their absence to geographical, historical, or technological considerations, or simply lack of intention on the part of the power organizing the empires to unify. The likelihood of such conditions is increased by size, and that is doubtless why contrast between states and empires has been connected to consider-ations of size.

There are some modern states, of course, so large and internally diverse as to put this hypothesis to a test—such as the USSR, China, and India, for size and diversity, and the United States of America, which adds geographical dis-continuity as well. While, however, we do presently recognize these unhesitatingly as states, some writers still wonder at the appropriateness of this recognition. In the case of the United States, one might note that the in-corporation of distant lands into the state has been quite recent, and occurred at a time when technology made communication nearly effortless, even at such a distance.

Sensitivity to some of these same issues may underlie the widespread opin-ion that the concept of a world-state is defective—though here the defect may amount to incoherence resulting from the fact that status as a state is depend-ent upon recognition by other states, which could not be forthcoming if there *were* no other states.

The upper limits on the size of aggregations of persons and territories eli-gible to be political communities depend both upon the natures of human be-ings and the technologies available to them. But the limits depend also upon the natures and intensities of the patterns of mutual responsiveness and coordination required in political communities. In the Greek city-state these patterns were relatively intensive and pervasive. In the Alexandrian empire they were considerably less intensive and pervasive, again necessarily due, at least to some degree, to geographical discontinuity. The former were surely political communities, but the status of the latter might be challenged.

One must be careful not to jumble what is required to be a political commu-nity and what is desirable for it. Hopes or expectations that the relations of people to one another will achieve certain degrees of intensity and pervasiveness may all too readily get expressed as requirements concerning what can be a political community. Apart from such hopes and expectations, the ranges of acceptable intensities and pervasiveness may be quite wide. How wide? And what considerations ought to be counted relevant in determining how wide?

Here the other requirements for political community play a role, for they are joint requirements and should not be considered separately. The task of answering these questions is, however, premature, since they require us to draw on many of the topics discussed in this book. At many junctures, indeed, our interests and preferences will present us with options.

(3) The preceding chapters on political community have already discussed the rationale for refusing to count tribes and clans organized along blood lines as political communities. If these aggregations are not political communities, it follows that they are not states.

(4) It is generally thought a characteristic of modern states that they are not personally ruled. Each makes use of a governmental apparatus whose admin-istrators, though perhaps appointed by a person who is the supreme ruler, are not considered merely the personal representatives of that ruler. Indeed, the modern distinction between the person of the ruler and his or her office sup-ports the same point. The point is probably connected to developments in our

ideas of legitimacy and sovereignty, and will be discussed extensively in Part II. If we are going to remain sensitive to the nuances of the word *state* in modern times, we should not forget that many kingships of the past have not fully and clearly satisfied this condition of modern states.

(5) Another feature of modern states is that they do not attempt to administer their relations with citizens exclusively through intermediary bodies, such as did the states of prerevolutionary France. This development has altered our understanding of what a citizen is and will be discussed in Part III. Citizens of modern states are regulated in some respects, at least, directly by the state, and not by traditional or intermediary institutions, as was generally the case in the predecessor political communities.

These five contrasts, then, expose important features of the historical peculiarity attaching to the modern use of the word *state*. They consequently also expose some of the ways assumptions that states are the basic units of political community may prejudice political philosophy.

WHAT OUGHT STATES TO BE?

Discussions of the essence or nature of states are often extremely difficult to distinguish from discussions of what states ought to be. The difficulty arises from a tendency deeply embedded in Western thought and appearing in many fields besides political philosophy, namely, the realization that the clearest examples of a kind of thing are examples of a good one of its kind— that is, one that is what it ought to be. Thus, we are tempted to smuggle features of a state that it has just because it is a good state into the list of defining characteristics it must have to be a state at all. In any case, discussion of what states ought to be has occupied a major portion of the history of political philosophy, and it has had two principal focuses: (1) What is required for the powers and activities of states to be legitimate or justifiable? and (2) Which forms of the internal organization of states are to be preferred?

These questions have sometimes been telescoped into each other in such a way that they have been difficult to sort out, and the first question has been conflated with the additional issue of what is required for there to be genuine states (for which see the immediately preceding section). Given these cautionary remarks, one may, though not without risk, say that most every major school or tradition in the history of the field has occupied itself in a central way with providing answers to the first of the two preceding questions. Both it and the second will be considered at length in Part II.

WHAT OUGHT STATES TO AIM AT?

There is substantial overlap in many accounts of what the state, law, and government, respectively, ought to aim at, but there seems little or no danger of any resulting consequential confusion. Each of the inquiries encourages us to see the institution in question instrumentally, and to ask to what ends it might usefully and appropriately be directed. It would not be unreasonable to think that the main aims for the state, law, and government might be the same or nearly the same. The overlap is substantial, even if not complete.

One might hold that states ought to aim at producing the greatest happiness for the greatest number of their citizens, for all persons, or for all sentient creatures, or at least that states ought to aim at making some specific and constrained contribution to that end. The utilitarians, who tend to talk more about the proper aims of law and government than about the proper aims of states, may be understood to take such a position if one supposes them willing to regard the proper aims of government and states as the same thing, and to view government as acting principally through the promulgations and enforcements of law.

Utilitarians, however, divide on the means to the utilitarian ends in question—for instance, on whether to advocate welfare or laissez-faire states. Generally, they do not believe that states ought to assume sole responsibility for *producing* the greatest happiness, and the like. Seeing states (law, government) acting principally and characteristically by means of general rules, effective because backed by systems of coercion (see Chapter Five), they recognize limits on the capacity of such means to contribute to maximizing general happiness. They think states ought to aim at maximizing general happiness only when both the costs and effectiveness of doing so have been computed.

Not surprisingly, they differ with one another on how these means may be used, and in their estimates of the effectiveness and costs of using them. These differences produce the differences among utilitarians previously noted. Some, such as J. S. Mill, believe that the contribution of states to happiness ought, out of consideration of effectiveness and cost, to be limited to preventing persons from harming other persons, and thus he advocated something like a laissez-faire state. Others—for example, some modern welfare economists—estimate effectiveness and costs differently, and advocate types of welfare states.

Another major orientation is associated with Kant, who rejects the idea that the state ought to aim in any way at producing happiness. His view is that the coercion-backed law through which states characteristically act is an inappropriate instrument for contributing usefully to happiness, given that the material and personal conditions essential to happiness for different persons are so diverse. According to Kant, the proper aim of states, and the laws through which they act, is to create conditions under which all persons (citizens? see Part III) will have as much freedom as is compatible with a like amount of freedom for all other persons (citizens).

Kant saw freedom as essential to each person's development and dignity as a person, and as each person's right. He also held that the proper aim of states is to protect that right as right—that is, simply because it is a right and protection of it is thus right, and not because doing so will contribute to anybody's happiness. This account, because of its focus on the equal distribution of a (basic) right, supports and draws support from the view that states ought to aim at producing and maintaining the reign of justice in the world.

As with utilitarians, political philosophers accepting the basics of this Kantian position divide on whether to advocate welfare or laissez-faire states. Among Kantians (in this broad sense), welfare states are advocated, when advocated, not because they contribute to the fullness of human happiness, but rather because they contribute to raising economically depressed people to an economic level by providing the minimum help, nutrition, and so on, necessary for human dignity and the development of distinctive human capacities. And laissez-faire states are advocated not because they can make especially adroit though limited contributions to general happiness, but because they can protect people's rights and are thereby essential to personal development and dignity.

The Kantians making these different advocacies are separated from one another by differing views on what human dignity and distinctively human capacities are, on what is necessary for their development, and on the dependence of this development on economic conditions and prospects.

Utilitarianism and Kantianism together provide an organizational framework sufficient for understanding most modern positions on what states ought to aim at. One often finds a mix of various utilitarian and Kantian elements that may usefully be examined separately. But appeals of other sorts have also been made in our cultural and intellectual histories and have left their mark on us.

For example, there are theologically oriented views that states ought to aim at promoting eternal salvation for all mankind, and historicist views of widely different sorts that states ought to express, in ways varying with the times and places of their existence, the forward movement or culmination of long and perhaps inevitable historical processes. The former sort of view is associated, for example, with Calvin and the Spanish Inquisition; the latter sort primarily with Hegel and Marx.

The principal state-types advocated as ones toward which we ought reasonably to aim are usefully understood also in terms of the distinction between laissez-faire and welfare states. Again, recommendations may involve elements from both types. And again, there are other views that have left their marks on our thinking; for example, the fascist corporate state, which is certainly not a laissez-faire state in any respect and can hardly be called a welfare state either; and the views of Plato and Aristotle, which are seriously distorted if analyzed solely through use of the distinction between laissez-faire and welfare states.

SKEPTICISM ABOUT THE STATE

In modern times the state has commonly been thought the fundamental unit of political organization. At the very least, philosophers have treated it as the principal locus of important problems of political philosophy. Some reasons for this prominence are easy to see. For most regions of the earth's surface in modern times supreme formal political authority has been wielded in the name of one state or another. Most other units of political organization are either formally subordinate to, instrumentalities of, or even parasitic upon the authority of this one, or they lack the systematic coercive backing characteristic of it. States also appear as gray eminences in our political life, seeming to stand behind and support all else.

The intimate connection between states and human law (discussed in Part II), and the belief that states are the legally autonomous and supreme units of legal organization underwriting all remaining phenomena of human law, both support the view that states are the fundamental units of political organization. We shall, however, find reasons to question this belief.

To say of the state that it is the fundamental unit of political organization is not to say that it is the building block out of which other units are constructed. Cities, commonly, and counties, always, are units of political organization, and they clearly do not have states as constituent parts; it would be more plausible to say the reverse. Indeed, in cases where one might say states are constituent parts of other political organizations, political philosophers declare resolutely that these are not the sorts of states they are talking about. Examples would be the states of the Union of Soviet Socialist Republics and the United States of America, though not the member states of the European Economic Community or of the North Atlantic Treaty Organization (the relevance of the last two depending on whether they are units of political organization or instead units of economic and military organization respectively).

The claim rather seems to be that the state as the fundamental unit is either (a) our most fully representative and central case of what it is to be politically organized, (b) the culminating development and fullest realization of political organization, or (c) something whose existence is a necessary condition for the existence of any clear case of political organization whatever (and also a sufficient condition for the existence of at least one political organization; namely, itself).

No one of these three is likely to be true of the state, but if any one were to be true, its truth might well justify the preeminence given in political philosophy to it. Even if it were true, one would not need to make the state the centerpiece of political philosophy. One might instead argue that the ideas of government, human law, the adjective *political,* or the ideas of authority and sovereignty could all be reasonably given equal or superior prominence in the analysis of the phenomena. Each of these, for example, could provide a starting point for understanding the topic range of political philosophies in contrast to the topic ranges of other fields of philosophy. The merits of each would lie not only in the economy and comprehensiveness of accounts based on it, but also in such elusive achievements as being illuminating or helpful or affording insight. These reduce to matters of how each starting place collects its data, which data it collects, the basis on which it collects them, and how each fits into what we (currently) need to know and be reminded of.

The decision to start with and give a central role to the state, as most political philosophers currently do, is thus discretionary (not arbitrary); there are other possibly rewarding ways of proceeding. One makes a kind of wager that this will be a helpful way of proceeding and as good a way as any, though perhaps with a different set of strengths and weaknesses. Numerous examples of other ways of proceeding are available and many of them are useful supplements to works in the style that currently predominates.

In addition to this, there is a difficulty attaching to the assignment of such a key role to the state. Political philosophers, throughout the history of their work, have variously identified the fundamental unit of political organization as the state, the commonwealth, civil society, the *polis,* the polity, the body politic, and so forth. In the eyes of many, these expressions are terms of the art of political philosophy. They are thus seen as merely alternative ways of referring to the same highly abstract thing; namely, something that can roughly be characterized as what would be left standing if any arbitrarily chosen politically autonomous unit of political organization were stripped of all the features attaching to it in virtue of its setting in time and place, leaving only those features that make it, or are consequences of its being, a politically autonomous unit of political organization.

Despite efforts of political philosophers to neutralize the various ways of referring to the "fundamental unit" by rendering them all into terms of art meaning the same thing, we should consider whether each contributes its own peculiar flavor and import into the discussion. Each, at least when used in modern times, gives to the discussion an air of modernity, quaintness, or esoteric technicality that, for good or ill, focuses our attention on the phenomena somewhat differently. If this is so to any significant degree, then relying on one of these expressions alone introduces temporal cultural partialities into the discussion. These expressions have histories outside their uses in political philosophy, and some are terms of art elsewhere. These careers cling to them.

For example, when the *poleis* of ancient Greece are labeled *city-states* by modern translators of Greek texts, and ancient discussions of these units of political organization (such as Plato's *Republic*) are arrayed alongside discussions of modern states by Hegel and Mussolini as presentations of differing views concerning the nature and ideal condition of one and the same unit of political organization—namely, the state—we may feel that a dubious attempt is being made either to divest the notion of the state of its modernity (that is, its association with the technological and ideological accoutrements and aspirations of the modern world) or to divest the *polis* of its antiquity, something in any case psychologically difficult if not impossible.

It would be better to mark the differences in scale, condition, and potential between the political communities of Athens and Sparta of the fifth century B.C. and those of Italy or Russia of the twentieth century A.D. by open recognition that they embody radically different conceptions of the groupings on which political organization can or ought to be based and on the aims of these groupings, and not different views on the fundamental nature, potential, and aims of the same or even similar groupings.

Something important about the discipline of political philosophy emerges from this discussion. The idea of the state, along with many other key notions relied upon in this field to describe the phenomena and articulate the problems, is subject to strains and stresses produced by the vicissitudes of human experience. Political philosophers aim to focus our attention upon certain aspects of broad ranges of social experience as these aspects occur, recur, and persist over widely different temporal, cultural, environmental, and technological conditions. They are seeking to bring into focus, reflect upon, and assess what explains and what justifies certain persisting or recurring features of that experience. They thus seek to develop ideas general enough to encompass large chunks of that experience—for the sake of economy of thought and the reduction of such vast expanses to something within our capacity to grasp—and yet still specific enough to be useful in focusing our attention on aspects of that experience. The idea of the state is one such idea.

But though this idea itself has influenced the course of human history by influencing how the phenomena have been perceived and thus what has been done about them, it has not and will not control that history. History (for instance, the history of international relations) constantly threatens to outrun it by producing forms of social and political life and organization that render the idea of the state otiose or lessen its importance because that idea no longer picks out the important or the only important and fundamental units of political organization.

Political philosophers may respond to such events by eventually jettisoning the idea except perhaps for its enshrinement as a relic of history. But another likely response is to rethink the idea with the hope of modifying and expanding it to accommodate the newly important phenomena, something we have already said is not likely to be fully successful. Why take the trouble in any case? There are two main motivations for doing so. First, we may wish to emphasize the continuity between the concerns of past thinkers and our own concerns. This can be achieved—though, as we have noticed, at a risk of underemphasizing the discontinuities—through a kind of terminological (or ideational) conservatism that favors stability in our basic stocks of descriptive and evaluative categories. We thus may prefer stretching old categories to fit new facts, instead of repeatedly and disquietingly abandoning old categories in favor of new ones. Secondly, and supplementarily, in seeing these ideas as instruments for focusing and trying to cope with certain persisting concerns, we seek by this conservatism of terms and ideas to keep these concerns in view.

Because the state has been the focus of so much attention in modern political philosophy, and because the state is after all an important political community, many of the principal issues of political philosophy can be discussed as attempts to answer the questions serving as headings for the first few sections of this chapter. We should remember, however, the reasons brought forward in the later parts of the chapter for why we should not try to stuff *all* the issues of political philosophy into this mold. The distortions of history, culture, and aspiration likely to result from such confinement of perspective are too various to be simply sketched. They range from misperceiving our histories and potentials, to grappling with pseudoproblems, and neglecting significant features of human experience.

FOUR

Nations and Nationalism: Ideological Foundations

There is a use of *nation* in which it is roughly synonymous with understandings of *state*. This use is supported by the use of *international* law to refer to law intended to govern the relations among states and between states and their "nationals." It is also supported by talk about the member states of the United Nations and its predecessor organization, the League of Nations.

If these were the only uses of *nation*, a separate chapter with the heading of the present one would not be needed. But there is another use of *nation* that has been highly politically significant and controversial, especially during the past two centuries, as it gives interesting meaning to two intensely popular ideas of that period. The ideas are that (1) every nation should be a state and the companion idea that (2) every state should consist of one and only one nation. The first of these ideas is by far the most popular and the most explicitly expressed, but the second has also had its day. Together they are important, though not the only, constituent ideas of nationalism. (Other occasional constituents are the idea that one's nation's demands have absolute priority over every other demand made on one, and *its* companion idea that unlimited aggrandizement of one's own nation is appropriate.) This chapter consists of an exploration of the pair of ideas (1) and (2).

NATIONS AND NATIONALISM

The general understanding of *nation* undergirding that pair of ideas also supports the conventional labeling of certain items in the contemporary world as *nation-states,* and thus has links with the uses of *nation* first mentioned here. Nation-states could be distinguished clearly from earlier items in the politica

46

aviary such as city-states and feudal-states when states became ideologically tied to an item called the *nation*. But what is the nation?

Debate on this topic has been widespread from the start of the tie-in. Things known as nations have been identified as early as ancient Israel. Substantial consensus on the existence and importance of nations in Western Europe, however, was not reached by historians for any period earlier than the last half of the nineteenth century, though many commentators think they were important somewhat earlier. In that century many people (Europeans in particular) came to believe that each nationality should form a state and that the state should include the whole nationality and perhaps even only that nationality.

These ideals were not often, if ever, achieved then or now (and may, as we shall see, not even be achievable). For one thing, nationality is not easily identified. There is, of course, an understanding of *nationality* in which it means the same as citizenship in the country that does or would issue one's passport. So understood, it is a term of art, the art of international law.

This is not, however, an understanding that would make our pair of constituent ideas of nationalism interesting. For this we need an understanding of *nation* as something that exists independently of the political entities that do such things as issue passports, and by reference to which the appropriateness of the scope of these political entities can be judged.*

Common genetic heritage, language, customs, religions or traditions, and territorial integrity or determinateness have all been suggested individually as criteria for the individuation and individuality of nationality so understood. But none of these quite seems necessary or sufficient, at least if one accepts the ordinary understanding of what things count as nations.

The criteria do not seem necessary because, for example, the United States of America is agreed to be a nation, but its citizens lack a common genetic heritage. The Swiss lack a common language. Lack of territorial integrity or determinateness has not been considered an obstacle to the nationalist claims of advocates of pan-Asian, pan-German, pan-Arabic, or pan-whatever movements. The United States of America early on made a big thing of denying that common customs, religions, or traditions were necessary for their nation, at least at the start: America was a "melting pot." (Of course there was a "pot," consisting at least of common customs, into which immigrants were received. See later in the chapter for more discussion of the point.)

Nor have any of these conditions just mentioned or any others put forward been sufficient. Common descent was claimed by Hitler as a sufficient reason for regarding many persons German whom the world has persisted in regarding as nationals of other nations—for instance, Austria, Czechoslovakia, France, and Poland. Great Britain, Canada, and Australia are all English-speaking nations, but their unity of language does not make them a single nation. There is likewise no particular territorial integrity or determinateness providing grounds for distinguishing between Canada and the United States,

---

*The appearance earlier of the word *country* is worth noting. The term's virtue is that it is neutral between *nation* and *states* and does not commit us to the overinflated understanding of *state* that would lead one to say that only states issue passports.

or between Spain and Portugal, and so on. The customs and traditions of various Germans differ more from one another than the customs and traditions of many Germans differ from those of many Austrians. Spaniards and Italians have the same religion but are different nations. And so on.

One may take the heroic measure of denying that various "countries" are nations, while agreeing that they are states. But no one I know of has yet proposed that, though some commentators are inclined on occasion to deny that some of the countries listed here are nations.

We are not denying that the satisfaction of some large accumulation of these conditions may be sufficient for nationhood, though perhaps we could. They all seem relevant to establishing the existence of some sort of cultural unity, and this is the (very vague) sense in which nations are discussed in this chapter in relation to nationalism. *Is* anything else needed? Would full nationhood, for example, be achievable without statehood? Why might commentators disagree about this? What might reasonably underlie this disagreement?

At any rate, one may see why some accumulation of the conditions already discussed might underwrite ideas of nationalism in which we are here interested. The guiding inspiration for these ideas is doubtless the view that it would be desirable for political communities generally to aggregate persons having a great deal culturally in common. In proportion to what they have in common, the members of such aggregations will be more likely to understand one another, be like-minded, and have many interests in common. That, at least, is the dream. The remainder of this chapter will be devoted to examining some aspects of the desirability and practicability of this ideal.

THE IDEAL OF THE NATION-STATE

Even in modern times there are regularized exceptions to the idea that the single best form of organization for new territories is the nation-state. Various political communities recognized neither as nations nor as states nor as parts thereof have been the protectorates of the third quarter of the nineteenth century, trusteeships initiated after World War I, and the mandated territories initiated after World War II. Regard for the economic and military security of smaller, unattached political communities in the world played a role in the formation and recognition of these communities.

Further, as already noted in passing in Chapter Three, communities that are already nation-states have sometimes decided that they could not rest content with that form of political organization alone. For example, confederation has a modern as well as an ancient history; we have already mentioned the European Economic Community. Again, with such nonnation-state communities as the EEC and NATO, economic and military considerations have also played a role. As commentators increasingly remark, the conventional nation-state organization of political communities becomes less attractive as states (1) must boost their capacity to defend themselves in the face of modern weapons technology, and (2) lose their capacity to be economically viable because of the rapidly increasing technological, financial, and economic interdependence of persons across state lines. The impact of such confederations and alliances as the EEC and NATO upon the idea and ideal of the nation-state is not yet clear.

If such exceptions to the idea that the nation-state is *the* desirable form of political community are recognized on military and economic grounds, what, other than mere historical lag, explains the continued vitality of nationalism? In some cases, granting a territory status as a nation-state may render the territory militarily and economically vulnerable by cutting it adrift from previous military and economic ties. In other cases, insisting upon existing full and uncontroversial status as a nation-state disables a community from taking steps toward effective military and economic security in the modern world. Still, however, the nation-state is currently the most widely accepted and aspired-to ideal of political community on the world scene.

Some aspects of its continued popularity can be dealt with only after a discussion of sovereignty (for which see Chapter Eight). Other aspects, those emerging clearly in the case of territories aspiring to, but not yet in possession of, status as nation-states will be dealt with here.

We should notice first that recognition as a *nation*-state is the currently conventional form of recognition on the international scene as a state. Here we see an effect of the second of the two constituent ideas of nationalism on which we are focusing—that every state should consist of one and only one nation. In the recent past, recognition as a state and recognition as a nation have been virtually indistinguishable. Such recognition is these days a matter of being admitted membership in the United Nations General Assembly. Admission to the assembly is accompanied by acquisition of various significant rights and privileges on the international scene and the power of having a voice, however small, that will be heard on that scene.

The standing of a territory and its citizens will thereby be increased to an extent that may be highly significant to those people. The increase in standing may bring advantages, including military and economic, that may, in the eyes of those people, more than counterbalance the possible losses. Many of those advantages result from recognition as a state, to which recognition as a nation just happens to be incidental. Other advantages may result from the special merit in being a *nation*-state. Those advantages are the ones in which we are here especially interested.

NATIONALISM AND SELF-DETERMINATION*

Though commentators have faced great difficulty and frustration in trying to specify the constitutive unities of nations (Henry Sidgwick suggested that the unity in question is similar to that formerly provided by kinship), political communities that are nations are most probably united more extensively and intensively than merely politically (for instances, linguistically, culturally, and the like).

Commentators have thought that these communities would thus be able to

*See the footnote on self-limitation in Chapter Six, page 102.

express fully the culture of their members and to maximize the unfettered development and expression of their own cultures by those members. Via this last consideration, nationalism has become identified as a vehicle of human freedom, self-determination, and self-development. The identification is clearly made in many nineteenth- and even twentieth-century discussions of the importance of nations.

Gathering people together politically who are unified in the ways previously suggested, one would conclude from reading these discussions, contributes to their liberties, as well as to their happiness, their power, and who knows what else. Some of these claims are doubtless partly confirmable or disconfirmable by empirical investigation, for example, of whether grouping in these ways advances, and failing to group them in these ways hampers efforts to advance the liberties, prosperity, power, and general happiness of peoples. We can look carefully at what human experience teaches us of such matters.

A useful prolegomenon to this examination is to notice that though the full range of advantages mentioned earlier is generally thought connected to material welfare, although not fully dependent upon it, many commentators believe that some of them—those concerned primarily with what has been called "the human spirit"—proceed quite independently of human material welfare—or at least that they ought to.

This last proviso presents a problem. For in discussions of such matters, a common hazard is unnoticed transition between what *is* the case (which, with respect to human spirit, is probably partly an object of empirical inquiry), and what *ought* to be the case. One often gets the impression that commentators have started out by talking about the first but are soon talking about the second.

A further difficulty in discussions of this matter consists of the undoubted fact that what people say in them makes a difference to the truth or falsity of the claims made *in* them. This is because feelings important to the human spirit can be engendered or discouraged by such discussions. Thus, for example, the presence through the nineteenth century of a multitude of claims about the importance of feelings of nationhood and the contributions of these feelings to the greatness of individuals and communities clearly promoted the growth of feelings of and pride in nationality and nationhood that were not present at the start. The importance of and value attached to nationality and nationhood grew during the course of the century, and the political importance of the idea of the nation was much enlarged as a result. Though, as we have noted earlier, developments in military and economic technology have somewhat reduced the importance of nationhood in recent times, we are still feeling the effects of that earlier heritage—a matter to which this chapter bears witness.

Three distinct though related applications and understandings of *self-determination* figure importantly in discussions of nationalism. First, a community is self-determined when it is not effectively governed or subject to government by some force from outside, as would be colonies, protectorates, and the like. Self-determination on this understanding is compatible with local tyranny, and it is debatable whether so-called "satellites" of more powerful states are self-governed. Second, a community is self-determined when its policies and decisions are largely determined by the wishes or intentions of the majority of its members. On this understanding of *self-determination* a community may be self-determined though a substantial minority of the persons resident in it have no "say" in the policies it pursues and decisions it makes. Third, the persons in a community are self-determined when, taken individually, they have a "say" in the policies and decisions of the community.

This last understanding of *self-determination* differs most strikingly from the others by being applied to *residents* of the community rather than to the community itself. It is the most troubling of the understandings (try, for example, to get to the bottom of what is understood by "having a say") and is less fully exposed than the other two in discussions of nationalism.

The invocation of the merit of self-determination for nationalism has been central to the popularity of the movement. Virtually universally during the early part of the nineteenth century, and in some quarters still, an attachment has commonly and firmly been made between the ideas of nationhood and some unspecified self-determination. The view eventually became that at least through achieving the status of states, peoples constituting the nations then identified could achieve a greater degree of, and perhaps their only passing acquaintance with, self-determination. Seen from this perspective, the drive for nationalism seems to be a drive to be governed by persons "representing" or in some way giving expression to one's own cultural, genetic, religious, and/or linguistic heritage. The motives for this desire may include a wish to be governed by persons who "understand one" and an often related though sometimes autonomous wish to be governed by "one's own."

Because of the geographical orientation of political control and the common histories of geographically localized distributions of genetic, cultural, religious, and linguistic similarities and heritages, expressions of the nationalist idea of control have thus often been intermixed inextricably with aspirations merely for local control. We shall examine this mix in the last section of this chapter.

The self-determination attached to nationhood has only gradually, however, become associated with popular sovereignty ("universal" suffrage) and "the people".* This association has not always been supposed and is not inevitable, even now. At the start of its development, the idea of nationhood was not generally supposed to have anything to do with popular sovereignty or "the people."

On its first modern appearance, the idea of the nation was of something embodied most fully in the king alone or in the king and the first and/or second estates (to use the expressions common in France at that time); that is, the king, the parliament, the church, and so forth—what were in fact various elites—rather than what we have come to think of as more central; namely,

---

*The distinction between these two is this. Popular sovereignty can be characterized as "universal" suffrage—which is not universal (that is, it doesn't include children, mental defectives, felons, and sometimes women)—and is expressed by (a) majority rule or (b) some kind of plurality rule. Minority rights may be included but are not a necessary part of it. "Rule by the people" (a) *may* be the same as popular sovereignty, but (b) may be understood to contain some minority rights as a necessary part.

"popular sovereignty" and what we now call "the people." The latter ideas developed later in the nineteenth century and gained precedence slowly. Even when the self-determination connected to nationalism has been associated, for example, with popular sovereignty, it has contained a potential for the oppression of minorities—a matter we shall discuss later.

But when the association is not made with even popular sovereignty, nationalism is quite consistent with tyranny. We see this clearly in the early history of the idea, but we see it also in the newly emergent nations and in recent fascist versions of old nations. The latter, for example, regularly overrode the liberties and self-determinations (at least on our common view of what these were) of the majorities therein. The fascist elevation of duty and discipline above self-expression led directly to this. Duty and discipline thus elevated were imposed by the persons who happened to be in power and were claimed in the name of the nation and/or state.

Therefore, in order to understand its persistent connection with nationalism, we need first to understand self-determination as something possibly quite *dis*associated from popular sovereignty. The resulting rule, no matter how tyrannical, has not been regarded as alien rule. If persons can identify the source of the rule as "their own," relative at least to what precedes it, they are apparently readier to consider it, no matter how undemocratic it is, as self-determination than they would if they perceived it as operated by alien force. The point may indicate only what is a curious feature of human psychology, or may instead indicate something fundamental to and entirely understandable about the human condition.

But just as experience revealed only gradually the disconnections between the first and second understandings of *self-determination,* so it only gradually revealed the disconnections between the second and third. Some critics of nationalism saw the latter disconnection early and clearly. For example, Lord Acton did. Because he also believed that single-nation states were likely to suffer from that singleness of purpose that invites oppressive rule no matter whether the purpose is to produce the greatest happiness for the greatest number, to promote the superiority of some particular class or race or religion, or whatever, he also thought that the nationalist ideal was a mistake.

He thought that turning individual nations into states would produce illiberal states by encouraging the oppression of minorities. A truly liberal and nonoppressive state, he thought, would be devoted to sheltering and sustaining more than one nation (substantial cultural minority), and thus tolerate and work within the limitations of the presence of cultural diversity. We see the third understanding of *self-determination* entering into his thought when he says:

> A state which is incompetent to satisfy different races condemns itself; a state which labors to neutralize, to absorb, or to dispel them destroys its own morality. The state which does not include them is destitute of the chief statute of a basis for self government. The theory of nationality, therefore, is a retrograde step in history (Acton, p. 298.)

His concern has been confirmed by the separatist movements of the recent past in mature nation-states.

Thus, whether nationalism has as a merit the promotion of self-determination depends on how one conceives of self-determination. Though each of the foregoing is a plausible construal of the concept, each also raises additional issues about whether it is a merit.

NATIONALISM AND MINORITIES

The principle of national self-determination has foundered on the fact that most of the states to which we have wished to apply it have been arguably composed of more than one nation (culturally speaking) or at least have had very large minorities; for example, minorities composing as much as 30 percent of the total population. This fact has created an embarrassment for nationalism especially when self-determination has been associated with popular sovereignty, as Woodrow Wilson associated it after World War I and as we have associated it largely ever since. The embarrassment results from the fact that the minorities in these states were commonly racially or culturally identified, and thus were permanent in a sense in which minorities within democratic states in the Western tradition are not supposed to be.

In consequence, they had no hope as a group of ever becoming majorities. In a system of popular sovereignty, they thus had no hope of ever controlling the government, and played out a role of permanent opposition never to accede to power. Their minority status was a politically desperate position to them in case the majority, a permanent majority, sought to oppress them.

The doctrine of national self-determination would appear in these cases to prohibit external intervention; at the same time, liberal principles, principles generally shared by persons espousing the doctrine of national self-determination, counsel some sort of assistance to those (hypothetically) oppressed minorities. There is still much rhetoric in the world about coming to the assistance of minorities in emergent nations, but very little guidance.

Apart from the problems confronted by some minorities because of their susceptibility to oppression, there is, secondly, their frequent desire to remain apart—racially, culturally, linguistically, religiously, and so on—from members of the majority. They sometimes, at least, wish to retain their difference. They may value their own ethnic or religious heritage(s) and wish to preserve and continue them.

The richness of the issues here can be suggested by noting the various qualifying terms we have used in connection with *minority*. We have said that there are ethnic, racial, religious, cultural, and linguistic minorities, and we might well add that there are also ideological ones. Some of these may be alternative ways of indicating all or part of the others. When we look at the minorities creating these problems with respect to the relationships between nationhood and nationality, we commonly find that they have clusters of these characteristics. For example, there are cultural *and* linguistic minorities, and possibly also religious minorities, and so forth.

The embarrassment that the minority constitutes in connection with nationalism is greater when the size of the minority is considerable relative to the size of the majority, and the minority has a large cluster of these characteristics; and it is smaller when the size of the minority is smaller and has fewer of these characteristics. This, however, is not invariable; much will depend upon the intensity of the attachment of minority members to their minority characteristics.

Further, membership in the minorities would in some cases be possible through choice, whereas in other cases it could only be a matter of inheritance. The clearest instances of the former are ideological or religious minorities; the clearest case of the latter is a racial minority. Our attitudes about the extent to which the existence of the minority produces a problem might possibly be influenced by our perception of whether membership in the minority were a matter of inheritance or choice; and whether, if a matter of choice, we believe that the choice made was either reasonable, fitting, or proper.

Problems with such matters are not just occasional and isolated difficulties in nation-states or difficulties especially to be found in newly-formed nation-states. A large number of modern states, some of decent age, still suffer sharp problems of separatism. For example, in Spain there is still a Catalonian and a Basque question; in Italy there is a Sicilian and a Tyrolese question. Scottish and Irish nationalism are still alive and fairly well in Great Britain. In an example from somewhat newer states, but still ones of reasonable age, Serbian and Croatian nationalisms are still vitally significant in Yugoslavia. And, of course, tribal affiliations are still much more important than state affiliations in many of the newer African countries.

Thus, the problems of nationalism are exacerbated by identifying national self-determination with popular sovereignty. The fundamental difficulty arising from that identification is its encouraging the use of nation-state-building as an instrument of popular sovereignty. If the benefits of popular sovereignty are seen to lie in the capacity it provides to "do things one's own way," as they are generally seen, then the presence of large, permanent minorities within national boundaries becomes an embarrassment when those minorities are systematically denied the expected benefit of popular sovereignty.

One may think the problem is merely how to draw the boundaries. Remembering the American experience with gerrymandering, one may imagine the twists and turns of national boundaries that might result. Such twists and turns of national boundaries are by no means unprecedented, but is the idea of a "nation" determinate enough to help us? Would it help, for example, not only with where to draw the boundaries between nations, but also to decide another matter of urgent current interest, how to distinguish between true nationalist struggle within a nation and mere civil war masked as nationalist struggle; that is, where each party declares itself to be the agent of the nation and the opponent to be a foreign agent, provocateur, or the like?

Cobban has argued that Woodrow Wilson's attempt after World War I to formulate and then apply a criterion of nationality promoting national self-determination, identifying the latter with popular soverignty, failed not only because of a multitude of political considerations but also because by altering frontiers in setting up new states, it proved impossible to avoid creating substantial new minorities. A minority, even a large minority, is of course not a nation. But when it is permanent and easily identifiable, it can create grave problems for any attempt to connect nationhood with self-determination in the form of popular sovereignty.

How is the nationalist ideal to incorporate the fact of substantial, seemingly permanent minorities? Whether these minorities are racial, religious, cultural, linguistic, or even ideological, the nationalist ideal seems to have a potential for attaching importance to them and thus posing them as problems. These reflect some of the requirements for nonparasitic political community in general discussed in Chapter One.

Minimum Size

Presumably, there are lower limits on the size of the populations with which we can be concerned. Some minorities will be too small to constitute themselves viable nation-states. As we remarked earlier, economic and military considerations in the modern world seem to require that communities be larger and larger if their independence is to be viable.

Nevertheless, some commentators will say that intensity of the desire to be independent, or, which comes to much the same thing, the priority given to that desire, must be considered. While this is no doubt true, there comes a point where the issue is not merely its own toleration of inconvenience, but whether a community can survive *as* independent. Survival of the life styles, religions, languages, and so on, of small minorities may at some point be beyond our capacity to assure. The location of that point may depend upon the ingenuity of the people involved, the toleration of them by persons who find them offensive, the control that can be found or exercised over persons tempted by their situation, and other such considerations.

The case of the Native American, or American Indian, is instructive with respect to the kinds of issues that might arise. The problems are not merely that the minority in this case is small and internally culturally diverse. One feature of the "minority problem" in this case is that at least many Indian cultures embody views about how to live that are at sharp variance with the majority views in the United States and large areas of the remainder of the world. Maintenance of the former views will make members of those Native American cultures unable to operate effectively in a world dominated by the latter views. On the other hand, assimilation to the latter will leave those Native Americans without what presently constitutes a substantial source of their feelings of cultural identity.

A prominent virtue of "reservations" is supposed to be that they provide environments in which Native Americans may continue their particular minority life styles. These life styles could be and have been subsidized to a great extent, but this idea of "wardship" has been found psychologically and culturally ruinous by many Native Americans as well as by others. Alternatively, Native Americans could become self-supporting on reservations through exhibiting themselves and their wares as tourist attractions. But, whether they support themselves in this way or not, the idea that they have *become* tourist attractions is a blow to the pride of many of them.

Such difficulties as these may arise in connection with any cultural minority anywhere. A minority not large enough and not so situated that it may become economically viable and independent may always have to consider the extent to which it will assimilate to the cultures of the people surrounding it in order to become economically and even culturally viable. If we set out to preserve the minority culture and the capacities of members of that culture to achieve what they recognize to be well-being, then we will perceive this as a significant human problem. How can cultural diversities of minorities, whether by choice or by heritage, be best preserved at reasonable cost? Considerations of human pride and psychological well-being, as well as economic and military considerations, will have to be noted.

Geographical Contiguity

Native Americans are a culturally diverse lot, and in this respect it is misleading to speak of them as though they were a single minority. But even if they were not so culturally diverse, their present geographic dispersal over a whole area presents a problem for some theories of nationalism. If the idea behind making nations (culturally speaking) into states is at least the idea that people should be "governed by one of their own (culturally speaking)" and if permanent cultural minorities are an embarrassment because they are not, the prospects of gerrymandering or relocation may seem promising. Perhaps the boundaries of the prospective nation-state can be drawn so as to exclude the minorities in question. Perhaps, on the other hand, the minority can be relocated so that it no longer resides within the state boundaries or so that it is concentrated and becomes itself a candidate for statehood. The wide dispersal of native minorities in America renders the gerrymandering of national boundaries unfeasible. And we have noted already the lesson taught by our experience after World War I of making serious efforts to redraw state boundaries so that they would coincide with national (culturally speaking) boundaries: political and other practical considerations made it impossible to do this redrawing without creating substantial new and troubling minorities.

Could the embarrassing minority problems connected with the formation of nation-states be "solved" by relocation? If the relocation is not welcomed by the relocated persons, it can present an unlovely picture of the nation that remains. That nation may appear and be illiberal and narrow, certainly subject to Lord Acton's stricture. There are well-known reasons why the relocated persons might not welcome the relocation. It does violence to reverence for the land of their forefathers, where they lived and are buried. Furthermore, traditional life styles (and it is certainly one of the aims of the whole nationalist movement to help preserve and promote traditional life styles) are sustained by particular locales and climates, and frustrated by others. A matching of minority-eliminating relocation with melioristic locales and climates would be especially fortunate and surely nothing that could be widely depended upon.

Another Phenomenon

There is a further phenomenon difficult to place in the preceding discussion. Racial, religious, linguistic, and other cultural similarities among people have come to be regarded in some quarters as sufficient to promote the creation of state boundaries in accord with them. So we have the pan-movements of various sorts, such as pan-Germanic, pan-Slavic, and pan-African. It is not always clear whether resulting national boundaries are supposed to coincide with the boundaries of the principal locales of, say, German-speaking people no matter where they presently live, or whether the boundaries are supposed to coincide with the locales of these people when relocated in some way to the approximate locations of the bulk of, for instance, German-speaking people, for example, in or near Germany. What is proposed along these lines would of course make an enormous difference in both the feasibility and in the potential for political power of such movements.

Indeed, we have to get clearer on the matter in order to determine whether these movements are straightforward forms of nationalism at all—or, rather, forms of imperialism. It has generally been on the minds of people promoting such movements to promote the dominance or at least the increased power of persons sharing the similarity in question vis-à-vis the world political scene. Nationalism and imperialism seem, however, to have different thrusts. Nationalism aims at political unification of persons having certain similarities; the unification may increase the power of these persons on the world scene, but that is not its principal aim, which is instead to make a state of that aggregate of persons, and thereby makes them politically self-determined. Imperialism, on the other hand, aims directly at the increase in world power of persons having the characteristics in question; the political unification of those persons remains a fortunate consequence of the movement rather than its purported and explicit aim.

ALTERNATIVE BASES FOR NATIONALISM

If, as experience following World War I shows, extensive and generally well-intentioned efforts at boundary drawing will fail to avoid creation of new, troubling minorities while eliminating old ones, and relocation most likely runs afoul of some of the ideals fundamental in the aspiration toward nationalism itself, nationalist ideologues might do well to cultivate views of nationalist foundations and aims eliminating or mitigating the "minority problem."

One way of doing this would be to create an Acton-type liberal state a part of whose ideology would be tolerance of minorities. Another would be to characterize the "nation" on which the nation-state was to be based in such a way that minorities of the sorts we have been considering would be fully identified as members of the "nation" and not, virtually automatically, be excluded from it.

There are promising bases throughout the history of nation-states for the latter idea. Indeed, concerning the facts about the formation and foundation of nation-states, many persons have been headed in the wrong direction. Much too great an importance has been given to common genetic heritage, common culture, common language, and so on. Perhaps, as Ernest Renan told us, for any group to constitute a nation, it is important to have a good capacity to forget.

To take the French nation as an example, as did Renan, the French may talk about their common heritage, but this requires a capacity for them to look back only so far. If they go back further, they find diversity rather than commonness. Another commentator (Cobban) declares that common languages and cultures have more often been results than causes in the nation-states of today. So some modern commentators jettison the idea that the roots of nationalism are in some presumed preexisting unity of the sort we have heretofore been discussing.

Some commentators have also pointed out a way in which the idea of a preexisting unity may be avoided in nationalist ideology. K. R. Minogue, for example, suggests that there is only one single criterion of nationality: the sharing of the grievance identified as "the national grievance." Whether this sharing is autochthonous ("sprung-from-the-earth") or fabricated should not, I imagine, make any great difference. Another commentator (Ernest Gellner) faces the latter prospect fully: he says that nation-states are not products of the awakening of nations to self-consciousness, but of an inventing of nations where they did not formerly exist.

The important thing about nationalist feelings, he says further, is that they have a capacity to inspire people to action. Along this line, Alfred Cobban sums up a great deal when he says that "a nation is a community that is, or wishes to be, a state." States have been created out of territories where nothing previously identified as nations existed, but where we now persist in trying to identify nations. Following World War I there were examples of this in the Middle East. In the mid-twentieth century there are numerous examples in Africa. (Some commentators assert that the decision should be put to a vote, but a difference is made by who is given the franchise. How is *that* decision to be made, and by whom?)

Moving in one of these directions may take us past nationalism's difficulties with minorities, but not without creating further difficulties. Questions now needing answering are: by what procedures should the wishes of the community be determined? How are the boundaries of the community in question to be determined? How large must it be? Is merely the wish to be a state (as determined perhaps by certain specified procedures) enough to support a claim to a right on the part of the community to self-determination, or is more needed? If so, what more? If nations, the raw materials out of which nationalism would construct states, are themselves the products *only* of wishes by communities to be states, then it becomes urgently important for applying the ideology of nationalism to have a precise and plausible way of determining the presence or absence of that "communal wish."

The way of dissolving the embarrassing "minority problem" we have just examined might be thought to be present whenever a community becomes a state. Some commentators think of all states as nations (contrast the quote from Cobban two paragraphs earlier). If they are correct, then every member of the community, at least every citizen of the state, is also a member of the nation and therefore cannot be a member of some "minority" of members of the community who are not members of the nation. This dissolution of the problems, however, makes puzzling the nationalist *ideal* that every state should consist of one and only one nation. Unless another characterization of *nation* is utilized in these discussions, that ideal could not fail to be realized.

In fact, both the understandings of *nation* as equivalent to *state* and as essentially involving genetic, cultural, or linguistic heritages have proven difficult to eliminate entirely from discussions of nationalism. The most promising move toward making *nation* independent of these ideas is suggested in the views of Cobban, Minogue, and Gellner alluded to previously. The basis of nations would there appear to be something roughly like the possession by a community of a reason (of which they are aware) or a desire to become a state (or, in some recent discussions, a largely, though not precisely delineated, self-determined region or segment of a state).

This understanding of the substance of *nation* does not, however, avoid completely the possibility of identifying troubling minorities within a nation. It would do so if the "communities" in question aggregated only like-minded persons; but they do not. Like minded persons can constitute communities of a sort, but we also frequently persist in understanding a "community" to aggregate persons living within the boundaries of specific geographical territories. When discussing political movements and ideologies, it is all too easy to slip from one of these understandings to the other without noticing that we have done so. It is easy, when talking about nations, to focus on like-minded persons. But when we talk about nations becoming states, we understandably shift to talking about communities as the persons resident within certain territories, because states *are* territories.

Most of the persons within a given territory may be like-minded and even have common grievances; they may, for that matter, have common genetic, cultural, and linguistic heritages, and the sharing of these may be connected quite understandably to their like-mindedness. But there may be embarrassingly large numbers of persons living within the boundaries of the territories in question who do not share the desires or possess the grievances of the majority. Some of these nonlike-minded persons may be like-minded relative to one another, especially if numerous. They would or could then constitute an embarrassing minority relative to application of the ideology of nationalism to that case. Thus, even the suggestions we have drawn from Minogue, Cobban, and Gellner would not suffice to dissolve the problems of nationalism with minorities.

These problems must not inevitably be faced; they are contingent upon the distribution of people over the earth's surface and on how these people regard one another. There may be some regions where the minority problem is a minor one or no problem at all. But our consideration of it does show that the vision of nationalism does not suffice to point the way always to clear and wholly acceptable resolutions to problems of self-determination.

NATIONALISM AND "MELTING POTS"

The United States of America is surely a nation on the understanding of *nation* first distinguished in the present chapter, where it is roughly synonymous with *state*. But is it a "nation" on the other understandings we have been scrutinizing, where it identifies some linguistic, cultural, genetic, and other commonalities? Our difficulties with *nation* can be illuminated by considering its application to this case. Here the central issues can be reached by considering alternative understandings of the "melting pot" idea so prominent in American experience and political and social ideology.

The early prominence of the melting pot idea in American history was due to the assumption that, while unities of genetic heritage and religion could be dispensed with (though how far we were willing to go in either matter was not clear), unities of language, culture, and, to some extent, political and social ideology would be sufficient for national unity. Though they were not, with some exception of political ideology, present initially, they could be grown and fostered here. It was this growing and fostering that was referred to picturesquely by the melting pot idea.

The declared hope of members of the already resident majority, and the aspiration of the immigrants themselves and their immediate progeny, was that the immigrants would assimilate to the point where they would become "truly American"—indistinguishable outwardly from members of the already resident majority. The attitude to be appreciated by members of the majority was the patience with which they held this hope and expectation. As the blueprint had it, the desired assimilation could be expected within a generation or two, and not immediately.

Supporting this expectation, and thus supporting the melting-pot idea, was the notion that the political forces operating in an established political community have substantial potential for "melting down" outward diversities. Every established political community doubtless has this potential. The expectation of members of the community that it *would* do this may have been especially explicit in the case of the United States of America. In accepting for membership what was to them such a wide diversity of cultural, linguistic, and racial types, the established citizens of the United States may be said to have made especially heavy demands upon themselves of this sort. Not that they were ever entirely free from anxieties on this score. They maintained, however, a picture of the United States as a sanctuary from political oppression and economic misfortune. (For further discussion of this issue see Part III.)

The importance of this matter for our present discussion is that it presents the idea that political unity or ideology can *create* a national unity and thus a "nation." The idea that statehood can in this way produce nations rather than merely recognize and conform to the prior existence of nations is foreign to, but not inconsistent with, the aspirations of nationalism that we have been examining. Those ideas suggest that one finds the nation and on that basis decides what the state is to be. The present interpretation of the melting pot idea in American experience, a suggestion congenial to some of the writers whose views we have noted, is quite otherwise. But notice that the unity of a nation in this new view does not involve either religious or genetic unity.

The jettisoning of religious unity as a constituent one for nations may be historically significant, but the jettisoning of genetic unity suggests broad horizons for nation-building. And if political unification is supposed to be one of the fostering conditions of nation-building, then certainly the aspects of nationalism on which we have concentrated in this chapter would need refashioning. The drive toward nationalism might become difficult to distinguish from a mere drive toward local government—a matter we shall consider at the end of the present chapter.

In some quarters, in recent decades we find a weakening of attachment to the traditional unities aspired to in nation-building. It may be that there is now especially wide appreciation among the majority of the importance to our peculiar national experience of the diversity of languages and cultures to be found among our immigrant populations, and the consequent richness of our national life resulting from this diversity. Widespread appreciation of this diversity and richness is nothing new in the rhetoric of American ideology, but may have reached new heights in its practice. The innovation apparently is that we no longer promote heavily the idea that we should try to melt down these diversities into something common and homogeneous, but rather the idea that doing so quite thoroughly would be losing something important, namely the richness and diversity otherwise embedded in our communal life. America is seen as a "tossed salad" rather than a "melting pot."

There are, of course, still lively debates about how far we should go in this matter. For example, think of disagreement about education in public schools. There are many grounds for favoring or opposing the practice unrelated to our present concern, but the spread of interest in the idea, as well as of interest in "ethnic cooking" and other types of ethnicity, suggests a lessening of the urgency formerly attached to cultural assimilation.

I have suggested earlier that immediate acceptance of some elements of a particular political ideology was expected of immigrants. Attempts to specify the exact content of that expectation, and even that there was or is one, are likely to be controversial. The idea, however, that the nation, insofar as there is a nation, is united most basically by political ideology is sustained by the idea that it was populated by immigration. (This idea, of course, overlooks native American Indians, slave "immigrants," transported convicts, and possibly some classes of indentured servants.) In combination with the idea that the country is a democracy, the notion that it was populated by immigrants sustains the view that the members of the political community here are legitimately united by their acceptance of elements of the ideology of that community. They are certainly not marked by any other communal unities apparent to the immigrants themselves, who were impressed by the cultural, linguistic, and religious diversities of their several origins.

The idea that the United States is a nation united by the common adherence of its members to a particular political ideology receives support from the common political rhetoric of the country, but is also subverted by that rhetoric. "The American Way" labels a rather particular political and social ideology, but is also supposed to describe extreme tolerance of differences in political and social ideologies. The tolerance may appear to be an element of the country's ideology but also makes difficult the description of a "national" ideology in the acceptance of which the people are united—unless, that is, arguments can be given for not tolerating intolerance.

Praise of "freedom of association" may convince us that the voluntary association of ideologically like-minded persons into political communities, and even into "nations" if they are numerous enough, is acceptable. But common understandings of this freedom do not illuminate what is to be done about dissenters who wish to remain on or even proceed to the site of a particular community (presumably for reasons unconnected with the unifying ideology of the community). Illumination on that point is an essential constitutent of satisfactory nationalisms having an ideological base. Whether it be a "melting pot" or not, as long as the unifying characteristics of the nation are made and not found, it will have to deal with attempts to "remake" them in a new light.

NATIONALISM AND LOCAL GOVERNMENT

The antiimperialist and anticolonialist sentiments so often giving impetus to nationalism are motivated by some of the same concerns motivating local government. Examination of this connection can expose some roots of the continuing call for nationalism.

The "localness" of local government is relative to a more extended governmental unit. Federated states and provinces are local governments relative to nations; counties and districts, cities and villages are local relative to states or provinces; and wards and precincts are local relative to cities. In each case the contrast is between something distant or remote or even alien and something nearby and familiar.

But local government is not merely government through the political apparatus that constitutes a subdivision of a larger political community. If the persons in local control are determined by processes outside the smaller community in question, it will not be fully and comfortably a manifestation of local government. The two conditions of local government whose presence is being felt here are that (1) the persons controlling the government be "home grown," in the sense that their identity is determined by events occurring within the community, not outside it, whether these events be elections, coups, or whatever; and (2) the principles and policies of the government likewise be determined, at least in part, by events occurring within the community.

But why should local government be preferred to (or as an addition to) government by a more extended governmental unit? Several possible advantages can be seen to follow, though it should be understood that none of them is an inevitable result of instituting some system of local government.

First, when the two conditions for local government given earlier are fulfilled, the likelihood (unless special precautions are taken) that the rulers will be responsive to the problems, desires, and aspirations of (at least the majority of) the members of the community is increased. It might be a useful exercise to imagine and describe plausible circumstances where this likelihood would not increase. Second, because the rulers are on or near the sites where their decisions will be effected, they will be more likely to observe the effects of, and receive response to, the decisions they have made. Third, given the likelihood that decisions will be in accord with the views of the locally predominant political power, these decisions are more likely to be implemented by persons who understand and are sympathetic to them. Fourth, there is the benefit of diversity or variations among local governments. Such variation provides, at least in theory, an opportunity for individuals to choose the type of local government or other schemes they wish to live under. Further, political experiments may themselves be seen as valuable, whether they succeed or not, since then one community can learn from the experiences of another. (The other side of the coin of diversity is the sameness produced by imitation, which in turn results from many human motives, among which are: (a) the copying of apparent success and (b) the copying because of the prestige of the persons or things imitated. Supporting inferences are sometimes made that (a) what another person or agency has will be successful or otherwise satisfactory for oneself, and (b) that one's own needs or desires are enough like those of others that what is successful or otherwise satisfactory for them will also be so for oneself.)

Fifth, if not only what is done but what manner of people do it matters, and if enterprise and initiative are admirable human character traits, then one may see local government as valuable because it encourages local initiative (and not just on the grounds that government will thereby be more responsive and understanding). (Contrast this with J. S. Mill, *On Liberty*, Chapter 3.) (The other side of the coin of initiative is the apathy induced by the unwillingness of those who must pay for schemes of improvement to pay for them. Since these are also often persons with power, the threat that nothing will be attempted is a serious one.)

Disadvantages to local government, in addition to those already mentioned, are generally recognized to be three: (1) the local government, because of its comparatively small size, may lack resources (such as revenue and technology) adequate to cope with problems (for instance, air and water pollution); (2) local government may lack a sufficiently global view of the problems at hand (for example, because it doesn't experience some aspects of the problem); and (3) the powers that be in local government may have views that are provincial and unrepresentative of the views of the bulk of members of the larger community of which the locale is a part.

How does the advocacy of nationalism differ from that of local government? Apart from the fact that nations that are candidates for being states must have a certain minimum size, there is the relativity of local government to some larger community (in the United States, *local* has a more specific use in which it contrasts with *state*). Local governments are not autonomous: their "localness" is identified with respect to some remote government of which they are a part and to which they are at least in part subordinate.

The precise nature of the subordination is often controversial and may even purposely be left somewhat indefinite. For example, each of the federal states of the United States of America is said to be "sovereign," yet the effects of the federal government's supremacy in some matters on this "sovereignty" are hotly debated. Though considerations motivating nationalism and local governments may be quite similar, the responsibilities, powers, and challenges of local governments may consistently be somewhat narrower than those of governments of nations that have become states. (Consider, for example, the discussion of the importance of resources to ensure military viability of nations versus local governments.)

But the more important differences between advocating local government and nationalism depend on what is identified as the basis of either. At the extremes, a nation may be thought to be a particular cultural or genetic group having only part of the members of a given community as its members, or as a group consisting of *all* the members of a given community insofar as they, by virtue of their communal residence, share a certain spirit or social bond. In the first instance, nations and local governments could be quite different, be in different hands, and serve different interests. In the second instance, the rationales for local government and national government show striking similarities. Only when the basis of national character is taken to be distinctively different from the basis for local government can the grounds for the former be clearly distinguished from the grounds for the latter.

Local government does not require the identification of a "nation," and hence its rationale does not involve consequent difficulties. There are still questions, however, about where to draw the jurisdictional boundaries, and over the way the location of these boundaries determines the presence or absence of minorities or majorities of opinion on various issues. Thus, the prospect of gerrymandering echoes one of the most sensitive issues in the formation of nations. In the case of nations, the boundaries of jurisdiction have sometimes been thought to need merely to conform to the boundaries of the nation. As we saw, this supposition readily breaks down.

Whether equally severe difficulties must be met in drawing the jurisdictional boundaries of local governments depends upon what the criteria are supposed to be for determining where the boundaries are to be. As the boundaries will often unavoidably determine who is in a majority and who is in a minority on any given particular issue, emphasis upon local control cannot be expected, any more than attempts to develop nations, to avoid confrontation of delicate and serious boundary-drawing problems.

In some cases the geographical distributions of persons may make more or less obvious some decisions about boundaries. But this in reality creates more problems than it solves, since the "natural" boundaries may not conform to the criteria that express the rationale for breaking off into nations or local political governments. The criteria could be respected by relocation of politically embarrassing minorities, or by some vision of creating a community (either local or national) by some process of acculturation, though this requires a clear understanding and acceptance of the criteria for locating boundaries in either case. Without these, there is little chance that the ideals of nationalism or local government can be given very thorough expression.

The attractiveness and viability of both local and national governments must be considered from the standpoint of their access to resources needed to make them economically, and, in the case of national governments, militarily, viable. Local governments will presumably have some access to resources beyond those gathered in their own territory, but nations may also have such access through friendships and agreements. Geographical and population sizes must be considered alongside access to resources needed to make the unity in question economically and militarily viable.

These determinations will, moreover, have to be made relative to the aspirations at a certain time in their history of the people being considered. Thus, rational determination of boundaries appropriate to the ideals of local and national control will be relative to particular historical circumstances and cannot expect to be made for all time.

The comparison of nationalism to local government in the respects considered here fixes especially on each as providing appropriate units for political independence. But each is supposed to be especially supportive of something else—a sense of communal unity. Nationalisms are supposed to *identify* the bases of that unity as well as to foster it. Local governments are supposed to provide a *basis* for it (but not identify it) and foster it as well. Again, there are deep similarities between the two. If nations, culturally speaking, can be created *by* creating political community, there will be no difference in principle in the kinds of considerations marshaled to support either.

Nationalism, in its modern form, appears principally to be a movement on behalf of local autonomy. This appearance is reinforced as noticed earlier by its antiimperialist and anticolonial contributions. The trouble with local autonomy is knowing how far to press it. The economic and military challenges accompanying political independence in the modern world may perhaps be ignored to a point in favor of depth of feeling, but they cannot be ignored utterly. Though technological considerations appear to change things from time to time, this sets, more or less roughly, a lower limit on the sizes of territories and peoples that can be viable candidates for statehood. Perhaps this consideration is what underlies the increasing talk in modern nationalist circles of nationalist movements having no aim at all to autonomous existence on the international scene, but rather to a *relatively* autonomous existence as a region of the state already on that scene.

In this case, local government and nationalism may telescope, or something entirely new may be created. The development may work a change, and possibly even an improvement, in the nationalist ideology. The autonomy demanded seems relative at present only to certain issues that have developed between the region in question and the nation-state in question. This seems to be the case, for example, with Basque nationalism relative to the government of Spain. The development, and the potential for improvement, cannot be fully understood before a study is made of many such cases and the pattern of understandings emerging concerning the respects in which the region will remain *without* autonomy relative to the nation-state of which it remains a part. The phenomenon may be a sign of the waning of the importance presently attached to the idea of the nation-state. That idea may, indeed, be merely a passing phase of the world's political life.

In this chapter, we have noted some of the stresses on nationalism and developments of the idea. The chapter has sought to explain both why the idea of national self-determination is so politically influential in our lifetime and why it presents such difficulties. There are some signs that it is being either abandoned or significantly refashioned.

FIVE

Government in Political Philosophy

Governments are organizations of officials charged with responsibility for directing and administering the political affairs of political communities. Almost every element of this characterization requires elucidation and supporting argument. Some are provided in the introduction and Chapters One and Two. The remainder will be provided in this chapter.

Governments fulfill their responsibility typically though not exclusively through the use of coercion-backed rules, regulations, orders, and commands. Early in Chapter Two, suggestions were made concerning the feasible outgrowth of such phenomena from the intensification and extension of our interest in, and demands upon, systematic mutual reliance (SMR). These suggestions were not intended as pieces of historical speculation concerning the actual origins of anything, but rather as explorations of some fundamental features of the commonly recognized functions of governments. That exploration continues in the present chapter, where we discuss further the connections between characteristics of government and the functions we have come to depend upon it to fill.

This discussion of the usefulness of government and the suppositions supporting our idea that it is useful will be accompanied eventually by a discussion of the *legitimacy* of government and the way in which legitimacy enters into the very idea of what can constitute a government. The remaining chapters in this part will be concerned in one way or another with these latter questions. As in Chapter Three, but to a lesser extent, the following four section headings separate questions that so far as I know are not separated in the literature.

WHICH THINGS ARE GOVERNMENTS?

By and large, political philosophers have not much disputed about which things are or are not governments. Theoretical discussion of the issue—that is, discussion of the principles in accordance with which governments are or should be recognized—has been confined principally to scholars of international law. In practical politics, the issue sometimes arises after coups and revolutions, but time and recognition by other governments generally resolve matters sufficiently to bring disputes about that, at least, to an end. And the issue can arise also in connection with constitutional questions, such as in cases where the outcomes or the legitimacy of elections are in doubt. But while such occasions as these and those formerly cited may interest political philosophers for various reasons, they have not, except derivatively, been the focus of any substantial attention.

In anthropology there have sometimes been doubts expressed about whether the coordinative usages of some preliterate or nomadic societies amounts to government. But these occasional doubts have not had noticeable effects upon political philosophy. Lastly, political scientists in pursuit of answers to the question "Who governs?" have sometimes provided answers that *could* create doubts about where the *real* government is. But such doubts have not played so much a role as one might have expected in discussions among political philosophers of which things are governments.

On the other hand, the last has a large potential to do so. If we ask, at the start, "Where is the government?" it may appear easy to find. In the United States, we look to the White House, the Capitol building, the state government offices, and so on. But if we ask, instead, "Who governs?" and then let the bewilderment this question creates when it is hard-pressed reflect back upon the question about where the government is, things will get muddier. For the question "Who governs?" is in some quarters not thought to be answered correctly or realistically by looking solely or even at all at government officials. Instead one is advised to look to "plutocrats" or to labor unions, or to "leaders of the community"—anywhere but to government officials per se. The inclination to look elsewhere need not be confined to the wilder reaches of political rhetoric. It could appear in political philosophy proper and in proper political philosophy. Powerful reasons can be given to deny that our government officials "really" govern. It may be claimed that they are merely front figures for the people who really govern, the persons of considerable economic and/or social influence in the community, or even persons from outside the community. But then, if these latter people govern, why not consider *them* the government? And so on.

In opposition to such thinking it may be asserted that the way to find the government is to find not whose word is sufficient to determine courses of political action, but rather whose word is necessary. There is good reason to identify those people, despite who influences them or "runs" them, as the government. We have a way of speaking that appears to manage the situation neatly. The other persons may perhaps be behind the government and perhaps even run it, but they are not *the* government. They are not like the driver of a vehicle, but at best like persons giving the driver instructions. In reply, one might say that though the former person is controlling the vehicle, it is not quite right to say baldly that this person is the driver of the vehicle.

When one insists on asking what the *real X* is, as it is here asked what the *real* government is, and it is insisted that the *real X* is not what it generally seems to be, watch out! What is happening is that a potentially illuminating but also potentially obfuscating move is being made. The ground of discussion is very likely being subtly shifted, and a new identification of what is important is being made. This may on occasion be worth doing, but we must be aware that it is happening. Thus, instead of merely asking, "Is the allegation correct or incorrect?" we should ask whether the attempted reidentification of what is truly important is in fact an improvement over what was previously treated as important. Our way of answering that question does not deal with anything so firm and "objective" as criteria of correctness and incorrectness, but rather with assessing and evaluating what we ought to be attending to.

So, to put the matter simply, we can ask whether we ought to be attending to whose word is *necessary* for issuing and effecting governmental proclamations and regulations, or to whose word is most powerfully effective in this regard. Does it appear that answers to questions such as these depend upon the matters we have been pursuing? What are we or should we be interested in pursuing? What problems are we or should we be trying to solve? What human concerns are we expressing? Are we trying to identify and learn to operate the machinery of government, or how to touch the wellsprings of power? Without knowing which interests we have, we will not be in a position to decide whether to go along with the claim about what government really is.

WHAT IS THE ESSENCE OR NATURE OF GOVERNMENT?

Governments, depending upon the context, are ordinarily thought to be either the people and parties at the top reaches of those who operate the political machinery, or they are the aggregation of roles and positions occupied by those people. As suggested in Chapter One, a government is commonly thought to have more or less the four following essential features: (1) it issues regulations and directives to which conformity is generally obtained; (2) it claims priority in obedience wherever regulations and directives are issued by it, whatever the context or subject matter (the cash value of this being that it claims the right to penalize nonconformity); (3) it claims legitimacy; and (4) the regulations and directives it issues and to which it demands conformity are commonly coercion-backed, either directly or indirectly, through coercion-backed remedial rules, regulations, or directives. Together, these four features constitute what is commonly regarded as the fundamental nature or essence of government. Some of these features have already been dealt with; others will be dealt with in succeeding chapters (see especially Chapters Six, Seven, and Eight).

Here, however, we can usefully draw attention to some of the places in political philosophy where these matters are likely to be discussed. The general issue of the nature or essence of government can grow out of concerns of, for instance, Thomists, Hobbesians, and anarchists. With Thomists it can grow out of their characterizations of the qualifying or identifying characteristics of rulers of communities (with reference to the common good), or in speculation about the need for government and whether government need be essentially coercive (compare with Yves Simon). With Hobbesians it can grow out of an interest in the connection between the existence of commonwealths and sovereigns. With anarchists it can grow out of their insistence that their critics have confused government with society, and that they (generally) advocate elimination only of the former and not the latter. Concern for the issues also appears to some extent in remarks by political philosophers on the importance of distinguishing the government of a state from the state itself; but these latter discussions have not to my knowledge raised any major issues in political philosophy. In these cases, the government is taken to be the people or parties currently in charge of the state apparatus, or, in a curious reversal of some moves discussed in Chapter Four, the state is taken to be the same as the nation.

WHAT OUGHT GOVERNMENTS TO BE?

This question has not, as with the parallel question about the state examined in Chapter Three, been substantially conflated with its close relative, "What is the nature of government?" (see the discussion of comparable questions in regard to the state), though of course inquiry into the latter has most often provided an important basis for conclusions about what government ought to be. But discussions of what government ought to be are not always easily distinguished from discussions of what the state ought to be, and from discussions, in particular, of which forms of internal organization of the state are to be preferred. Governments can be seen as *constituting* the internal political organization of states or at least the major element of that organization. Thus, we might equally expect to hear claims that governments ought to be democratic or monarchical or constitutional or whatever, and that states ought to be democratic, or whatever. This parallel need not either result from or produce confusion. We must, however, keep in mind that this closeness is underwritten by two suppositions: (1) that our present interest is in the political character of states, rather than in other aspects of their characters, and (2) that the political character of states is determined mainly by the kinds of government they have.

Though these suppositions may be both reasonable and harmless, there is good reason to separate inquiry concerning what government ought to be from inquiry concerning what states ought to be. Governments can be representative, states cannot, though of course we could arrive at some special understanding of what it was for a state to be representative. The legitimacy (for instance, the constitutionality) of a government is also something very different from the legitimacy of a state. Further, for a government to be popular may be something quite different from, and even under some circumstances inconsistent with, the state's being popular. And the government's being wise may be quite another matter from a state's being wise; the former may be a judgment about domestic policy, whereas the latter may be a judgment about foreign policy.

These differences provide sufficient justification for a separate inquiry into what governments ought to be. This separation is the only way to provide a place for some topics of undeniable importance in the history of political philosophy; for example, whether governments should be popular or representative; the importance of knowledge, justice, or magnanimity in rulers; the relative merits of rule of law and rule by discretion. (Consideration of these topics is spread throughout Part II.)

Consideration of which forms of government are to be preferred was given direction by Plato and Aristotle. They were followed by Aquinas, Hobbes, Montesquieu, and other major figures in the field of political philosophy who discussed the relative merits of monarchy, aristocracy, democracy, and the like. For centuries this shaping so dominated inquiry into the matter that governments not fitting the typology very well (such as the Roman and German empires, the Netherlands and Swiss confederations) were either rejected as unacceptable or crammed into the typology with its departure therefrom obscured (compare with S. R. Davis).

Gradually, however, though nominal use of the typology was continued, as Sidgwick noted at the end of the nineteenth century, there were significant alterations—for example, modern use of *monarchy* denotes governments in which only a share of power is possessed by a person called the *monarch*. Fascists, socialists, and communists have departed completely from reliance on the typology in their discussions of which governments are to be preferred, as have numerous modern political scientists who have been concerned with the practical merit and workability of what have been recognized in this century as basic styles of political organization. Some persons both inside and outside the field of political philosophy have regarded discussion of this issue as *the* principal job of political philosophy, but once that interest is distinguished from the others we have considered, it is seen to be considerably less important than that. Indeed, since the days immediately following World War II it has not received substantial attention from political philosophers proper.

WHAT OUGHT GOVERNMENTS TO AIM AT?

Among responses to this question, political philosophers have cited both the achievement of positive goals and the fulfillment of negative constraints. The most prominent among the positive goals have been (1) being representative, (2) promoting the well-being (or moral development) of citizens, (3) protecting individual rights (something that could also be seen as the fulfillment of a negative constraint), (4) promoting the glory or fulfilling the historical destiny of the state or the nation, and (5) destroying the remnants of the bourgeoisie (the task of the government of the proletarian state). Among the negative constraints, the most prominent have been (1) acting constitutionally where there is a constitution, (2) enforcing the rule of law rather than the rule of people, (3) observing and being respectful of individual or minority rights (see number 3 in the preceding paragraph), (4) acting not inconsistently with either human or divine justice, and (5) acting only in accord with the actual or hypothetical consent of "the people."

This discussion of government has mentioned many more topics than it has investigated. Many of these can be illuminated by discussions elsewhere in the book. In any case, the objective here has been merely to suggest the contexts in political philosophy in which they may arise. The question headings provided here separate topics most often jumbled together in the literature, even though they are significantly different from one another.

THE NEED FOR ORDERS AND COMMANDS

We noted in Chapter Two that a use (and possibly even a need) for government can arise out of extending our dependence upon SMR geographically, temporally, culturally, or technically past the point where mutual understanding alone can suffice for its successful operation. Where the more or less lasting goodwill of friends or relatives, common understandings of persons with the same cultural heritages, and relatively familiar and uncomplicated tasks that may characterize the lives of some aggregations of humans are absent, mutual understanding may also be absent or at least insufficient to sustain the demands made upon it by SMR. The insufficiency of mutual understanding in many matters has long been widely assured by enlargements of knowledge, technological capacities, and ambitions. Reliance on mutual understanding has thus long been insufficient for many people and in many places, and additional bases for coordinating our mutual reliances have been required.

We are supposing, for reasons given in Chapter One, that some extensive or intensive coordination of human activities is aspired to. We are also supposing that, among the persons whose activities are to be coordinated, there are persons who are either not related to one another, or not previously friends, or without similar cultural heritages. We are also supposing that the tasks confronting them do not include only tasks that are familiar and simple. Is it likely that wordless understanding will suffice for the needed coordination? If not, what *will* suffice? Proposals? Advice? Requests delivered by whomever feels like delivering them?

Experience does not give most of us much hope that such devices alone will work. *Present* experience has led most of us to believe that human desires, inclinations, and opinions are too diverse. (The emphasis on "present" hints at the importance of anarchist views. Experience has not led everyone to this conclusion, and some are unwilling to reach conclusions on the matter solely from present experience.) In view of likely diversity, most of us will believe there must be provided some more definitive and decisive way of determining who does what, when, and how. It is here that orders, commands, rules, and regulations find their roles. If they are univocal and persons are sufficiently motivated to conform to them, they *can* coordinate human behavior. Problems peculiar to rules and regulations will be considered elsewhere, and orders and commands will be considered here.

Behind orders and commands lie phenomena of authority and authorization. Without at the moment considering the possible roles of these in motivating persons to conform to orders and commands, consider momentarily their roles in identifying spoken words *as* orders and commands. Orders and commands may, of course, be authorized or unauthorized, but without *some* structure of authority, spoken words could not be recognizable as either orders or commands.

This truth has become obscured by the fact that certain intonation contours have come to be associated with these spoken words. Consequently, we may be tempted to identify any spoken words having such contours as an order or command. When appropriate authorization is absent we sometimes say such things as, "Stop ordering me about; you have no authority to do so," or, "It was amusing to see the child issuing commands to his parents." But we also say, "The child was pretending to deliver commands." And we all know that persons with authority sometimes deliver orders or commands with very different intonation contours from those just suggested. For example, many orders and commands are delivered with the intonation contours typically associated with suggestions, questions, advice, and the like. Clearly, the intonation contours typically associated with orders and commands are not necessary to make them orders or commands. The question is whether these contours are sufficient to do so. In sum, without some recognizable structures of authority there might be leaders, but there could not be people issuing orders or commands.

Authorization enters again into the story when we consider how orders and commands are to be made univocal. To be univocal they must at least be internally consistent, allowing for some but not a great many changes of mind, even if only one person is to deliver them. If more than one person is to deliver them, the deliverings of the different deliverers are subject to the same constraints and thus must themselves find some way of coordination.

The need for univocality is premised upon a desire to utilize SMR in situations in which orders (commands, and the like) are relied upon instead of more or less wordless mutual understanding to *coordinate* human behavior insofar as it is to be coordinated. If not univocal, the orders and so on will be unreliable instruments for this purpose. (The univocality, it should be noted, has nothing much to do with unanimity. In fact, its appearance as a requirement here suggests the contrary—that the need for it arises precisely in situations in which unanimity is not expected.)

A common means of safeguarding the required internal consistency is to restrict who is to deliver orders, and so forth. The restriction is indicated and brought about by *authorizing* some person or group of persons, and only them, to deliver the orders in question. The requirement of authorization does not make univocality or even internal consistency certain, but increases the likelihood of the first and thus the second, through the limitation thereby placed upon the sources and settings of orders, and so on. Authorization will be discussed in Chapter Six. It appears here only as a familiar instrument contributing toward the univocality needed or probably needed, we commonly believe, for effective large-scale coordinations. With these, people must know *where* to look for the definitive information on what to do and when to do it. Whether more than one person will be needed to give this information is merely a technological problem. In any case, the need is the same. (Of course, the more elaborate the technology supposed, the more probable it is that extensive coordination has already been achieved.)

Second, problems of coordination are not met completely merely by the *delivery* of univocal information (unless, perhaps, the information is considered to have been delivered all the way to the cerebral cortex). One has also to check on how the information is being understood. This is important because if it is understood differently by different people, then coordination will not, except by accident, be achieved.

It is important to observe that the problem so far is merely one of understanding, not one of goodwill or intention to perform. The sufficient presence of the latter disposition cannot, perhaps, be supposed without taking special measures to provide it. We will soon discuss the matter. But even with respect to getting uniform understanding alone, more than merely a delivery system will be necessary. There has to be some provision for observing the results of the receipt of that information and for correcting misunderstandings of it. We do not yet have sufficient technological resources for this to be achieved with respect to any large-scale enterprise by any one person. Thus, more than one person will be needed, and some person(s) will have to be authorized to make any corrections that are necessary. At this point, the potential for the growth of a fledgling administrative enterprise becomes apparent. We have here, in fact, the lineaments of government.

This discussion should not be taken to suggest the inevitability of centralization. When a number of people have been authorized to deliver orders and commands, the needed coordination among these orders and commands does not necessarily itself occur through the issuing of and conformity to orders and commands. Certain specific conditions have been mentioned earlier as giving rise to the need for orders and commands as instruments of coordination; these conditions or a significant portion of them may not be present among the persons authorized to *issue* orders and commands to the society generally. They may be sufficiently united in opinion, cultural breeding, or aspiration to coordinate their activities well enough through the other instrumentalities mentioned previously.

Further, we are talking here only about situations in which coordination is needed. Coordination is not always needed. People may sometimes be permitted without answering to anyone to go their separate ways. There are thus many enterprises in which decentralization is feasible. These may be enterprises in which coordination is unneeded, or in which coordination may be achieved by methods other than orders and commands, or in which a mixture of these considerations is present and thus have elements of both centralization and decentralization. Much of the debate surrounding centralization and decentralization concerns the nature of the enterprises in question, whether they are enterprises of one or the other of these sorts.

A further consideration is the following: whether persons can reach agreement and thus coordination without orders and commands depends not only upon their common backgrounds, and the like, but upon the time they have to reach agreement and also upon the pressure under which they are to reach agreement. Unlimited discussion or extreme urgency could produce agreement where more limited discussion or less pressure to reach a decision would not. Thus, even where coordination is required and backgrounds are strikingly dissimilar, and so on, leaving the matter decentralized may produce certain desired effects. It may profoundly affect the quality of discussion and of social relations we have.

We have spoken so far in this chapter only of the aspiration to create schemes of mutual reliance. In Chapter Two, however, we discussed further the pros and cons of an aspiration to specialize. That further aspiration intensifies our need for administration of our efforts to coordinate our activities. For mutual affairs will become more complex, our dependency upon one another will increase, and our knowledge of precisely what other people are doing on our behalf and even our knowledge that they are doing it will decrease. This provides us with yet a third basis for that administration of our affairs characteristic of government. The first arises out of our aspiration for fairly extensive schemes of mutual reliance. The second arises out of presumptions concerning what is needed to secure coordinated compliance (univocality). The third arises out of our interests in intensifying the reliance in order to permit specialization.

THE WISH TO CONFORM

Now consider the obstacle to coordination provided by the fact that some persons may not *wish* to conform. Lack of such a wish need not be solely the result of ill will toward authorities or anybody. One *may* feel that the principal benefits of coordination will redound only to one's enemies or to at least persons with whom one feels no sympathy. But there are other sources of a disinclination to conform. A person may have alternative, more valued, activities in mind, or may feel that the required activities are in some way ineligible for performance (immoral, too costly, or otherwise badly mistaken). Or a person may be simply too lazy, too distracted, or too apathetic to engage in the required performance. These obstacles to coordination include selfishness, ill will, and weakness of will. They also include ignorance and inattention. But it is difficult to believe that they refer only to defects in human nature or human knowledge on the part of the ruled. This last is clearly so if the rulers are not supposed to be infallibly wise, moral, considerate, and so forth. And the fact that rulers are *not* all these things cannot reasonably be considered a defect in *them*. It is the human condition, and quite consistent with being well informed and well intentioned.

This last point is of some interest in political philosophy because the contrary has often been asserted. The attribution of a need for political authority to defects in human beings is a well-worn theme in political philosophy. The most complete opposition to it that I have seen is the following argument (by Yves Simon): authority would be needed in communities of creatures even if these creatures were perfectly well intentioned and perfectly well informed.

For in such communities there might be two or more ways of achieving a given goal between which there was nothing to choose with respect to excellence of result, and no more than one of these ways could or should be adopted. In this case, there would have to be a way of determining which way to adopt; perfect intentions and perfect information would not suffice. Authority would have its use in determining what to do in such cases.

If, as we indicated earlier, the supposed lack of intention to conform to requirements of coordination has so many potential sources, how are we to correct it? Clearly, we must motivate people to intend to conform. But how we do this depends upon the explanation for why they fail to conform. Political philosophers, with the exception of the anarchists (discussed later), have thought that coercive backing for the orders and commands, rules and regulations, will always be necessary in order to achieve the coordination required. It may not always be sufficient and it may not be necessary in the case of every individual person, but it will be *generally* necessary. Coercive backing, it is thought, will reliably contribute to conformity depending upon the stiffness of the coercion in question relative to the strength of the reasons or causes for nonconformity. Putting together the considerations adduced here with the discussion offered earlier, one finds an additional rationale for the coercive backing characteristic of government. Coercive backing is thought to play a major supportive role in a central aspiration of government—to have large-scale coordinations of human activities in order to achieve the rewards of extensive SMR.

Not every scheme of SMR is governmental, and government may itself not always seem to be engaged in the operation or support of such schemes. But government does offer important support to nongovernmental schemes in modern life through the laws it promulgates and the courts it operates, all of which can underwrite the aspirations of operators of nongovernmental schemes to obtain conformity to their own efforts at coordination, and to settle disputes among themselves and other persons. Many governmental activities that do not themselves seem to constitute operations of schemes of SMR thus are nevertheless supportive of such schemes. Other governmental activities not seeming to fit into our discussion can be treated as serving (note: not *intended* to serve) SMR by clearing the decks for (by enlarging the areas of our lives in which it will seem feasible) or as actually the operation of a scheme of SMR—for instance, that involved in our significant (though not complete) abandonment of reliance upon self-help in personal defense (more on this last later).

Thus, starting, as we saw in Chapter Two, with a need for food, defense, and a few other basic goods and services that we may each plausibly try to provide for ourselves, we may seek to improve the reliability, quality, and delivery of these goods and services. Without assuming in any way that we *have* gone down this path toward government, we can see that this path leads toward government. And this is without considering wide ranges of common human needs and desires clearly "social" from the start, such as to propagate, to befriend, to be "accepted" in various ways by others. As most of us have these as well as "solitary" interests, aspirations, and beliefs, our collective arrivals at and maintenances of the administrative institutions characteristic of government are understandable. These institutions can potentially bestow benefits that we are prepared to recognize *as* benefits. This is not also to say that we do not recognize a potential in the institutions for damage to our interests: it is also there. We will discuss it later. It has led some, though not yet very many, to abandon reliance on institutions having such a liability.

RULERS AND EXPERTS

So far we have mentioned only our interests in having univocal orders and commands by which we may coordinate our activities, and in obtaining compliance to them. But we have also other interests in the content and character of the orders and commands. In part, that interest is in their legitimacy, a matter considered in Chapter Seven. Presently, we shall consider another facet of that interest. If the content or character of the orders and commands in question is inappropriate, then our coordination may be to no purpose, at least less effective than it might be, and possibly even counter-productive to our interests. We should examine here the means by which the orders and commands are to be generated. Are these means likely to generate generally reliable and fruitful as well as univocal orders and commands?

An enormous variety of generating schemes has been invented, many of which have been adopted at one time or another and in one place or another. We have wide historical experience available if we will but consult it, though it is not often definitive. Political philosophers have often argued in support of one generating scheme or another. Their arguments often seem to have been drawn from consultations of experience, but sometimes have an a priori flavor. As an example of the latter, consider Hobbes's argument that monarchy is preferable to "aristocracy and polity," on the grounds that monarchy provides a single person as sovereign of the commonwealth and thus the sovereign's commands and laws are more likely to be univocal than would otherwise be the case.

Concentrating now especially on the reliability and fruitfulness of the orders and commands, supposing that they will come from some persons or other (not necessarily monarchs or aristocrats, but perhaps "the people" expressing themselves in some recognizable form or other) we would want them to be well informed, skillful in the use of information they possess, and well intentioned. We might, depending upon the situation, desire them to possess other characteristics as well. As mentioned in the Chapter Two discussion of ideals and utopias, differing characters of peoples and locales may make differing styles and policies of rule desirable in those places. Also, the character and intelligence potentials of the "rulers" will make a difference in what we can hope for from them.

A fundamental question is, "Who should rule?" Plato's answer, sensibly enough, is that it should be the most intelligent, knowledgeable, and best-intentioned people who can be found or developed. There are two important things to notice about this answer. The first is that *several* characteristics are to be sought in rulers and that we want a combination of as much of each as we can get. The second is that persons having these characteristics optimally are to be found or *developed*. Large portions of the *Republic* are devoted to discussing how the rulers are to be selected and trained.

The idea that we should select and train our rulers may sound "elitist"; nevertheless, there are also traces of the idea in almost every democratic practice and theory. The popularity in democracy of the diffusion of power to rule affords no reason to abandon interest in the quality of rule or these modes of attaining it. In democracy we do not commonly extend political rule to infants, mental defectives, convicted felons, and we often express concern for the intelligence, knowledge, and character of the persons to whom political rule is extended. Plato had no interest in the *Republic* in diffusion of ruling power; he staked much more on the advantages of selecting and training rulers than do proponents of democracy. His ideas on the matter are, however, relevant to the question, "Who should rule?"

Plato believed that many years of further selection and training will be needed after an initial selection of potential rulers, and that this should be started very early in the lives of those chosen. But Plato wanted rulers not only to be well intentioned and knowledgeable, but also to be physically healthy, vigorous, strong, steadfast, and well balanced. Perusal of the *Republic* may turn up other characteristics as well. Surely we, along with Plato, would like our rulers, whomever they may be, to have such characteristics. Difficulties may occur, however, when we consider how to *get* such rulers. We should be concerned with who is available to be selected, the precise mechanisms for selection and training, and also *who* is to do the selecting and training. Putting aside for the moment important questions about the capacities of the persons available, our concerns should be how to get the community to accept and perhaps even cooperate with the processes of selection and training, and with the reliability of the processes used.

Unless one wishes to take "pot luck" when it comes to rulers, some mechanisms of selection *or* training will have to be utilized. This furthers our dependence upon administrative devices. But, unless our rulers are godlike from the start (Plato doesn't much consider how to deal with the fact that they might not be, until the *Statesman*), there will be some important things of which they are not aware and they will issue at least some maladroit orders and commands. These possibilities give Plato an interest in providing opportunities for the orderers and commanders to "learn" on the job. Providing them with opportunities for feedback on their efforts to rule may be one of the most significant steps that can be taken to improve the quality of their rule. Thus, concern for such feedback is not an interest confined solely to democracies. Even tyrants may have an interest in it. But provision for it will increase the need for administration of communal affairs. If one is serious about it, and about the available feedback actually getting to where it will do the most good, one will want to provide some mechanisms for it. And the mechanisms will have to be administered.

Two further interesting points concerning knowledgeability and good intentions of the rulers, whomever they may be, are discussed by Plato in the *Republic*. First, concerning knowledge, what do we wish our rulers to be knowledgeable about? Stamps or butterflies? Given the way the world currently operates, we do not consider knowledge of such matters to be important or even relevant in equipping persons to rule. We would like our rulers, of course, to have expert knowledge about ruling, but what sort of knowledge is this?

It would seem desirable that our rulers have expert knowledge of human nature and the human situation, at least insofar as they exist in the community they participate in ruling.* Various aspects of each are subjects of special studies of some extent and depth. Resultingly, while there are no persons recognized to be experts concerning the *whole* field, there have come to be recognized experts in parts of it.

Modern political life in particular presents us with problems of such complexity that we often rely on the special knowledge of such "partial" experts. Their knowledge is often so esoteric with respect to the knowledge or insight of the rest of us, however, that the challenge is often how to consult them without being controlled by them. In our efforts to make use of the special and relevant knowledge they have, we and our political leaders often try to consult them and end by feeling or finding that they have become our rulers. But the partiality of their knowledge relative to knowledge of the scope we believe we need prompts us to believe that our formal political leaders should not rely solely on any of them. An "overview" of some sort is apparently needed.

What knowledge equips a person to take such an overview or to synthesize one out of many partial views? Many commentators have felt rather helpless in the face of this question, and generally only some technocrats and theologians have felt they could provide an answer.

But pressure from the question creates an urge in many commentators to seek escape routes, for example, by recommending the diffusion (or at least the appearance of diffusion) of decision-making responsibility by which we are so captivated in this country. Their hope is that this can be carried to the point where decision makers normally need to know only what normal persons can be expected to know—for instance, what everyone commonly knows about his or her own locale and personal situation. Some such recommendations travel under the titles *democratization* and *decentralization*. However, diffusion of decision making affords no good reason to be unconcerned with its quality. Democratization and decentralization each have other rationales, some of which have already been suggested (as in the discussion of local government) and some of which are to be discussed in this chapter. Some varieties of democratization and decentralization may even *be* solutions or partial solutions to the problem posed earlier.

Unless there is some a priori way of gaining the desired general knowledge of human natures and situations, it is presumably to be gained through experience and observation. Hobbes said that experience is bestowed equally on all persons. But whether or not this rough claim is convincing, humans differ from one another in the insight their various experiences afford them.

What gives insight? Even the experiences of fairly sheltered persons may be so multifarious as to appear chaotic. On the other hand, persons of very wide experience may rightly or wrongly see the important facts about the

---

*The following thoughts were prompted by reflection on Plato's discussion of the divided line in the *Republic*.

world as few and simple. It depends upon the capacity of persons to see a pattern or patterns in their onrushing experience. It may simply be a matter of seeing what the experiences "add up to." A person who is good at doing this would, on grounds of knowledge, anyway, be a more competent ruler than one who is very bad at it. And we might reasonably hope that our decision makers have well-developed capacities of this sort. Plato's discussion in the *Republic* of the knowledge he wishes his rulers to have can be understood as sympathetic to this account.

Second, concerning good intentions, Plato stressed careful selection, periodic testing, and rigorous training in attempting to produce decision makers with good intentions. But he did not suppose that they alone would be successful *enough* to produce well-intentioned decision makers. He structured his ideal society so that it would have institutional safeguards assuring the good intentions of the decision makers. Thus, for example, the decision makers were not allowed to have private property, and they were not to know who their biological children were. Such enticements into well-known forms of supposed corruption were thus absent, and the decision makers could be counted on to be free from them.

Some modern institutional safeguards against misrule through corruption seek to protect rulers from temptation only indirectly, but to protect the public directly from the effects thereof. This is the point of public-disclosure laws concerning the assets of public officials. Consider also the checks and balances so much a feature of American constitutionalism. The overall point in such institutions is that, even with programs of careful training, testing, and selection, one should not hope for too much success in the production of important character traits in the decision makers.

There are, of course, commentators who hope for nothing at all along these lines. Some teach us that, in political as well as in economic matters, if each person pursues one's own interests, the interests of all will thereby be furthered. The ensuing confusion is supposed somehow to balance out in everyone's favor. It is the operation in the political realm of the "unseen hand" of classical economics. Such suppositions aside, our conclusion might reasonably be that, though we must provide institutional safeguards against the probable lack of complete success in programs of selection, testing, and training, we cannot design institutional safeguards so powerful that we can safely do utterly without programs of selection *or* testing *or* training. In considering this matter, we should remind ourselves that our concern at this point is with the character of the decision makers, and not with their knowledge and skills. We need, therefore, to isolate the potentials of such programs with respect to character from their potential with respect to knowledge and skill.

ANARCHISM: THE ELIMINABILITY OF GOVERNMENT

Anarchists advise that we do without government. This, or something like it (their target is sometimes unclear—see the discussion further on), indeed, is their only explicit conclusion. They argue that our apparent need for government originates in the corruption of our natures by coercive institutions. Once freed from this corrupting influence, we or our descendants may live fruit-fully and harmoniously enough without such institutionalized coercion.

Anarchist theses should be taken seriously. Significant anarchist tendencies can be found in many political philosophies where their presence may be little suspected. Much democratic and Marxist theory, for example, contains significant expressions of such aspirations and hopes. Anarchism's target has variously been described as political society, the state, law, and government. The underlying difficulty anarchists find with each of these is the coercive backing (thought to be) central to it. Anarchists believe that coercive backing is a dispensable evil in that sufficient coordination among human beings can be achieved without it. It is not always clear whether they wish to rely on volun-tary compliance alone, or whether they will also permit persuasive devices, sometimes of rather severe impact, such as ostracism, scapegoating, or out-lawry (to be discussed in more detail later) to effect compliance. Further, it is not always clear whether they believe that anarchism is suitable to human be-ings with a rather short period of conditioning or only after a very long accul-turation process. We shall subsequently (in Part III) discuss the predominant reasons *why* they are opposed to coercive backing. At the moment, we are in-terested in their vision of our practical prospects without it.

Serious consideration of anarchism will require us to muster considerable insight into human nature. We should consider carefully what rational grounds there are for believing that our present coercion-backed institutions are having corrupting effects on human nature, that these corrupting effects would be removed by the removal of the coercion-backed institutions, that the coordinations needed for our present large-scale schemes of mutual reliance could be effected through unforced understanding and voluntary compli-ance, or that, if not, we could then irreproachably cut back to schemes of a modest enough size that such means of securing compliance would suffice. Of course, we should also trace carefully the claims of some anarchists that there are methods short of coercive backing for securing compliance that do not quite amount to simply letting all do as they please; we must be sure that these methods in fact are distinguishable from coercive backing *and* will not merely replace the latter with something equally or even more undesirable.

Some anarchists, for example, appear to countenance methods of securing compliance much the same as ostracism, scapegoating, and outlawry. Ostra-cism operates through a communal decision to have nothing to do with a per-son, not to communicate with or to have any commerce with that person. Scapegoating is a communal provision, as hostages for "blood" demanded by foreign enemies, of persons who have offended against the customs or standards of the community but whom the community lacks the power to punish—their offenses thus rendering them vulnerable to mistreatment of a special sort by enemies of the community. Outlawry is a communal declara-tion that certain offenders against the customs or standards of the community are outlaws whom anyone can destroy at pleasure—these persons are thus denied protection otherwise afforded by the community to members of the community against injury (broadly understood).

Historically speaking, these were mechanisms often used by communities relying extensively on "self help" for personal protection. Ostracism occurred in ancient Greece. Scapegoating and outlawry were familiar in medieval times, when kings were weak and lacked power to protect citizens. (Outlawry is recommended in a text familiar to political philosophers, Locke's *Second Treatise of Government*.) Are these devices coercive or noncoercive? Would reliance on them to back efforts at social coordination be preferable to the reliance on coercive backing typical of governments? How far, in the end, is reliance on one from the other?

If anarchists are right, much of the administrative apparatus sketched in previous sections of this chapter will still be necessary. If they are wrong, then our plans, aspirations, and tolerances should depend upon how and precisely where they are wrong. Perhaps we should be content with less extensive coordinative enterprises. Perhaps, on the other hand, we shall have to rely on the administrative apparatus and the coercive backing normally thought characteristic of government.

In any case, we should be clear about the mode of that reliance. This is necessary (if not sufficient) in order to assign appropriate weight to the anarchist's challenges. A position commonly accepted by many commentators on political phenomena and on the coercion associated with it is that coercion is merely the bottom line. It is not intended that political devices rely on coercion right off, but that it be available when much else has failed.

Indeed, some nonanarchist commentators have held that we should not rely too much in human affairs upon formally political procedures and operations precisely because they are coercion-backed, and that reliance upon them is a sign of the failure of much else that is highly desirable to attempt. The deficiency would be that politics, together with its coercive backing, is, or at least ought to be in the end, a backup to other ways of proceeding in human affairs.

Anarchists may be seen as so upset by our common reliance on political coercion that they wish to give it up entirely; perhaps we would be more reasonable to take the position that we should not resort to it so soon. Anarchists may then say that merely holding coercive politics at the ready makes a profound difference in what else occurs and what else can occur. Holding up and brandishing a fist will make a difference in allegedly voluntary, cooperative, and agreed-upon behavior. Some important issues in political philosophy to which *this* leads will be examined further in Part III.

Not all anarchists concentrate so fully on the coercive aspects of political society as I suggest here. Some anarchists appear to be complaining of any reliance whatever for social coordination upon devices not requiring the use of an individual's faculties such as perception, judgment, and responsibility. Thus they might be opposed to schemes utilizing any orders and commands whatever, regardless of how compliance with them is to be obtained. Evaluation of the views of such anarchists requires discussion of quite another sort than that provided here.

A second issue underemphasized in this discussion of anarchism concerns some anarchist contentions that they are attacking only *political* institutions, and not all social institutions whatever. They wish us to do without the former, and some are especially careful to note they do not expect or wish us to do without many of the latter. Thus, there are some devices of social control that some anarchists, at least, would leave in place. It is then incumbent upon them to state precisely what it is about political institutions that they find objectionable that is not found in the social institutions that they would leave in place.

SIX

Authority

AUTHORITY AND COORDINATION

As we have seen, the insufficiency of mutual understanding to coordinate at least some schemes of SMR has diverse sources (see Chapter Two). The question we now wish to pursue further is how, in view of this diversity, to obtain the desired coordination of activities. If coordination is to be achieved through proposal and acceptance of some one coherent, perhaps not perfectly precise, course of action out of the many possible courses, the problems become how to get *a* course adopted and how to get citizens to conform to it. A fairly blunt instrument is consequently often brought into play: authority.

Authority operates in various guises as a solution to both the coordination problems just stated. But it does this in so many different settings and ways that discussion of it has become rich, confused, and confusing. One must notice first that authority, via its contributions to coordination generally, affords avenues to personal power, preeminence, and wide enlargement of personal capacities, giving it importance in human affairs for reasons quite other than its contributions to public service. It operates too in diverse ways in contributing to coordination—sometimes relatively directly in the issuing and enforcement of orders and commands or the other ways in which policies and procedures come to be marked as authoritative, and sometimes indirectly—for example, in the granting of permissions, immunities, and empowerments, each of which, given astute use of it in the service of various human motives, may vastly enlarge coordinative capacities within communities.

Despite and even especially because of the nature of its contributions to coordination, authority has a potential to make things bad as well as better. No reasonably comprehensive discussion of it should fail to bring this capacity to light. Furthermore, we may readily see that this capacity is almost continuous with and emergent from precisely the features that make authority useful. For example, authority may aggrandize the interests only of the wielders of authority and their supporters. Altogether, authority has thus vastly enlarged the capacity of ignorance and insensitivity, as well as of sheer nastiness, cupidity, and self-aggrandizement, to do injury to human beings. Some commentators would claim that it has also foreshortened and distorted the "natural" course of human development through interference with the development of such important characteristics as perceptivity, sensitivity, and judgment; this claim, however, is more controversial than the others and will receive careful separate attention in Chapter Fourteen.

SENSES OF AUTHORITY

What *is* authority? In attempting to locate and describe it, philosophers have usefully distinguished several different idioms using the word *authority*. *In authority*, the idiom most closely connected with authorization (as distinguished from *an authority*, as in "she is an authority on butterflies," and some uses of *on authority*, as in "I got my tires replaced on the authority of Jones, who was in a position to see the situation better than I" [compare with G. Young]) is the one of these idioms on which we shall focus here. There is nothing inescapable about this. Headway could also be made through focusing on another of the idioms just mentioned, or by giving precedence to an altogether different, though related, expression—for instance, *authoritative*.

Before launching into our discussion of *in authority*, it would be worthwhile to exhibit the foregoing briefly. Consider *authoritative* and the headway that can be made through examination of it. First, consider its links with *in authority*. Straightforwardly speaking, though only persons can be in authority or can exercise authority, things other than persons, such as documents and utterances, can have authority. This does not mean that the latter are in authority or exercise authority; it means only that they are *authoritative*. Perhaps they are authoritative because they have been authored, endorsed, or uttered by persons in authority, perhaps not. (Alternative sources of authoritativeness are not well understood despite abundant discussions of them.) Further, just as what persons say (in utterances and documents) can be authoritative, so, perhaps by extension, the persons themselves can be authoritative. A person, for example, would be authoritative (as distinct from merely seeming authoritative or being authoritarian) if the person spoke authoritatively, either because he or she exercised authority or because he or she was a recognized expert in the matter at hand, and recognized experts were in agreement. Because persons *in* authority customarily *exercise* authority by means of *authoritative* utterances (understanding *utterances* broadly), authoritative utterances could reasonably be chosen basic to an understanding of what it is to be in authority. A person who is in authority normally is a person able to exercise authority; the normal means of exercising authority is issuing authoritative utterances or documents.

Utterances and documents are authoritative relative to conditions in the following ways: (a) relative to a given subject matter (for example, city clerks do not issue traffic tickets, and traffic police do not normally perform marriage ceremonies or register voters); (b) relative to a given population (the public-health officer of Johnson County cannot normally issue authoritative utterances of residents of Jackson County); and (c) relative to a given time or time span (if the sheriff or a deputy orders you to remove your car from the street, you may be able to appeal the order, but it is authoritative at least until the appeal has been made). Authoritative utterances and documents may or may not be relative to conditions in yet another way—to whether the authority system in question is religious, legal, fraternal, and so on. As various authority systems appear to coexist in many communities, this last relativization raises important questions about the ultimate impact of an authority system on persons within its ambit. If various authority systems within whose ambit a person finds oneself are not carefully adjusted among themselves, what resolution of their several supposed behavioral impacts is supposed to occur? The path to adequate understanding of these last relativizations is heavily contested, and we shall not enter directly into it here. (But we cannot avoid entirely making some remarks bearing upon these questions as we proceed.)

To bring out the relativizations about which we are comparatively certain, I offer the following schema: if some proposition, p, or some particular formulation thereof, fp (p or fp being contained in some utterance by a person in authority or in some authoritative document), is authoritative for a person Z, at time T, relative to matter Y, then p or fp plays a very special role in determining what is, shall, or must be done or professed about Y by Z, and no other proposition or proposition formulation shall or should be more important in determining for Z at T what shall (and so forth) be done or professed concerning matter Y.

Notice that this is an elucidation of what it is for a segment of an utterance or document to be authoritative *simpliciter*, and thus does not raise the question of what to do or profess when coexisting authority systems fail to coordinate, or even what to do or profess when one has any of a number of other kinds of reasons as well (for example, stemming from considerations of morality, prudence, or personal inclination) for not conforming to the workings of a given authority system.

Though attributions conveyed by the idioms *an authority* and *on authority* do sometimes contribute to coordination, these contributions operate quite differently from that of the attribution of authority in which we are interested here. For example, consultations with communally recognized experts (persons sometimes called "authorities") may contribute to the achievement of a desired coordination directly, indirectly, or not at all, depending upon what is true of the experts being consulted (for instance, do they agree?) and what is true of the persons doing the consulting (for example, how seriously dedicated and able are they to act on what the experts tell them?). However, the attributions of authority to persons, on which we shall focus here, contribute quite differently from this to the achievement of coordination, though their operation may on several different grounds be readily confused with the operation of attributions of authority of the sort just noticed. In both cases, "authorities" may be consulted to obtain reliable information on matters of con cern. But in the case on which we shall not focus here, the information is only *reported* by the "authorities" in question, whereas in the cases on which we shall focus here, though the intention of the "authorities" is often only to report on matters of concern to the persons doing the consulting (such as on what the relevant rules and regulations are and how they are likely to be administered—matters on which the "authorities" may very well be expert), the persons doing the consulting will normally be quite mistaken to suppose that the important issue will ever be only whether the "authority's" utterances were true or false. The "authority" is not so marked because he or she is an expert in anything or especially reliable in providing true reports on it, but because he or she is *in* authority. Being in authority gives one's utterances a special force in contributing to communal coordination. One's utterances, if made in appropriate circumstances and about appropriate matters, serve social coordination through social backing of opinion and supportive behavior—behavior ranging from the application of formal sanctions to the use of less formal expressions of disapproval, such as "snubbing." (Later there will be a more careful characterization of the "backing of authority.") Persons in authority thus have an unusual, though often sharply limited, capacity to get other persons to act in accord with their utterances. Persons in authority have this special capacity, and persons exercising this capacity are exercising authority.

We shall examine this capacity carefully from several different perspectives, gradually learning more of its (sometimes) controversial characteristics as we do so. We shall ask (1) what is it about being in authority that marshals this social backing? and (2) precisely what *is* this social backing? The first question will provide an opportunity to discuss the distinction between authority and power (discussed in the next section), the second question, an opportunity to discuss some aspects of the administrative effectiveness of authority, and the relation of authority to hierarchy (covered in the following section).

AUTHORITY AND POWER

As the earlier remarks on the underside of authority have already provided occasion to suggest, the contribution of authority to coordination and the motivation to conform to authority are not always fully voluntary or involve a belief in the benefits of authority. Nevertheless, its effectiveness does appear to many commentators to rest upon something other than the use of naked force. Indeed, its usefulness in human communities is widely thought to depend upon something other than naked force. This has led to the examination of the relationship between authority and power.

Controversy about the relationship between authority and power has concerned principally whether authority and power are distinct or whether authority is a kind of power—not that anyone's ideas about power are all that clear. It, too, is a troublesome idea, and controversey rages about what *it* is. We need, then, to specify the relationship between two ideas, neither of which is particularly clear. This is, unfortunately, not an uncommon situation in philosophy, but it is one of the features making it so captivating to some persons.

In any case, in view of coupled references to authority and power in discussions of the ways human communities do or should operate, it would be unfortunate if continued efforts to get clear about what might be meant by these references were not forthcoming.

Most understandings of power have it include the capacity to gain compliance through intimidation by brute force. Authority also sometimes gains compliance a similar way. But there is a difference. The capacity to use brute force in order to intimidate *is* the power, whereas the capacity (the power) is wielded or threatened *in the name* of authority. Unlike exercises of naked power, exercises of authority explicitly or implicitly invoke entitlement (or purported entitlement) to do what is done.* Unlike exercises of naked power, exercises of authority rest their hoped-for effectiveness in securing compliance upon the basis of (purported) entitlement.

Entitlement to order, command, permit, and so on, whether purported or actual, is at the heart of exercises of authority. Philosophical interest in the matter has centered upon exploration of the considerations that bestow entitlement and on precisely what entitlement is. Social scientists have been interested primarily in how entitlement works (if it works) to secure or contribute to securing compliance.

If a person or group is or claims to be entitled to issue orders, commands, rules, regulations, give permissions, or empower, that person or group has or claims to have special license and backing to do these things relative to acceptance by and support from some actual or ideal community.** Having license and backing in a community to do something is being able to do it without giving offense in that (actual or ideal) community (that is, it is not, given the circumstances, contrary to the practices and usages of the community), and (expectedly) receiving support from the community. This support is typically through (1) communal enforcement procedures such as fines or imprisonment, (2) the variety of ways in which the members of a community may express their disapproval of persons who do not accept the orders, and the like (such as the "snubbing" previously mentioned), or minimally (3) noninterference with (some of) one's own efforts at enforcement.

---

*The analysis in this chapter of authority, while deriving importantly from J. Raz, departs from his analysis in some particulars that I shall not detail here.

**The reader will be aware that heavy use has been made in this book of Hohfeld's format. Persons who think that every right must have a correlative duty will not like this. In my opinion, they are wrong, and I have argued a relevant type of case in my "Competition and Moral Philosophy." Other remarks about Hohfeld are offered later. To say that the community might be ideal covers, for example, the case of a rightful claimant to an office whose office is usurped by another. *Ideal community* here refers to the procedures and usages of the community if it were (which it is not) operating in accord with the standards on which the rightful claimant's claim is founded. Reference to an ideal community is intended also to cover cases of procedures and usages in dreamed-of communities not anywhere (yet) fully actualized. In either case, the ideal community in question will often be ideal relative to some actual community, and its ideality will have strong roots implicit or even explicit in the latter. These roots are exposed, for example, when careful analysis is given of the idea that the claimant's claim is rightful. They concern the standards and ideals adherence to which members of the actual community profess. Further pursuit of this topic would carry us far into discussions of the foundations of rights—a topic not dealt with in the book for reasons given in the introduction.

One or other of these kinds of support would, given the circumstances, be in accord with and called for by the practices and usages of the community. Further, the claim concerning actions of persons claiming entitlement relative to some communities so to act is not that these actions will never be challenged in that community but only that they will acceptably be challenged at most only in accord with the established limits and procedures.

This characterization of entitlement, even as so heavily qualified, is not exceptionless, but merely ordinary. Trying to formulate an exceptionless characterization would probably push too far in a direction where merely going some way would be salutary: recognizing that most of us live in intricate nests and webs of "communities" in which our entitlements will differ and sometimes even conflict. Exercises of our entitlements vis-à-vis one of these "communities" may not always be done without giving offense vis-à-vis, or losing backing in, another "community." And maybe, depending upon how we characterize communities, entitlements within a single community may, on occasion, conflict. If we made the characterization of entitlement relative only to a single community and, further, individuated communities so that each would have an entirely coherent set of practices and usages, there would be no such exceptions to the claim that entitlements in a given community could be exercised without giving offense in that community. But it will be less troublesome in the end not to suppose this. We should nevertheless continue to recognize that reference to practices and usages must play *some* role in the identification and discrimination of communities. This topic will be discussed further.

The key elements of our characterization of entitlement on which I shall focus are the ideas of "without (ordinarily) giving offense in that community" and "doing things that (commonly) receive backing from the community." The bases and natures of the practices and usage presumed in both "not giving offense" and "receiving backing from" may vary from community to community. Acceptance of them need not always be voluntary; it may sometimes be coerced. And acceptance may not even be fully actualized if, in the mind of the speaker, he or she is speaking somewhat more of an ideal than of an actual community, more of a community that, by some standard or other, ought to be rather than (clearly) is.

Authority is what valid claims to entitlement invoke—entitlement to issue orders, commands, permissions, and the like, to do so without ordinarily giving offense in the community in question, and to do so effectively. So, to have authority to do something is the be entitled to do it (from the viewpoint at least of the practices and usages in question) though not necessarily vice versa. It is this special setting that makes authority so distinctively different from naked power.

Problems are sometimes thought to arise because of the common distinction between de facto and *de jure* authority. *De jure* authority is thought to be authority in accord with the particular understood or cited practices and usages of some actual or ideal group, considered apart from whether or not the authority gets exercised and is fully recognized. De facto authority, on the other hand, is thought to be authority actually exercised and effective within some social group, considered apart from the question of whether or not that authority is exercised in conformity with the practices and usages understood or cited.

The problem is to distinguish de facto authority on this understanding of it from naked power. If effectiveness alone were the crucial idea of both de facto authority and naked power, they would not be importantly distinguishable. Some commentators (such as Raz) suggest, however, that de facto authority is distinguishable from naked power by its *purporting* and ordinarily (see Chapter Twelve, on obedience and obligation) to some extent being acknowledged to be in accord with the relevant practices and usages, while naked power carries no such pretension or belief. In de facto authority, consideration is absent only respecting whether exercises of the authority are (ordinarily) actually substantially in accord with the practices, and so on. The distinction between de facto and *de jure* authority now elucidated amounts to the fact that the former *purports* to be and to some degree is (ordinarily) thought to be (whether or not it actually is) in accord with the practices, and so forth, and *is* effective in the given social group; whereas the latter *is* in accord with the practices, and so on, whether or not it is (substantially) effective in the given community.

This amplification appears to resolve some of the former trouble, but continuing problems now prominently present themselves—substantial ones concerning how to think of and identify the practices and usages of the communities, and less consequential but tantalizing ones concerning the extents to which de facto authority must ordinarily be believed to be in accord with the relevant practices and usages and to which *de jure* authority must have acceptance (that is, be effective) in the community. We have already touched briefly upon the first, substantial difficulty earlier in the discussion.

Yet another range of difficulties on this point is also suggested by Roscoe Pound's popularly accepted distinction between "law in books" and "law in action." The problem he presents is the need to distinguish between the force and effect of formal and perhaps even official and "effective" statements of what the practices and usages of the community are (shall be), and what we can learn about the actual practices and usages of the community from examination of the behavior of officials and citizens.

The debate about the relationship between authority and power is not totally settled by resolution of those points of interest. The contest between views of authority as entirely distinct from power and as a species of power may still rage. But some of the difficulties giving rise to this debate and to the view that something important depends upon the outcome of it will have been met.

EFFECTIVENESS-CONDITIONS OF AUTHORITY

As the end of the first section of this chapter, we asked two questions. We now deal with the second of these: what *is* the social backing characteristic of authority? The preceding section touched only on how the social backing is typically achieved, not on what it is. This section will focus on the latter.

The activities to be backed are the issuing of orders, commands, rules, and regulations, and the giving of permissions and empowerments.* Backing these activities is not just promoting or encouraging them—though it doubtless does increase their incidence. Backing them instead centrally and directly promotes or increases their effectiveness-conditions, thereby creating an environment in which the point of performing them is enhanced. For example, compliance is the effectiveness-condition for orders, commands, rules, and regulations. Thus, compliance enhances the effectiveness of them, but there is no direct effort to increase the *number* of orders, commands, rules, or regulations issued; that is, directly to promote or encourage order-giving, and so on. (Effectiveness-conditions for permissions and empowerments are a bit more complicated to state and will be given later.) Promoting or encouraging order-giving, and so forth, would be, in addition to backing them, giving people motives to engage in them (for instance, rewarding them or penalizing their nonoccurrence). In contrast, backing them amounts to enhancing their effectiveness and thereby at most indirectly increasing or providing motives to engage in them. Enhancing their effectiveness would be of little interest to creatures who did not desire or could not be made to desire for one reason or another that the orders, and so on, be effective, say, in order to reap the fruits of their effectiveness; for example, the coordination that results from compliance with them. Without supposing creatures to have such desires, backing these activities cannot be supposed to increase their incidence.

Further confusion must be guarded against also by distinguishing between what is is to back these activities and how they are to be backed. The section in this chapter entitled "Authority and Hierarchy" will consider the latter issue. We are not here considering views concerning how the backing is to be achieved, but rather what it *is* to provide backing.

There are several different activities being backed, and we need to separate them in order to see each clearly. With respect to the issuing of orders, commands, rules, and regulations, backing these activities consists of promoting compliance. With respect to the giving of permissions, most broadly speaking, backing consists of not prohibiting the activities of persons acting on the permissions. A narrower case of permissions that, though surrounded by and involving much more complicated manifestations of authority and authoritativeness than this (such as, they are protected from certain kinds of interference) is the permission possessed by teams in competitive games to score if they can. They are not prohibited from trying to score, though their opponents are likewise not prohibited from trying (in certain ways) to stop them. That the opposing teams are so situated is precisely what makes the situation competitive. In contrast, some permissions are protected. They are backed not only by not prohibiting the activities of persons acting on them, but also, centrally, by prohibiting the attempts of others to interfere. These latter permissions do not, in themselves, generate competitive situations, though they are often found there (for instance, games ordinarily have rules delineating

*Wesley Hohfeld used the term *privilege* for what is here called *permission*. For explanation of the idea and of the term he used to describe it, see Hohfeld. For a fuller exposition of the idea, see Glanville Williams [1945].

what shall count as an offense by a competing team or its members against an opposing team or its members).

In protected permissions the central element is that interference is prohibited, and compliance with this prohibition is demanded. There are, however, problems arising with any claim that prohibited interferences are sufficient to prevent any interference whatever with the permitted conduct. Of these, two would be especially worth mentioning because of their typicality of the problems philosophers recognize. (1) When interference with the protected conduct is prohibited, what is to count as a prohibition? The problem arises in at least two ways: (a) What if interference is not formally prohibited but only heavily fined? (b) What if interference is formally prohibited, but the penalty is sufficiently light so that, as with the attitudes of many people toward parking fines, it is regarded only as "the cost of doing business"? And (2) when interference with permitted conduct is prohibited, what is to count as an "interference"? Here, we must recognize that protecting permitted conduct does not assure the success, continuance, or even indulgence in (of) that conduct.

There are at least three reasons why this is so: (a) The conduct may be unsuccessful, or whatever, because the person engaging in it lacks the capacity to succeed, and so on. If the lack of capacity is attributable to internal defects in no way attributable to the actions of other persons or institutions, then it will not be thought an interference. (b) The person may fail to succeed, and so forth, because conditions generally are unfavorable. For example, a person seeks to exercise freedom of speech in a high and noisy windstorm, and cannot be heard because of it. If the occurrence and noisiness of the windstorm and the incapacity of the person to be heard despite it are not seen as resulting from interferences by other persons or institutions, they will not be seen as the sort prohibited in protected permissions. And (c) if the person who would engage in the permitted conduct is prevented from doing so, and so on, even because of the behavior of other persons or institutions, these results may not count as prohibited "interferences" because they have not or are not shown to have precisely that intention (for example persons allegedly having a protected permission to attend unsegregated schools and cannot do so because they cannot meet the admission standards because, having lived in a previously segregated society, they are presently unequipped to do so). These rough arguing grounds delineated do not, in themselves, provide principles for settling debates, but only show the issues that often get argued.*

As can be seen, the effectiveness-conditions of permissions, whether protected or not, raise questions either of noninterference or compliance (with the prohibitions on interference). Empowerments raise nothing startlingly new. Backing them consists of backing whatever orders, commands, rules, regulations, permissions, or subsequent empowerments result from the exercise of the empowerments in question. Found here are some central issues in discussions by political philosophers about the relationship of authority to human freedom and, in particular, to personal autonomy. (*Personal autonomy* is

---

*John Stuart Mill's essay "On Liberty," Chapter 5, discusses applications of his Principle of Liberty that mature and rational adults are not to be interfered with for their own benefit. His examples exhibit problems about the dividing line between what is and what is not interference.

intended only to distinguish the autonomy under discussion from the autonomy of (political) communities, considered in Chapter Nine, "Sovereignty.")

To summarize so far, compliance is the effectiveness-condition for the issuing of orders, commands, rules, and regulations; it is also permissions and for enpowerments insofar as exercises of the latter do not result only in the issuing of permissions or in the endless giving of further empowerments. Empowerments sometimes result in these, but often result in the issuing of protected permissions, orders, commands, rules, or regulations in which compliance becomes an issue.

Compliance is sometimes investigated by asking, "Do persons 'comply with' the orders, and the like in question?" Alternatively, it is investigated by asking, "Are persons 'in compliance with' the orders, and so on, in question?" Insofar as there is a difference, the first question suggests that inquiry is about whether persons acquiesce or yield to the orders, and so forth, whereas the second question suggests that inquiry is about whether persons are, for whatever reasons, in accord with them. There are no sharp boundaries in either case, but the second expression, *in compliance,* is frequently used synonymously with *in accord,* which shows more clearly its lack of concern for the reasons for compliance. This suggests that, if as we have stated, "compliance" is the effectiveness-condition for orders, and so on, then the name of the game is to secure action in accord with the orders, for whatever reason or however explainable. There is nothing surprising about that, but one should note that consequently the reasons for acting in accord with the orders issued may not have figured importantly in practical understandings of authority. The important thing has been generally thought to be that the actions, for whatever reasons, *be* the ones designated by the orders, and so on.

The effectiveness of authority is supposed to lie in its capacity to make a difference in the way people behave. Exercises of it are supposed to get persons to do things they would not, in the absence of these exercises, do. Since these exercises involve issuing orders, and the like, the effectiveness-condition of them—that is, compliance—must involve more than reliance on mere happenstance to produce conforming action.

However, if excluding happenstance excludes only the idea that compliance is brought about through mere coincidence between the orders, and so forth, and the whims and fancies of the persons whose behavior is in compliance, this would be profoundly consistent with conclusions about authority to be reached later. But there are numerous ways in which acting autonomously may be consistent with *not* acting merely out of whim or fancy. This is important because the potential for conflict between authority and personal autonomy will be a major concern of later discussion.

There is a further important question about compliance to be asked. Do commands, and the like, require for their effectiveness "compliance no matter what"? Commentators have frequently answered this question with a resounding yes. They have done so largely on the grounds that if the exercises of authority in question did not require unqualified compliance, that would be ineffective because compliance would then become discretionary and a matter for personal judgment. This would be unacceptable because authority, as is widely believed, is of use precisely because it avoids reliance on personal judgment in situations in which that reliance would be insufficient to produce the needed coordinations of human activities.

In trying to evaluate the foregoing claim, you might look first at actual exercises of authority. The most proximate and notorious examples of "compliance no matter what" occur in the military, fire departments, and police departments. These are all cases in which failure to get perfect coordination may be fatal to the enterprise and may even be fatal to one or more of the participants. Under certain dramatic and unusual circumstances, entire civilian populations are sometimes subject to such a discipline even by relatively "liberal"—that is, not totalitarian or authoritarian—systems of political authority. We understand the reason for this very well: the urgency of the situation in which we find ourselves may put a very high premium on immediacy of compliance, and the mutuality of the reliance may put a high premium upon certainty of compliance.

We do not always face such situations; consequently, we do not always demand "compliance no matter what." There are, however, situations in which compliance is expected to be more or less automatic, as with respect to automobile traffic regulations. Compliance there is expected to be more or less automatic because (a) these are commonly cases in which the cost of compliance is relatively low and attempts to determine whether to comply on the basis of judgments in individual cases are notoriously fallible and risky, and (b) large economies of effort and relief of anxiety are achieved through more or less "automatic" compliance.

It is clear in many legal systems that noncompliers, if detected, risk confrontation with the administrators of the legal system. Though there are these risks, detected noncompliers may escape confrontation and thus penalty. Prosecutorial discretion can be exercised in failure to prosecute them, jury discretion or judicial discretion in failure to convict them, and judicial discretion in suspending sentences of them if convicted. Or they may actually find vindication in their confrontation—their noncompliance may be found formally to have been justified, excusable, or done under conditions justifying mitigation of the normal penalties thereof. Such phenomena do not occur in every legal system with equal frequency, in every jurisdiction of any legal system, or with equal frequency concerning every subject matter of the laws. But they are familiar.

This point is fleshed out in Joseph Raz's convincing claim that authority operates to exclude some, but not necessarily all, reasons, for doing other than as authority directs. The exercises of discretion and the vindicating circumstances whose effects have been just mentioned operate justifiably just in case there are "nonexcluded" reasons for failing to do as authority directs; that is, roughly, reasons not excluded from consideration by the authority scheme in question, and that outweigh whatever accumulated reasons there are for doing as authority directs. This account gives a theoretic base to the idea that the "requirements" of orders, and so on, issued under authority schemes are often understood not to be fulfilled "no matter what." These "requirements" are not to be fulfilled, in particular, when there are nonexcluded reasons for failing to fulfill them that outweigh the reasons there are for fulfilling them.

A classic discussion of a consideration that may sometimes be understood not to be excluded occurs in Hobbes's *Leviathan*. Hobbes says that compliance with the commands of a sovereign or sovereign's agent is not understood to be required by commands leading to the complier's immediate and certain death, mutilation, or dishonoring. His reasoning is as follows: the subject's compliance is required to any commands only because of a previous consent on this complier's part to comply. This consent must be understood—that is, it would only be reasonable to understand it—as given with a view to some benefit or other to the consenter. The consenter's immediate and certain death, mutilation, or dishonoring is of no conceivable benefit to the consenter. Therefore the consenter can by no means be understood to have consented to obeying a command leading immediately and certainly to such consequences. Hobbes has here said something congenial to Raz's understanding of authority. One's immediate and certain death, mutilation, or dishonoring may be considered nonexcluded reasons for nonconforming actions. One may find, among other, too few, congenial discussions, Richard Wasserstrom's article on obeying the law.

It is not always easy to discover these or other nonexcluded reasons applying in practice. For example, suppose that there is a platoon of recruits being marched by an officer who at one point gives the order, "Left march!" To turn left at this point is to march directly into the route of oncoming traffic. May we suppose that the sergeant has made a mistake and that compliance is not "required" in this case? One might perhaps suppose that the order has been given with effects not fully foreseen by the officer and that he or she had no intention to endanger the recruits. Further possibilities, however, might be suggested by contrasting this with the situation in which the recruits are being ordered to do something leading to their marching off a dock and falling into the water. May one suppose that this is not intended? The answer here does not seem so clear as in the previous case. We can here easily imagine legitimate goals an officer might have had in giving the latter order even foreseeing the stated consequences. Second-guessing administrators of a system of authority is at best a risky business, and the conclusions one reaches—understood as conclusions about what reasons for noncompliance are not excluded—may be based, as critical examination of Hobbes's remarks eventually suggest, upon debatable conceptions of the probably polyvalent nature of the enterprise in which authority has been accepted.

What if compliance to an authoritative command requires someone to do something immoral? Depending upon the nature and extent of the presumed immorality, some commentators believe that it can weigh against reasons for compliance (is nonexcluded), and other commentators believe that it cannot do so and cannot count against compliance at all (is excluded). Discussions of civil disobedience and revolution have sometimes seemed to hinge on this issue; the matter will be discussed later.

Raz's position gives a theoretical base for responding also to the argument that authority demands compliance "no matter what" because otherwise compliance would be discretionary and we would fail to avoid precisely what authority is supposed to avoid—reliance on personal discretion. Raz's point clearly allows a place for admitting that there is one important respect in which there is no discretion to be exercised at all—that is, in the exclusion as reasons against compliance that one has a wish, desire, whim, or inclination not to comply. There is no discretion whatever about this. Generally, it is to be excluded, and that is all there is to it.

Concerning what other reasons might be excluded by various systems of authority, Raz is not so clear. This is not surprising, as systems of authority differ here. As the previous discussion of the avoidance of confrontation and the obtaining of vindications for noncompliance suggested, however, there is considerable variation among legal systems and even within various legal systems (with respect to jurisdictions, administrators, and subject matters) in terms of what reasons for noncompliance are excluded and which are not. It is within this residue that important differences between very "liberal" governments and "totalitarian" and "authoritarian" governments are found.

Lastly, we may remark upon the distinction between compliance and obedience (see Chapter Twelve). A person may fail to comply with an order and yet not be disobeying it. This is so when the noncompliance occurs in circumstances in which the order was never intended to apply. For example, if our drill sergeant is issuing marching orders to recruits, civilian onlookers would not be regarded as disobeying his orders when they fail to comply with them.

ORIGIN OF AUTHORITY

Concerning how the practice of authority gets started among human beings, it is unlikely that we can show its initiation to be via consent, such as is often now supposed necessary for it eventually to be legitimate. (See the next chapter for a discussion of legitimacy and the sort of consent supposed to operate in establishing it.)

We can, given our present historical understandings, easily believe it highly probable that important and successful early roles in the origin of authority were played by conquest and intimidation—phenomena having very little to do with the relevant practice of consent, being based on coerced acquiescence. We need not suppose the coordinative results of the conquest and intimidation to have been long-lasting or fine-tuned; but we have seen coordinations "get started" in history again and again through such devices—such as various tribes and nations that have come to have long and highly developed histories.

Discussion of the origin of authority in connection with various important social relations such as the practice of consent may be taken to suggest a chronological ordering of the presence of the two. No such suggestion is intended. If the presence of authority of some sort is a necessary condition for the presence of the social relations (or vice versa), even then the most required is that the latter not appear before the former (or vice versa). Their appearance could be simultaneous and could also be gradual. Indeed, many historians and anthropologists believe one or both likely.

Philosophers have, by and large, made no special investigations of what has in fact been the case here. Whereas social scientists debate the history of the matter and the practical necessity of authority to large aggregations of persons aspiring to achieve social coordination, philosophers are more likely to inquire into whether authority is a constituent of the relationships between any aggregation of persons so related as to constitute a society. There is thus a difference in subject matter as well as in focus.

Philosophers also debate over the contents and coherence of suppositions operating at the base of the most influential modern view of the source of entitlement to authority, in particular whether entitlement rests on consent. Much of their attention is focused on whether creatures having the moral attributes and capacities required for entrance into morally significant consensual relations can coherently be supposed to exist under the asocial (or "social") conditions presupposed by the view that societies or political societies can *begin* with consent.

A further example indicating the thrust and flavor of philosophical interests in this problem area is provided in the following critique of a statement by Sebastian DeGrazia in his article, "What Authority is *not*": "[a]ccepting . . . authority gains . . . admittance to public life within a community" (p. 330). This statement is in need of modification, but does contain something important. If, as some anthropologists and others have argued, every community has a structure and that structure embodies authority, communities would be unlikely to exist or be recognizable if a substantial portion of the persons claiming to be members did not accept in some way or at least profess to accept the authority embedded in the structure of the community.

But acceptance of existing authority (for that is what DeGrazia is talking about) is neither sufficient nor necessary for gaining admittance to a community. It is not sufficient because the community may not be open and may not admit all who seek admittance; it is easy to imagine that other qualifications for admittance might be required. Neither is it necessary to gain admittance; if *gaining admittance* means merely being treated by other members of the community as a fellow member, all that may be necessary is the *appearance* of accepting the authority. That has already been suggested. If, on the other hand, *admittance to the community* is taken to mean something more complicated, neither acceptance of the authority nor the appearance of acceptance of it may be necessary; some communities accept persons as members despite how they behave and what they appear to believe.

Whether or not some acceptance of some authority is conceptually "necessary" for the existence of society, it is, some commentators may believe, not necessary in practice for the coordination we have been discussing. Frequently mentioned alternative instruments of coordination are leadership, influence, and power. (The conditions we have specified under which coordination is to be sought exclude the possibility of relying also or instead on spontaneous cooperation or moral consent. If either cooperation or moral consent were to be relied upon, it would initially have to be absent and manufactured through the exercise of leadership or at least of influence.)

Consideration of leadership, influence, and power as alternatives to authority is, however, bedeviled by the fact that none of them is very clear or clearly distinct from the others. It is controversial just how leadership, influence, and power are related to one another, and also how each is related to authority—the latter being a crucial issue here. Authority has seemed to some a form of leadership, a kind of influence, or a species of power (this last allegation has been examined in some detail in an earlier section of this chapter). When isolated from authority, any of the three may have some capacity to coordinate human behavior; all commentators seem to agree that there are plenty of examples of exercises of leadership, influence, and power unconnected to authority. We should be careful to ask, however, whether any of the three, when correctly and carefully isolated from authority, has an appreciable capacity to coordinate human behavior in situations such as those consideration of which has led to our introduction of the device of authority. A justifiably positive answer to this last question is not immediately or obviously in the cards.

The cards do show that leadership, influence, and power each has diverse sources. Many of these sources are exceedingly difficult to disentangle from their bases in authority. For example, leadership may come about through the wielding of economic or military influence, each of which is shot through with reliance on authority. Or instead, leadership may perhaps come about through the force of a particular personality as exerted in face-to-face relationships. Does leadership from the latter source operate in utter isolation from reliance on authority, and can we perceive the results of its isolated operation? Appropriate replies in both cases may be unclear.

Influence, in turn, could result from economic or military status, intelligence, force of personality, or even good looks. Can we be confident of our capacity to monitor the results of these influences when uncontaminated by any reliance whatever on authority? Similar troublesome difficulties with the sources of power are well known. There is no need to deny utterly that important roles are played in coordination by leadership, influence, and power, but we should consider just how substantial any of these roles would be if it were purified of the reliance on authority with which it is ordinarily shot through. An accurate account of the issues is by no means easy to come by or likely to be uncontroversial when offered. Thus, the status of any of the three as an alternative to authority remains unclear.

AUTHORITY AND PERSONAL AUTONOMY

As mentioned earlier, modern political philosophers have been concerned with the impact of authority upon personal autonomy.* A discussion of this concern will further clarify authority. Unfortunately, as should not be surprising by now, neither of the key notions in this relationship between "authority"

---

*A brief exploration would be worthwhile concerning the considerations apparently influencing whether one talks here about *autonomy, freedom, liberty, independence,* or *self-determination. Autonomy* is often limited to political communities or to the "moral autonomy" of "natural" (not corporate) persons. (These "persons" are not always what are straightforwardly identified as persons, but rather noumenal selves—a Kantian heritage is sometimes detectable here. Such selves are much different from, though connected with, phenomenal selves.) *Freedom* and *liberty* are sometimes treated interchangeably and are sometimes sharply distinguished. When distinguished, *liberty* (or sometimes *freedom*) is sometimes said to have a peculiarly political or economic reference, and *liberty* is sometimes said to have a contrast with *license,* whereas *freedom* has no such contrast. For yet another popular view see, for example,

and "personal autonomy" is uncontroversial. Thus, not only must we hope that an attempt to discuss the impact will illuminate the idea of authority, but we must hope that our efforts to get clear about the impact will clarify the idea of personal autonomy.

Most everyone discussing the matter agrees that persons who are not permitted to exercise their personal judgment or discretion do not have personal autonomy.** So persons having personal autonomy must at least not be prohibited from exercising their personal judgment or discretion, though much else may also be required.† Consequently, a task of anyone wishing to examine the relationship of authority to autonomy is to examine carefully how authority prohibits one from exercising personal discretion and whether the prohibition results in a clear violation of personal autonomy.

It might seem obvious that (effective) authority prevents people from exercising their personal discretion. After all, even in this book we have introduced authority as useful precisely because it does this. But even casual reflection may seem to reveal that there is at least one circumstance in which authority does not prohibit a person from exercising personal discretion: when a person happens for reasons (or in response to impulses) unconnected to the presence of authority to choose what authority directs. For example, if a person just happens to want to do what he or she is ordered to do, then he

---

Glanville Williams. *Independence* is applied to communities (not necessarily political ones) and to persons (not necessarily natural ones). Though it is applied in these ways, it probably is not confined to any of these, though it does seem confined by some speakers to formal (legal?) rather than informal political or economic considerations, and in that respect differs from *autonomy. Self-determination* confronts speakers with two rather special problems: (1) the way it seems to divide things into a self that does the determining and a self that is subject to the determination, and (2) problems about its relationship to nearby terms, *influence* and *control*. In discussing this important area, one should note several crucial relativities. There is first the easy relativity of the claims of independence and of authority to particular persons, populations, or jurisdictions. Secondly, there is the relativity of the claims of independence and authority to particular ranges or kinds of activities. Thirdly, there is the relativity of the claim of independence or of subjection to some force, control, or influence, either to contemplated raw power or to something normative, and even to a particular kind of raw power—for instance, political or economic, and to a particular kind of normativeness, either moral, political, legal, or whatever.

**Autonomous persons are different from autonomous actions, and both are talked about later. But there is nothing amazingly difficult about converting statements about one into statements about the other.

†The remainder is allowed for especially in the later broadening of our understanding of "personal autonomy." We characterize autonomy here in terms of prohibitions and the absence thereof. That characterization permits a sharp focusing of the discussion upon some presently crucial features of autonomy. Subsequently, we characterize autonomy in terms of what one has or has not the capacity to do. The reasons for this later broadening are as follows: we are trying there not to foreclose any important general controversies about autonomy. Though governments often play a role in determining action through imposing prohibitions and failing to do so, they also have other ways of making things impossible or making them possible—putting them out of reach or, further, making them inevitable. There are debates, however, about whether the effects, in order to count as important influences on personal autonomy, must be intended by the government or merely removable by the government. These debates, which are or should be prominent in discussions of freedom, independence, and the like, should not be foreclosed by anything we say here.

or she is, in a sense, only being permitted in the situation to act in accord with discretion. One might, nevertheless, stop short of saying that this person is being permitted to *exercise* his or her own discretion. The point is that no alternatives to the choice made are permitted. So it seems that personal autonomy requires that one have a choice. This enrichment of our understanding may be fixed by a rough understanding of personal autonomy as "doing *as* one wishes" (which implies that one actually has a choice), rather than "doing *what* one wishes."

There are, however, remaining difficulties left uninfluenced by either of the just-mentioned idioms. Some difficulties concern the number and quality of the alternatives that must be available. Is it enough that there be at least two alternatives of just any quality, or must there (at least sometimes) be many more than two, and/or alternatives of some very special quality? These questions must receive solid answers if we are to know how personal autonomy and authority might conflict. The questions are similar to questions frequently asked also in discussions of freedom and independence, and as we have suggested, those concepts are close to autonomy.

Unfortunately, the questions are no better answered there than here. With each of the terms, the parameters of discussion often are expected to come clear from the context of discussion—that is, from the kind of thing whose autonomy, independence, or freedom is being discussed (such as a person or a political community)—and whether we are discussing economics, politics, or whatever. But the guidance given by such context-considerations is not always sufficient to avoid serious trouble. In part this is because it does not always make clear enough whether the discussion is *limited* to political or economic considerations or whatever. This difficulty is exacerbated because, as we have seen, characterizations of the "political" and "economic" are often imprecise and controversial, and also because differing theories of the natures of the entities in question (such as persons or political communities) whose autonomy, freedom, or independence are involved sometimes operate importantly in the discussion although they are unstated there. For example, the "person" whose autonomy or freedom is in question may turn out to be, as we suggested in a note, something other than the phenomenologically identified person of which we normally think.

Apart from these considerations, and even in conflict with them, there is some temptation to deal with the crucial concepts ("autonomy," "independence," and "freedom") by founding an understanding of them contextlessly on general characterizations. The temptation presents us with an interesting choice between two radically different ways of proceeding: (1) instead of allowing parameters to be fixed by an understanding of the context in which the terms have been used, we see, for instance, some remarks about personal autonomy contextlessly and conclude that to be fully autonomous a person would have to be God-like in ways not fully enviable (fully autonomous persons would have then to be impervious to any external influence, and hence at best unfeeling), let alone ways that would allow any actual human beings to be truly autonomous (it would have to be true that nothing would be an obstacle to their doing what they had in mind to do). The former condition would fail to conform to our generally favorable attitude toward "personal autonomy," and the latter condition may be thought to be an unuseful understanding to apply to human affairs because any affairs to which it did apply would not be recognizably human. Analogously, politically independent communities are supposed to be independent of political forces outside themselves, but attempts to provide a contextless understanding of this condition might well produce a similar impression that politically independent communities must be quite isolated from and unaffected by political events in any other communities—this, to say the least, would sharply reduce the number of communities in this world that could correctly be called "politically independent."

Many persons think in consequence that such contextless interpretations are insane: the resulting understandings make it impossible to apply the expressions in question ("personal autonomy" and "politically independent") to the very things in this world to which the expressions are supposed to apply. Attitudes of distress over these consequences, however, are not inevitable. Some persons might maintain, in view of precisely the protested consequences, that these contextless understandings are exactly what is needed. If the expressions so understood turn out not to have application in this world, then we indeed lose our capacity to use them to divide and classify actual phenomena, but we arguably gain a capacity to perceive and comment profoundly upon the human condition. And if contextless understanding leads us to lose the common, wholly favorable attitude toward personal autonomy, this is all to the good, because we should understand anyway that personal autonomy is not entirely advantageous.

(2) Alternatively, we may wish to understand the expressions in ways that preserve our capacities to use them in dividing and classifying actual phenomena. If so, we must scale down our conception of what it is for persons to be fully autonomous and for communities to be fully independent. In doing this, we can be guided, at least somewhat, by the contexts in which the expressions appear and let these contexts focus our interests. In this, we will meet two principal kinds of difficulties. (a) We need to determine what is to count as a background condition against which action (whether or not autonomous) is carried out, and thus persons or communities can count as autonomous, and what is to count as a foreground condition the presence or absence of which would count toward an action's being autonomous or not autonomous. For example, we might count as background condition unmanufactured climate conditions preventing one from doing what one wishes, whereas we might count as foreground conditions all social conditions preventing one from doing the same. Contrariwise, concerning social conditions generally, we might count as background conditions social conditions not specifically intended by their perpetrators and count as foreground conditions only intended conditions. (b) We need to determine whether conditions that both prevent one from doing some things and enable one to do others (for instance, wind resistance, which prevents one from traveling more rapidly but enables one in winged flight to gain altitude) should be counted for or against autonomy. Such difficulties as these may be expected, and, unfortunately, consideration of the way in which the context focuses our interests will not alone be sufficient to surmount them.

Such parameter problems must be largely settled before we have a solid base from which to judge how many and what kind of alternatives must be available for persons to act autonomously. The latter judgment, in turn, will be needed if one is to give careful examination of possible, likely, or inevitable conflicts between personal autonomy and authority.

That problem is alleged to be that the exercise of authority extinguishes personal autonomy. Most everyone agrees that it can do so. Some commentators, however, believe that it always and inevitably does so. Our present concern is with this more spectacular claim. The pesky parameter problems just considered appear, for example, as follows: utilizing for the moment the rough understanding of personal autonomy used previously (not being prohibited from exercising personal judgment or discretion), authority exercised, for example, in governmental control involves limits on one's continued capacity to do as one wishes or even perhaps to do as one thinks best. But, then, so does nature. If we have trouble seeing that nature does this too, this is because limits placed by nature on us are ordinarily built into the background against which we set out to act.

Turn now to closer examination of the two popular rough understandings (sufficient conditions) of personal autonomy just mentioned in passing: doing as one wishes and doing as one thinks best.* Though they must eventually be dealt with separately, some remarks may be made about them jointly. As suggested by earlier discussion, whether one can in fact do as one wishes or thinks best is an empirical matter. We must remember as well that experience has taught us that what people wish or think best is sometimes quite insane or unreasonable. We have two alternatives in dealing with the latter point: the first is to bite the bullet and argue that forbidding people from doing insane or unreasonable things (or both) is nevertheless still infringing upon their autonomy; the second is to argue instead that prohibiting them from doing insane or unreasonable things (or both) is by itself no infringement of the autonomy of these people.

Concentrate next on the idea that these people can or cannot *do* as they wish or as they think best. This can reveal that, for one thing, claims about autonomy or the lack thereof include some understanding of the qualification "in this situation," even when not explicit. Thus, claims about personal autonomy would, when fully explicit, read "doing as one wishes or thinks best in this situation." We thus would benefit by pressing to have the situation specified—at least somewhat. "The situation" may be understood to include only background conditions (against which one is supposed to consider what is wished or thought best). For example, it may include our understanding that one is an ordinary human and not a superman or superwoman. Challenges to such understandings of the situation may have much the same effect as challenges to the sanity or reasonableness of one's wishes or thinkings best so far as challenges to one's conclusions therefrom about autonomy are concerned. Alternatively, "the situation" may include some "foreground" conditions—including some such that consideration of one's wishes or think-

*The sufficiency of either doing what one wants (wishes) or what one thinks is best is controversial. What does one do when what one wants or thinks best is immoral or the like (see the following paragraphs)? The question needs to be considered.

ings best would be relevant to judging whether one is or is not acting autonomously.

Considering the two rough understandings of "autonomy" separately, the first ("doing as one wishes") seems to be an especially strong candidate for suggesting conflict between personal autonomy and authority. As Raz has remarked, acting for the reason that one has a wish, whim, urge, or the like, so to act, is always an excluded reason under schemes of authority for so acting.* Thus, if acting as one wishes is what it is to act autonomously, there must be a conflict between autonomy and authority. Doing as one wishes, however, is only sufficient for acting autonomously; it is not necessary—unless persons really *doing* something are always "doing as they wish." (Because they are doing it indicates that they "wish" to do it. Compare this with the discussion in Chapter Four about how *really* can refocus priorities). Persons performing unpleasant duties are not, in any ordinary understanding, doing only as they wish, yet there is in some circumstances no doubt whatever that they are acting autonomously—"on their own" and unprompted by anyone else—in performing an unpleasant duty. (Doing as one wishes is sufficient for acting autonomously only when personal autonomy is not identified, as it often has been, with some "higher" or "moral" portion of the person's nature or character. The fact that a wish was irresponsible, selfish, or in some way not sufficiently dutiful has in these latter cases been taken to indicate decisively that an action determined by that wish could not be truly autonomous.)

The occasional sufficiency for acting autonomously of doing as one wishes, on the other hand, is precisely what shows that our third rough understanding of acting autonomously—namely, "doing as one thinks best"—won't do either as a necessary condition in the account. Acting on what one regards as irresponsible or selfish wishes is ordinarily not thereby regarded as having failed to act autonomously. One need not, therefore, *always* be doing as one thinks best in order to be acting autonomously.

Still, in the light of earlier discussion of the two understandings together, a further difficulty appears, especially prominently in connection with this third understanding. For example, a wild, unmanufactured storm preventing one from visiting a sick friend may be considered a background condition against which one determines "as one thinks best" (and, less clearly perhaps, as a background condition against which one determines to do "as one wishes"), and confrontation with an armed robber demanding that we hand over the funds held in trust for a friend might ordinarily be counted an inter-

---

*At this point a commentator argues that medical authority does not operate as described, and that the analysis consequently probably should be restricted to political authority. In hospitals, the wishes or impulses of the patients have weight against the orders of the doctor. I disagree with the conclusions expressed in the first sentence, though not necessarily what is asserted in the second. A plausible and convenient, though not inevitable, analysis of the situation is as follows (I don't believe that any analysis here is inevitable). Relative to many of the activities of nurses, technicians, etc., the doctor is "in authority." Relative to many of the activities and expectations of the patients, the doctor is "an authority," a notion that has not been much analyzed here. Relative to some of the patients' activities—such as with respect to "what goes on in the doctor's hospital"—however, the doctor may be, depending on how the hospital is organized, "in authority." Both manifestations of "in authority" just mentioned operate just as described in the text.

ference with our personal autonomy. But why should not the latter be counted instead as a background condition against which we determine "as we think best"? Perhaps we can say why, but doing so would require more assumptions and arguments than have here been made.

Such parameter problems are often confronted in political settings, and the difficulties to be met in coping with them are, if anything, amplified there. Consider, for example, the limitations placed by political tyrannies on what one does. Such limitations are customarily considered limitations on personal autonomy. But in some circumstances and for some (nonpolitical) concerns, some of such circumstances may best be considered *faits accompli* and part of the background conditions against which one considers doing "as one thinks best." It seems easy to say that for other circumstances and other concerns, these same limitations are to be considered "foreground" obstacles to "doing as one thinks best" and thus infringements of one's autonomy. Some of such limitations are after all the very models of what we think of as infringements of personal autonomy.

Considered in the abstract, this may appear to be an easily resolvable matter. But, in the richness of actual situations and problems, where the division between public and private problems is often not easily made, and the distinction between *fait accompli* "background" and conditions considered changeable "foreground" is targeted by heavy rhetorical guns and uncertain hopes, both public and private matters are not likely to be so clear. Furthermore, in actual situations, whether a particular governmental regime is actually a "political tyranny" will be hotly contended and seldom as clear as we might hope. When the appropriateness of the attribution must be debated, we may have a very long road indeed to showing that the governmental limitations in question are appropriately considered obstacles to our personal autonomy.

All this applies plausibly also to "doing as one wishes." But there is one respect in which this understanding of what is there sufficient for acting autonomously constitutes a sharp departure from what was offered earlier. It shows, as the other does not, that self-limitation is consistent with acting autonomously.* This, as we shall see, is something important if we are to uncover the possibility of personal autonomy and authority being consistent.

Remember that, with any system of authority, acting on "mere" wish is an excluded reason for acting on any matter directed by authority. That is the one excluded reason that is always clear. But personal authority and authority may both be understood as perfectly consistent with self-limitation, limitation that is by one's "better self," or even, in some opinions, by one's representative. In societies generally there are fully recognized and standardized ways of limiting one's capacity subsequently, rightfully, and perhaps prudently, to do

---

*Especially here, in the following treatment of self-limitation, but also in the discussion of "self-determination" in Chapter Three, the treatments are hardly exhaustive. Controversial questions remain concerning the natures of the selves doing the limiting and determining (and for that matter the selves being limited or determined). Careful treatment of these issues would require a book that is much too long. Instead, widely used intuitive or preinstructed notions of the selves involved are relied upon. Self-limitation (and self-determination) are (forms of) consent. Many people believe that consent authorizes or legitimates, and so I discuss these matters here and elsewhere. But I nowhere argue that consent or any particular act(s) of self-limitation or self-determination either authorizes or legitimates.

as one might otherwise have wished. Large literatures in political and moral philosophy focus on this issue.

But what about the consistency with personal autonomy of limitations on one's doing as one thinks best? My reply at present is merely, What about self-limitation? What that question leads us to see is that basic questions may be asked about the role that self-limitation plays in our social life, and how far we may safely extend the socially recognized and standardized means by which we can achieve it.

Self-limitation is an essential feature of moral life. Humans who themselves place no limitations whatever on the occasions on which they act solely from desire, mood, or inclination could not lead moral lives. Furthermore, given the importance of some such limitations to capacity for mutual undertakings it is difficult to understand how social or political life could occur without them. Thus, if personal autonomy is to be consistent with leading a moral and social life at all, some forms of self-limitation must be consistent with personal autonomy. The difficulty is to determine the fully plausible range of self-limitation. If there are mechanisms by which self-limitation can be achieved through the use of representatives or other political means, than it would not be clear that the operation of the resulting institutions must infringe the personal autonomy of those subject to them even when these persons are in some respects not being permitted to do even as they think best. Persons who make promises, contracts, or swear oaths may be acting autonomously and yet henceforth be unable rightly or prudently to do as in some respect they think best. If we have difficulty recognizing this state of affairs it is only because we understand the promise (or whatever) to be part of the "background" conditions under which we calculate doing as we think best, and not part of the "foreground" conditions where its effects upon what would be right or prudent for us to do could be considered obstacles to our doing as we think best. Analogous difficulties have been, of course, suggested earlier in our discussion.

Some inabilities to do as we think best are perfectly ordinary parts of our moral and social experience, and, far from being thought impairments of our personal autonomy, are central expressions of it. Therefore, the mere fact that the mechanisms of politics sometimes limit in some respects our capacities to do as we think best does not in itself demonstrate that they impair our personal autonomy. Perhaps many, and even all, mechanisms of politics do indeed impair our personal autonomy; but nothing that has so far been said here can demonstrate or provide a basis for demonstrating that they do. The fact that our political life places limits upon our capacity to do in some respects as we think best shows, in itself, nothing. How these limitations are brought about in individual cases, whether through coercion or persuasion, and so on, and by what means they come into being, whether by conquest, common agreement, or the like—these questions are left open so far as our discussion has yet gone. The only conclusion supportable at the moment is that there is nothing about political authority per se as we so far understand it that brings authority inevitably into conflict with our presently rough understandings of personal autonomy.

One further frequently used understanding of personal autonomy will be rewarding for us to look at here. This is the understanding contained by presenting, as a condition inconsistent with personal autonomy, that one does what one does "just because someone else says to do it." The question I wish to raise about this understanding of autonomy is whether it exhibits, as it is supposed to, a plausible construal of the operation of authority.

The picture of someone doing something merely because someone else tells him or her to do so founders on any of a number of considerations as an account of how authority operates. In many organizations of authority (though not all—we shall consider later the case of so-called absolutist kings in premodern "states"), it is simply false that someone can tell another person in any manner whatsoever to do anything whatever, making that person believe that it was wrong, and where it would in fact be wrong not to comply. The principal difficulty here is the expression *just because*. Modern political authority is often not addressed to anyone personally ("told 'that' person to do so") and is often not issued by a readily identifiable person (" 'someone' told that person to do so"). So to understand of authority so grasped would be insufficiently broad to be fully useful.

But *just because* is troublesome in a deeper way. Suppose that I do in fact do something "just because" someone else tells me to do so. Who *is* this person? Understood from the standpoint of explaining my compliance, it cannot be "just anyone." Authority does not work in that indiscriminate fashion, and the circumstances of compliance to authority do not characteristically permit it. On the other hand, from the standpoint of a person determining whether or not my autonomy has been infringed, no difference at all is supposed to be made by who the authoritative person happens to be. The mere fact that it is another person is supposedly sufficient. And yet, to say that this other person may be "just anyone" is likely to obscure any grounds that might be present for claiming that my compliance to the orders, commands, and the like, of this person might plausibly be seen as pieces of self-limitation. That is, in obscuring what might possibly explain my compliance to the order of this person in particular, we make it impossible to detect any grounds, if there are any, for holding the outcome to be a piece of self-limitation and not a piece of autonomy-infringement.

We have so far stopped short of asserting baldly that cases of purported "self-limitation" found by extending political mechanisms to some point of purported "self-limitation" are genuinely so. There will always be some grounds for asserting that the autonomy of some participants in the process is being infringed. But then, there will be some grounds for such assertion even in cases where participants are trying to coordinate their activities and trigger their own actions so as to coincide with the actions of certain selected others—which is, I should think, a full case of self-limitation. Though in cooperating they are perhaps acting autonomously, they are not, in the determination of what they do and when they do it, presumably acting "on their own." Thus, in the arena of which we speak, there will most always be reason to deny that persons are acting autonomously and some reason also to assert that they are doing so.

The case of cooperation, however, may have special characteristics. It is admitted on all sides that a person may comply with the commands of another person consistently with acting autonomously if the complier does so because of believing that compliance would be beneficial (to whomever the complier has in mind). The complier's reasons for believing this may include anticipated compliance to these commands of most other persons present where the compliance of all (including the person whose autonomy is in question) will be beneficial. In such circumstances, the complier may believe him- or herself to have sufficient reason to comply. Such compliance, supposedly, is not an infringement of the complier's autonomy. What other nonautonomy-interfering reasons are available?

Some discussions by scholars of how authority works proceed, then, without raising to sufficient prominence the importance of proper pairing (proper in terms of the authority structure) of persons to offices, and they thereby suppress any recognition at all of the rationales supporting the exercise of authority. The importance of proper pairing *is* widely enough recognized by the public generally to be fodder for comedy; consider Groucho donning judicial or academic robes in a Marx Brothers movie. Sometimes even in actual practical affairs there are serious cases of mistaken identity or of controversy concerning who legitimately occupies a given office. As such actual and comically fictional cases show, we do not ordinarily do something merely because someone with red hair or someone named Jones has told us to do so but because we believe ourselves to have sufficient reason to believe that the person with whose commands we are complying occupies a given office in a relevant authority structure and therefore is empowered to issue, say, directives commanding compliance from us. It is in the further rationales of this, which is something likely to vary from case to case, that we can uncover whatever grounds there might be in the case at hand for talk about self-limitation. It is certainly unwise for us to allow the rather indefinite directing of our attention attempted by *just because* to obscure this.

There are other places in the modern operation of authority in which entrance points for self-limitation are to be found. Unless a political regime claims absolute authority (and not all do), what is ordered, and so on, might not receive compliance, and the like, until, for example, more sacred obligations or urgent dictates of prudence are met. Further, as already mentioned during our discussion of compliance, unless ultimacy is effectively claimed for the authority in question, compliance might not inevitably be required if, for example, the order (or whatever) is eventually judged on appeal to be invalid; noncompliance is sometimes necessary in order to get a test of validity, and systems purporting to provide for such appeals cannot afford to extinguish utterly noncompliance for that purpose.*

As this small collection of types of cases suggests, authority structures can provide a rich variety of occasions on which not only personal judgment is called for, but the nature of the judgment can reveal to us some grounds for compliance. These grounds need not reveal any reason at all to say that the limitations in question are self-limitations, but there is no reason to suppose from the start that they cannot do so (a matter we will examine further). Thus, on this fourth understanding of *personal autonomy,* having found in it

*This point is often not well understood, and the subject should be approached carefully.

occasion to push a little further into understanding how authority operates, we still find no decisive reason for believing that the conflict between authority and autonomy is inevitable.

AUTHORITY AND HIERARCHY

Historically, authority has been associated with inequality. Our discussion of authority has doubtless reinforced the strong general tendency to suppose that a command-relation is the central aspect of authority. Viewing authority as hostile to equality is promoted by viewing authority as establishing most essentially command-relations. As we shall see, this is only a part of the story. But even here authority does not lead inevitably to hierarchy. The intimate connection between authority and inequality can be retained while still denying an association between authority and hierarchy.

A convenient way of characterizing hierarchy here is that the persons being commanded do not have an opportunity to command those persons who have commanded them. The mere generation of command-relations does not require hierarchy. Aristotle noted, for example, that persons fit for ruling are accustomed both to ruling and to being ruled. Thus, some alternation of ruling, violative of hierarchy, is not only consistent with command-relations, but has been thought advisable.

Human history has seen clearly hierarchical authority systems. The absolutist monarchies of seventeenth-century France and Hohenzollern rule in Prussia furnish clear examples about which a great deal is known. Nevertheless, even in these cases there are difficulties. The king's will and power need even there to be wielded through some instrument, in each of these cases, an administrative apparatus whose effectiveness required the stability and respect stemming from regular use of certain procedures (see the discussion of deSeysel in Chapter Eight, on constitutionalism and rule of law). This constituted no limit on the nominal extent of the king's authority, but it did constitute a limit on his effectiveness. This raises the following issue: to what extent were the inequalities generated relative to the functionaries mitigated or controlled by this administrative dependence?

There are also limits on authority to command. These appear in two radically different ways. First, as we observed earlier in this chapter, jurisdictional limits, both geographical and topical, are commonly placed on the competence of any given authority. Also, the actions of authority are subject to reversal or invalidation by other authorities in the same system of authority (and sometimes there is no authority in the system whose actions are not so subject). Thus, systems of checks and balances operate in connection with command-relations. These systems are possible because some authority is not either unlimited or ultimate. Subject matter, jurisdiction, temporal extent, and systems of appeal all offer occasions when the commanded may become commanders of the very persons who formerly commanded them.

Second, when a system of authority is placed in its setting in the life of a people, we understand that its requirements are not the only ones, normative or prudential, being made of many of these people. In consequence, provision must be made for when the requirements of authority conflict. A frequently considered question among political theorists, for example, is whether there are any requirements over which the political requirements do not take priority. The issue is frequently posed as though there were a perfectly general answer for all political regimes per se, and it may be that a claim of absolute priority is endemic among political regimes. But, though some political regimes have done so, few insist upon this priority. The matter is handled in various ways; sometimes requirements imposed by religious affiliation or family ties are explicitly permitted to take precedence over what would otherwise be legal requirements. Sometimes, instead, failure to comply with legal requirements is excused at law, for example, by a legal defense of "necessity."

Authority can play a role in carrying out executive functions in ways not involving anything so personally oriented as commands or orders. We noted this earlier in our discussion of *authoritative*. Apart from consideration of how documents, for example, become authoritative (there may be no clearly identifiable persons responsible for this or the persons responsible may be long dead), the documents may "rule." Dorothy Lee's book *Freedom and Culture* offers material from many different cultures to this effect. Thus, that a system of authority plays the role of carrying out executive functions does not in and of itself make inequality inescapable. (There is, however, a warning in the statement of a British judge who said, "I care not who makes the law, just so I can interpret it." The import of this statement will be examined somewhat in a later chapter.)

Another indication of how executive direction need not generate inequality is in executive direction through majority rule. Especially if there is no set of conditions or circumstances making the identity of majorities constant or relatively so, the shifting identities of the members of majorities might block inequality, at least insofar as authority per se is concerned. (But this issue becomes complex and difficult when studies of the oligarchical tendencies of groups are introduced.)

So much for the command-relation and related executive functions. Those are not the only relations generated by authority. As noted earlier, valuable privileges, protected liberties, immunities, permissions, and empowerments may also be generated. Authority thus appears in distinctly unhierarchical modes of coordination, such as those proceeding in accord with unforced cooperation or consensus. So the reaching of consensual agreement on an issue may (under certain understood conditions) be required and settle the issue for all participants.

Insofar as social structures in which differences in authority are apparent are significant in a given society, differences in authority may result in significant differences in power as well as in status among persons. The capacity of persons in authority to issue permissions, immunities, and empowerments is highly important (in addition to the command-relations) to the eventual production of differences in power and status among persons. Further, the differences accepted in the system of eligibility conditions either for issuing these orders, or whatever, or granting these permissions, and the like, or for having them bestowed upon one will result in further differences in the power and status of persons. These differences in power and status may be associated, both because of their natures and because of their consequences, as significant indices of inequality among those persons. But, as is not surprising, the social structures in question may be nested among multitudes of other social structures distributing authority differently. In any case, authority, traveling with entitlement or purported entitlement, is not the only dimension of power relations needing examination when equalities and inequalities are being considered. Therefore, inequalities engendered by any single social structure or any limited set of social structures, though perhaps significant enough when taken by themselves, should not be taken in isolation when the overall question of the qualities and inequalities among persons is being considered.

Political communities have social structures, and within these structures differences of authority will be apparent. These differences further mark, according to many political philosophers, who are rulers and who are ruled. This distinction is undeniably important, but it is not always possible to draw or draw well, and, depending upon the basis on which it is drawn, it may or may not include consideration of all the important bases of power differentials in the society. Concerning this latter point, it is important to recognize that the distinction between ruler and ruled is relative to a given social structure or perhaps to a grouping of social structures. The consequent distinction between rulers and ruled, if possible to draw at all, should never be considered to delineate a complete picture of power relations among any particular aggregation of persons. There may be other significant social structures generating or constituting different sets of equalities and inequalities, though political structures may be among the most significant of them.

The community, however, even respecting a single structure or grouping of structures, should not be expected to divide neatly into rulers and ruled. In the first place, there may be persons who have some authority in the structure but who are also subject to many of the rules, orders, or commands generated by that structure. We may not know whether to classify these persons among the rulers or the ruled. Secondly, the ideology supporting a structure may contain ideas making this classification (between ruler and ruled) or any other along these lines difficult. For example, consider the idea that the rulers are the "servants" of the people (that is, the ruled).

AUTHORITY AND ITS REQUIREMENTS

We earlier distinguished between the effectiveness-conditions of authority and the means used to obtain them. The effectiveness-conditions for some exercises of authority turn out to be compliance, for others noninterference. Our concern now is with how people seek to obtain the necessary compliance and noninterference.

Exercises of authority result in "requirements," "prohibitions," and "tolerations." We shall speak of these collectively as "requirements." A common move in political philosophy identifies these requirements so closely with the coercive means of obtaining them that purported requirements not so sought are not considered genuine. Consider purported requirements sought less coercively; for example, the "requirement" that a long-owed debt be paid. Courts may continue to claim that the debtor has an obligation to repay the debt, but at the same time refuse to do anything whatever to enforce that "obligation." It is common to say here that "the statute of limitations has run out." One finds commentators who, for what appear to be good reasons, deny that (despite what the court says) there is any longer a political-legal requirement that the debt be repaid. This is because these commentators identify the requirements of authority with the effectiveness-conditions thereof (for instance, compliance), a perfectly proper thing to do, and then go on to infer that the effectiveness-conditions are not to be taken seriously in a society unless that society backs them with compulsion. The idea underlying this move may be that the need for authority lies in the need for compulsion. This is more or less a "bad-man" theory of the need for authority, an idea we noted earlier, that through ignorance and/or lack of cooperation persons generally must be compelled if their actions are to be coordinated.

Against this, Yves Simon argued, as we mentioned earlier, that a community of perfectly well-informed and well-intentioned people still could have a need to determine a single course of action when there is nothing to choose between two or more actions on the grounds of their desirability. This need has nothing to do with the need to compel. According to this view, the need for political authority is not a consequence solely of deficiencies in human beings. Even though human beings *are* universally deficient, it is necessary to imagine this condition altered in order to isolate anything else that might be involved in the need for political authority and its conditions for successful operation. This can be accomplished only by appropriate "thought experiments," such as those carried out by Simon.

"Experiments" such as those are common in philosophy, but very often put off students in philosophy, who find them too fanciful and fail to see their use. In this case, Simon's discussion serves to give a useful perspective on political authority. Especially in the religious context in which Simon dealt with the matter, issues concerning the fundamentality of evil and other deficiencies of humans are of great interest. It is thus significant to show, if it can be shown, that the need for political authority is not traceable solely to the deficiencies of human beings.

Picking up our "statute of limitations" case, some commentators point to courts that declare that there continue to be "requirements" or "obligations" even when there are no sanctions for noncompliance, and conclude that such requirements still exist. Why would they claim this? They may notice that, in declaring that the requirements exist even though they are not enforced, the courts are sending a message of disapproval, though the message would be equivocal to someone believing legal techniques to be built on the so-called "bad-man" theory of law just adumbrated. It would be less equivocal to someone believing instead that the law is built on the so-called "puzzled-man" theory (H. L. A. Hart)—that persons subject to the law may often enough be seen as ready to comply if only it is made clear to them what they are to do. These two views present contrasting accounts of how the effectiveness-conditions of authority may be sought, and hence of the roles of authority in human life.

Remember that authority and the exercise of naked power differ in at least one respect: authority operates through entitlements or purported entitlements. Power may draw support from entitlement but does not require it. When it draws this support, it is not "naked"; to the degree that it does not draw this support, it is "naked." Law backed solely by naked power (if that is conceptually possible) is plausibly explained by the "bad-man" theory. But as the "bad-man" theory is more entrenched than the "puzzled-man" theory, we might do well to look for support for the latter.

Entitlement and purported entitlement surround claims to and exercises of authority with an invitation to normative judgments. This invitation is a special feature distinguishing appeals to and exercises of authority from appeals to and exercises of naked power,* and provides a basis for understanding the deep plausibility of the "puzzled-man" theory. Authority operates through the effects of these normative judgments on persons making them and other persons. Persons subject to legal authority are not in need of reasons to comply but rather are already equipped with such reasons since the judgment that compliance is "required" by the system of authority has normative impact. Whatever "normative impact" means, the "requirement" plays a role in obtaining coordination in human affairs solely through information concerning what is "required." In the "bad-man" theory, on the other hand, the presence of sanctions is critically important to the functioning of legal authority, so that what is not sanctioned cannot be taken seriously, since according to that view persons generally must be compelled if their actions are to be coordinated.

There is no need to suppose that either the "bad-man" or the "puzzled-man" theory of law is sufficient unto itself to explain ordinary human efforts to fulfill the effectiveness-conditions of legal authority. The latter theory can, however, combat the tendency promoted by the former to believe that if laws are not sanctioned, they cannot be taken seriously and must not be genuine laws. Legal authority *can* function in the way described by the latter theory on some occasions for some persons.

---

*Commentators on the distinction between law and morality offer conflicting opinions on what sanctions attach to moral judgments. So there could be disagreement about whether emphasis on the normative character of law can yield a "pure" version of the "puzzled-man" theory.

SEVEN

Legitimacy and Consent

LEGITIMACY AND AUTHORITY: PRELIMINARIES

Our earlier claims about authority assert that it is always accompanied by entitlement or at least purported entitlement.* Realizing that purported entitlement is parasitic upon both the operation and understanding of actual entitlement, our investigation now is, what *bestows* the entitlements identified with authority? This question is practically identical in significance with the question, what bestows legitimacy upon authority? Entitlement and legitimacy often amount pretty much to the same thing; where they do not, this is because the terms used are flexible, and the conditions of their uses diverge in specific contexts. Except for such divergences, being entitled to do something is being able to do it legitimately, and vice versa. In both cases, what is meant most generally and loosely is that the person's doing the thing in question on that occasion and in that manner and with respect to those people is okay.

There is more about this later, but for now it will be sufficient to launch a discussion to clarify an important matter before the foregoing issue can be taken further. When asking what bestows entitlement or legitimacy, we should note that there is no helpfully specific perfectly general account. Different accounts may be appropriate to different social structures, communal beliefs, and situations. Failure to admit this much would be unperceptive. We may, however, stop short of a thoroughly relativistic set of accounts. Can just any beliefs, practices, or usages provide bases for bestowing entitlement or legitimacy, or can some imaginable beliefs, and the like, even though relevantly accepted by the populace in question, fail to do so?

*Neither entitlement nor purported entitlement, however, is always accompanied by authority, for instance, where the entitlement is to do something not directly affecting other persons.

This issue is truly difficult, but discussions of it would be clarified if two things were done: (1) if sharp distinctions were made between, on the one hand, (a) "anthropological" views of entitlement and legitimacy-accounts that report the social consequences of the relevant practices and usages of some community or collection of communities, and, on the other hand, (b) "critical" views, in which thinkers and speakers are trying to describe (the limits of) entitlement—or legitimacy—conditions they themselves would freely endorse after reflection. An example of a view that is "anthropological" only would be a report by a modern Western European writer of the "entitlement" of slave owners and "free" humans vis-à-vis slaves in a slaveholding society. It would also be helpful if it were recognized and understood that (2) there are always ways in which a good "anthropological" description commonly has important bearing on the acceptability of any "critical" account of the community in question. This point needs careful discussion, and the present book is not a good place to explore it. We may at present note only that, just as we might be reluctant to agree that anything socially accept*ed* somewhere in the world is accept*able* for the place where it is accepted—for instance, witch burning—so we might think it unwarrantedly arrogant and unfruitful for persons adopting a "critical" view of entitlement to ignore utterly the views and practices of the persons who accept them. Given that one cannot, however, take those views and practices to be decisive, the difficulty is to state precisely how and why one should take them into account. The origins, scopes, and settings of institutions, and so on, are so various that no single general account of much specificity can be expected to emerge from a study of them. When we consider also how often it appears that scholars present a "critical" instead of a purely "anthropological" account, and also how poorly the two endeavors have been distinguished from each other and how difficult it often is to distinguish them, thus introducing the further difficulties just adduced, we should not be surprised that the pot of controversy has been boiling for so long. Though many political philosophers have tussled interestingly with the matter, too many persons working in this area fail to maintain the distinctions described in (1); failing that, they cannot deal except confusingly with the significant and difficult challenge in (2).

At least from the "anthropological" point of view, the considerations bestowing either entitlement or legitimacy may often be found explicitly in the rules, principles, and so on, supposedly controlling the formal or official practices of the particular community—for example, formal statutes describing how slaves are to be acquired and title to them transferred. We may also be guided to entitlement or legitimacy by inferences from these formal rules; for instance, an inference that parental authority entitles parents to determine a child's schooling if and because the parent is held responsible for delicts and tortious acts committed by the child.

If, on the anthropological understanding, exercises of authority are not always legitimate, it is likely because the authority is seen as stemming from one segment of the society's actual or ideal standards and the legitimacy or the entitlement are judged by another segment, perhaps a more encompassing one. On the other hand, "legitimacy" without "authority" may result from segments of a social structure that do not claim anything like rights or powers except perhaps remedially; thus, no one may be in authority over anyone else except in remedial response to the actions or behaviors of others. Inequalities of power are thus absent from these segments of these structures, at least in their nonremedial status. If one concentrates only on such a segment of the structures in question and notices only it or elevates it to supreme importance, one may fail to notice that the total structure (ordinarily) does bestow authority differentially. It is not sufficient to look only at a segment of a structure. One must look at the structure as a totality.*

The connection between authority and legitimacy (or entitlement) is rich. For example, authority via authorization often concerns the transferral of entitlement (and hence legitimacy of action) by someone entitled to do the thing in question to someone else, (a) sometimes thereby divesting oneself of entitlement to do the thing in question—as in transferral of ownership rights—and (b) sometimes not—as in granting permission to enter on one's land. On occasion, however, it involves entitlement by someone who, though authorized (empowered) to entitle, is not also authorized to do (empowered to do) the thing in question. For an example of the latter, a county clerk who is not able to cast the vote in question may authorize a citizen to cast it.

Commentators who believe that legitimacy of rule (entitlement to rule) is bestowed only by the consent of those ruled often suppose an invariable connection between authorization and legitimacy. The underlying idea here is that the ruler is authorized to rule only by those who, but for that authorization, would have the "right" to rule themselves. There are other views also associating legitimacy and authorization intimately. For example, one supposing that God had some initial right to rule and delegated that right to persons could build a story of legitimacy along the alleged divine rights of rulers.

But not every account of legitimacy associates itself closely or even at all with authorization. For example, how did the authorizers acquire initial entitlement to rule? Not, according to everybody, through authorization. Also, accounts of legitimacy founded on success or on charisma, "time immemorial," or succession may very well be able to do without the notion of authorization. The essential connection between legitimacy and authorization could be retained if it is thought that legitimacy authorizes, but this empties

*When speaking, as is so often done, of entitlement, legitimacy, or authority without scare quotes, we may be expressing normative judgments about the way we believe things ought to be. Suspicion that this is often so leads many discussants of these matters to a condition of high excitability. The "things" in question, after all, include various ways of telling people, directly or indirectly, how to behave, and doing this in ways that enlist or are likely to enlist extensive social backing and thus draw interest and be decisive, or at least be troublesome to resist. (This is a feature to which they are generally thought to owe much of their effectiveness in coordinating human behavior.) Interest and excitability often stem also from, for example, desires to arbitrate and settle contending claims to entitlement. The interest and excitability have centered in and around the way entitlement, or the like, to do things, does or can possibly fit into the value *our* culture places on equality, personal freedom, independence, and autonomy. As a result, philosophers have devoted considerable attention to exploring connections and possible conflicts between authority on the one hand, and equality, freedom, independence, or autonomy on the other. Our earlier discussions of these should be helpful in understanding some of the principal courses taken by treatments of the sources of entitlement and legitimacy.

authorization of the idea that it is a process in which someone with authority to empower other persons or agencies exercises that capacity with the result that someone or some other agency ends up having authority who clearly did not have it initially. Thus, a connection between legitimacy and authorization as the transfer and exercise of a power may well be acceptable, but an invariable connection between them is dubious.

Authority is, as we have previously seen, an important source of inequalities in power. It is both bestowed and supported by the ideas of "legitimacy" and "entitlement," making differences in authority possible and recognizable. "Legitimacy" and "entitlement," in turn, are bestowed by accepted social structures no matter why the social structures are accepted and no matter whether they are the minimum social structures in which the differences of authority being examined are embedded or more encompassing ones.

How important is legitimacy to the initiation and sustaining of authority and hence to power differences among persons? One popular view is that considerations of legitimacy are superfluous. It is said that the bottom line is always force. Force, it is said, can operate independently of any considerations of legitimacy, and even quite effectively counter to them.

The question here is the empirical one of how to obtain compliance to rules and regulations, orders and commands. This question, as we said before earlier in this book, should not be answered without careful consideration of (1) the extent of the technological resources available to the rulers, (2) what specifically is being regulated or commanded, (3) the quality of life acceptable to rulers and ruled, and (4) the extent to which the ruled can be intimidated, reasoned with, or co-opted.

Recognition of legitimacy, however, also plays an important role in facilitating compliance. It does so even independently of any role it may play in contributing instrumentally to motivate compliance by enabling potential compliers to identify what they are being called on to comply with. It marks certain sources or forms of rules, regulations, orders, and commands as the ones to which compliance is demanded in consequence of accepting the social structures in question. It integrates the issuance of directives, and the like, with the social structure legitimating them. The effectiveness of that structure is not dependent on whether most persons see either that unforced compliance contributes to aims they hold dear, or that failure to comply would probably meet with some communal disapproval or even opposition (or dependent on dispositionally willing cooperators—promiscuous cooperators—with most any scheme whatever).

If recognition of legitimacy were not integrated, and orders, and so on, did not obtain widespread compliance, compliance would then have to be considered anew in every instance, and this would threaten the survival of various schemes of coordination. To put a fine point on it, utterances and inscriptions could not or would not count as orders, commands, rules, or regulations (even purportedly) if they were not issued under color of social structures providing contexts in which they could be seen as authoritative and thus legitimate. In the absence of such integration, would reliance on force alone be practicable? Some may think so, but there is serious question of whether any rulers would have the determination and technological means to achieve anything like useful large-scale coordination, or to achieve it without disastrous consequences to their hopes for a good life.

Many commentators believe that force of some type is often necessary to compel obedience, but if force sufficient to compel obedience were necessary in every instance, rule would be unlikely if not impossible.*

LEGITIMACY AND JUSTIFICATION

Legitimate, in some applications, seems to mean something very specific—as in "legitimate child" or "legitimate theater," the former indicating "born in wedlock" and the latter "a theater doing plays rather than sketches (as in vaudeville)." If one presses for a broader understanding in each case, one may come up with something covering both cases—for instance, in accord with accepted conventions (the child was born in wedlock) or standards (the theater is of recognized merit). Not far away from this latter understanding are the understandings needed for "legitimate heir," "legitimate offer," and "legitimate business." One might, however, separate these latter three from the others and from one another into sometimes meaning "genuine," "serious," "lawful," as well as the other understandings already considered.

The understanding of *legitimate* that will do us the most good here is "in accord with (as directed by) accepted standards or conventions." This is sometimes conveyed more or less by an understanding of *legitimate* as simply "not in violation of accepted standards or conventions" ("not illegal" or "not fraudulent"). If "doing something legitimately" and "being entitled to do it" are both taken then in the broadest understandings of them normally available (roughly, that there is no objection to what is done based on standards or conventions that are or ought to be accepted in the society in question), they will be roughly equivalent.

There is thus an understanding of *legitimate* as, roughly, "okay." Even more broadly, however, there is an understanding of *legitimate* as "justified, all things considered"; that is, nothing against it in the end not counterbalanced by some positive consideration. There are also understandings of *legitimate* as meaning roughly that the thing in question transgresses nobody's rights, or that the thing in question is authoritative. The latter, in turn, can mean either that it can be done without breaching any of one's own obligations, or that one has been granted power to do it and it violates no one's rights under the authority system.

Questions of legitimacy, which are very important in political philosophy, may therefore require general consideration of rights and obligations. These concepts are discussed in Joel Feinberg's volume in this series. For the present, we shall consider these factors only insofar as they impinge upon the issues just raised.

Legitimating, on one understanding, consists therefore in acting so as to bring subsequent actions (or occupancy of offices) within the scope of what is

---

*As Rinehar Bendix says in *Kings or People,* "Psychologically, bank credit and governmental legitimacy rest on an amalgam of convenient commonplaces, inarticulate assumptions, and the willingness to let others take the lead and to leave well enough alone" (p. 17).

permitted or empowered by standards or conventions with no violation of anyone's rights. This demand for legitimating may be distinct from the demand for justifying. The importance of seeing this distinction can be shown by the following hypothetical case. Suppose that the official activities of a political community are thought justified by the vast service done by them to universal human interests. Still, the organization and operation of that community may not be thought legitimate because they fail in some way to accord with what, for example, God or the people have ordained or licensed. For human beings characteristically demand not only that something good be done, but that it be done by someone entitled to do it. This demand is crucially important to the origin, growth, and development of political communities. Thus, an understanding of the difference between justifying activities and their legitimacy is important.

Notice that *justify* and its cognates can have either normative or descriptive force. Normatively, the words focus attention on the availability or unavailability of good reasons for whatever actions, decisions, or policies are under consideration. Descriptively, the words focus attention on the presence or absence of reasons offered as good reasons by some particular person or group of persons for the action, decision, or policy under consideration. In the latter case, the reasons need not actually be good ones; they need merely be offered as good ones.

Whether taken normatively or descriptively, "good reasons" sometimes are considered with no accompanying suggestion about whether there are countervailing good reasons against the action, decision, or policy in question. But sometimes the "good reasons" are offered "all things considered." In the latter case, the suggestion is made that there are no countervailing considerations outweighing the "good reasons." On the first of these understandings but not always on the second, something may be justified with no suggestion whatever about whether the thing justified is also legitimate. Whether this suggestion is always or only sometimes absent on the second understanding depends on whether lack of legitimacy is always or only sometimes a reason against the thing in question outweighing any possible reasons in favor of it.

Confronting the question raised by this last remark, consider when and where lack of legitimacy outweighs good reasons in favor of something. Clearly, something may be justified and yet lack legitimacy. It can even be justified in the first understanding (no good reasons against it), and still lack legitimacy. For example, a person may intervene in the affairs of other persons "for their sakes" and yet be transgressing their rights thereby.

But can something be justified, "all things considered," and still lack legitimacy? Perhaps the good reasons on behalf of the thing in question are so powerful, they will outweigh the lack of legitimacy. A person may intervene in the affairs of other persons for their sakes in matters so important to them that the fact that the intervener has no authority to do so (and there may even be other persons who have this authority) will not be held to outweigh the benefits this intervention will bring about.

This matter is of great importance in politics. The distinction between the content of rules and orders, and so forth, and the question of who gives them has been used to manage this issue. Their content may, given the circumstances, make their delivery by *somebody* justified, but their delivery by whomever actually delivers them may not be legitimate. That is, the persons who deliver them may not legitimately do so, since they lack the authority to do so.

Readers should note, however, that "it all depends on where you put the wrinkles," as a philosopher friend of mine used to say. There are options here. The connections between *justification, legitimacy, entitlement,* and *good reasons* are such that, given the flexibilities, pressures may be placed on and complications appear in connection with one of these terms and resultingly not appear in connection with the others. There are choices to be made. One could have placed the wrinkles elsewhere.

DOES CONSENT LEGITIMIZE?

This section examines whether orders and demands for obedience are legitimated by consent. For political philosophers, the most fundamental issues concerning this matter are why consent of the governed should be *required* for the legitimacy of political community or government; and, quite differently, why consent of the governed should be *sufficient* to establish legitimacy of government or political community. Put slightly differently, the issues are: if the governed, by their voluntary acts, can bestow legitimacy on some government or political community, or, by withholding their consent, can render a government or political community illegitimate, whence is this power of theirs acquired?

Theories of Natural Rights are much relied upon to provide the answer, but either one must accept the historical theological basis of these theories (which is itself not without problems), or find an acceptable secular basis for them. H. L. A. Hart, in his article, "Are there any Natural Rights?" explores the relationship between the theory of natural rights and moral bases for political authority as rendering something morally permissible that otherwise would not be. Such discussion as his makes contact with political philosophy at a very fundamental level, being concerned not only with what *is* relevant in the justification, defense, and criticism of political institutions and political conduct, but also with why whatever does appear to be relevant is relevant. Most political philosophers concerned with natural rights do not challenge the view that consent is somehow relevant (though they should). They merely wish to understand why it is relevant from the standpoint of justification or legitimation; that is, not merely from the standpoint of explanation. (Explanation may itself evoke considerations relevant to justification, but the two processes are distinct.) These are topics of considerable controversy, though we shall not explore them in detail here.

Given the difficulties surrounding theories of natural rights, one may find it better to step back into the "anthropological" mode in attempting to answer these questions. A historical account may be given of how legitimating practices originated, and how a particular communal imposition of standards of legitimacy occurred. But while such accounts may be relevant to answering the questions of the philosopher's "critical" mode, their relevance to that question must be established by additional argument.

Further, numerous questions about "consent theory" remain, four of which will be dealt with here, even if the preceding "most fundamental" questions are put aside. (The "self-limitation" mentioned earlier will not suffice to answer the earlier two questions because it does not explain how we each got authority in the first place, though this matter is discussed again at the end of this chapter. Hart, in the article just cited, seems to promulgate, perhaps justifiably, the "anthropological" mode.)

In order to consider these questions about legitimacy in a way congenial to what has been said earlier in this book, we may begin by noting that a necessary condition of the existence of political community is some degree of coordination in the activities of the community members. Conformity to rules, and the like, is often the form this coordination requirement takes. A principal question here is whether people will conform to rules if the latter do not issue from some authority that the people regard as legitimate. We dealt with this question about legitimacy earlier in this chapter. If one presses for further specification, we must realize that what legitimates rules and orders for members of the community in question—for instance, "time immemorial," succession stemming from some particular family, God's word as interpreted by the priests of a religion, the charisma of a particular leader—might not do the same for us.

Problems also arise concerning the evidence that standards of legitimation, even on the "anthropological" view, have been met. What behavior confirms that rules, orders, and the like are regarded as legitimate? Should we accept as evidence that they were acquiesced in? Perhaps not, since legitimacy might be based, as we have seen, on totally different considerations. Yet, perhaps so, but with restrictions on the form the acquiescence must take. For example, if conformity were coerced, it would not do for us. But if only clear cases of coerced conformity were to be excluded, much that would be troublesome would remain: what if acquiescence were "grudging" or founded in deception? Would acquiescence of these sorts reveal an opinion that the rules were legitimate?

CONSENT

If consent is to be given importance, four problem areas emerge.

(1) *What kind of consent* legitimates and/or what behaviors constitute adequate evidence for consent that is legitimating? *"And/or"* indicates that there may not be two distinct questions here but merely alternative ways of putting what amounts to the same question.

(2) *Consent to what?* There are two aspects to this question. The first concerns whether consent is being given to some person's occupying an office vested with political authority (of some character and dimension), or to a constitution, by-law, or bill. The second concerns the character of the obligations or activities imposed by the consent. For example, as we have observed, Hobbes believed that one could not consent to one's own death, mutilation, or dishonor. His reason for this was that he viewed a person's consent as given only with the view to some benefit to oneself, and he did not see that this was possible in the cited cases. This provided Hobbes with at least a view of what one has not consented to.

(3) *Is unanimity of consent required at every stage or period* when communal decisions are made, or do some stages require less?

(4) If there are not, *what are the various stages,* how much less than unanimity is sometimes required, and what justifies the lesser requirement? This can help distinguish the various agreements (a) to form societies, (b) to adopt particular forms of government or (c) constitutions, (d) to choose authorities, and (e) to adopt particular rules, and the like. These issues also eventually encompass discussions of majority rule, rule by representatives, and even the ways that unanimity requirements can amount to minority rule by virtue of veto power thereby given to minorities.

Now let us take these issues in somewhat more detail, starting with the first two.

(1) and (2). The notion of consent has been roughly handled and vastly overextended, especially in connection with political phenomena. Also, the kinds of behavior that can be taken for appropriate consent have been the subject of vastly overinflated claims.

What, for example, is consented to when a person votes in a democratic election? Here we must distinguish between consent as a social act (open and recognizable—to which consequences are attached by social policy) and consent as a psychological condition.* If consent is a social act, voting certainly is a sign of consent, though the question remains, consent to what? But if consent is a psychological condition, then voting is clearly not always accompanied by consent. Motives for voting and intentions in voting may be quite diverse and have nothing necessarily to do with consenting psychologically to anything. Consent as a social act, however, could be a signal of some sort, a signal that may be delivered unintentionally, mistakenly, deceivingly, or entirely incidentally to some other aim or intention.

The social act and the psychological condition are not supposed, of course, to be unrelated. However, a psychological condition is not a piece of observable behavior, and the possibility of a lack of correlation between the condition and any particular piece of such behavior is shown by the occasional difference between what persons have thought themselves to be consenting to and

---

*What about tacit consent? Is voting a sign of consent? The difference between express and tacit consent is this. Both are actions or inferences based on courses of action. But express consent is an action taken (by observers for a mixture of empirical beliefs and social policy considerations) to signal the presence of the psychological condition (consent)—voting for instance—and tacit consent is an action or an inference based on a course of action that is taken (again, by observers again on the same mixture) to provide evidence of the presence of the psychological state (not that it's being signaled—for example, using the roads). Maintaining the distinction between signaling and producing evidence of the same psychological state, especially in the face of open social recognition of each, may be difficult. For example, supposing an act to be signaling a condition may involve per se supposing also that the act offers evidence of the presence of that condition. In this case, every case of express consent would also be a case of tacit consent. Hence, the foregoing exclusion in the characterization of that consent ("not that it's being signaled"). And the same behavior that is thought to provide evidence of the presence of the psychological state may, if the actor is aware that it will be so taken, be understood to signal the psychological state.

In the text, I've characterized consent as either (1) a psychological condition or (2) a social act. I characterize tacit consent either as (a) an act *simpliciter* (not necessarily a social act) or (b) an inference based on a series of acts. Either (a) or (b) provides evidence of the presence of the psychological condition (1). In short, tacit consent is not either (1) or (2) and is not therefore true consent.

what reasonable or thoughtful third parties may have taken them to be consenting to.

"Consent" as a social act is taken to legitimate what is consented to only when we suppose that the person consenting has a legal, political, or moral (depending upon the context of the discussion) power of rightful disposition over the things or events consented to. To say that a person has a power of rightful disposition over things and events is to say that the person is entitled by his or her voluntary act to determine whether the particular thing or event shall be wrongful or not. Some fairly good correlation is thus commonly presupposed between the recognized social act and "consent" as a psychological condition.

If this were not so, the account of consent as the exercise of a power of rightful disposition—to dispose of something by one's voluntary act—would be difficult to find plausible. And there must be at least some rough connection between particular social policies and psychological conditions of some sort; otherwise, the social policy would likely lack utility or justice. But the correlation is not necessarily perfect because the psychological condition(s) need not be identifiable psychologically as "consenting to" something. And, more importantly, the correlation cannot be perfect precisely because the act in question is a social one—(taken to be) a signal to other people—and mistakes, deceptions, and the other things already noticed are thus possible.

With perhaps some exceptions, and out of policy considerations, the act is normally taken to be decisive in signaling the presence of the psychological condition. It is like signaling at an auction. If bids are signaled by scratching one's ear, and you happen to scratch your ear at an inopportune time, you may have bid on a Chippendale armchair whether you intended to or not. Careful discussion of the policy considerations likely to be made here in such a simple case should be highly revealing of the issues raised and pressures generated by utilization of consent to legitimate.

In any case, as this discussion shows, even if the understanding of consent were to be as a social act, it would be entirely too hasty to say immediately and without argument that psychological conditions are irrelevant to the rights and obligations of citizens who perform the act. Nevertheless, if the conditions remain hidden, then other persons would presumably be unaware of them and could not cite them as a source of legitimation for their doing anything. One can thus understand why political philosophers sometimes object to the idea that consent legitimates anything.

But the spread of examples between cases where the psychological conditions of the consenter remain hidden and cases where they are expressed fully and explicitly in well-understood conventionalized social acts is broad, and the detected presence of the psychological conditions may very well sometimes be thought to make something legitimate. There are social policy considerations in favor of as well as considerations against the social act as obligating even when the relevant psychological conditions are absent.

What we are inclined to make in the way of social policy decisions when the psychological conditions are absent depends upon our understanding of why they are absent. If the absence is explained as a piece of deception on the part of the "consenter," we may not hesitate to impose the full range of obligations resulting from the "normal" case where both the act and the conditions are present; if the absence results from entirely innocent ignorance, our decision may be much different.

Another dimension of "kind of consent" is revealed when we notice that some commentators deny that consent, even presumably as a social act, can impose an obligation. D. D. Raphael, for example, agrees that promises and contracts can impose obligations but denies that mere consent can. He considers the effects of apathy, fear, and so on, and holds that consent due to them does not obligate. Discussions in medical ethics have recently had the same general import in focusing on "informed consent." This consent is distinguished from consent *simpliciter* by allegedly being what counts in medical practice for moral consent.

One can conclude from this discussion that there are consents, such as those mentioned by Raphael, that are not moral, and most probably do not oblige. At any rate, there are consents that do not carry with them the moral permissibility of what is consented to—for instance, consent to do something violating the presumed rights of the adult third party in the case. In medical practice, the most important borderlines are supposed to be between informed consent and coerced consent or consent based upon deception. One could, however, hold that all this multiplication of "consents" is unnecessary. One could merely refuse to call anything genuine consent that had any of these objectionable features, preserving the titles *consent* or *genuine consent* merely for consents that were free of them.

We have another lesson about choices in philosophy here. Such problems as these have been raised in political philosophy for a long time. The availability of alternative manners of discussing these problems, an availability capitalized on in these cases, may be disturbing and even confusing. Philosophy harbors many examples of this sort of thing. It is not that there are no rational means whatever of choosing from among them; it is rather there are no conclusive, decisive ways.

One mode of analyzing and understanding the problem at hand may be more illuminating than another. But our grasp of what is illuminating, more illuminating than something else, or unilluminating, though sometimes quite clear and definite, is not always shared by others and often does not lend itself to elucidation or "illumination." In any case, here is an instance of two alternatives from which there seems nothing to choose but that lead to the appearance of radically different results concerning the topic.

A principal use of consent to legitimate in politics has become to legitimate order-giving, and so on, by particular persons, and not especially to legitimate particular orders, commands, rules, or regulations. The former use raises all the more vividly our earlier question concerning what consent has been given *to*.

Few philosophers have supposed that unqualified consent has been ordinarily given to every order given by an order-giver. On the other hand, this particular use of consent would not be of much value if subsequent "free" (whatever that is) agreement with every specific order or command were also required. If one has consented to a particular person's becoming an order-giver, then the consenter need not forbear making judgments of any sort concerning the rightness or wrongness of the orders given. But the consenter may have committed himself or herself to obeying the orders even in some circumstances in which he or she would have felt free otherwise to disobey them.

One might suppose on grounds mentioned earlier (in Chapter Six, on authority) that disobedience for the reason that one has a simple inclination would be wrong. But other reasons for disobedience might also be insufficient in a given system of authority. Perhaps the consenter believes the orders given to be imprudent, unwise, or counter-productive relative to acknowledged common goals.

Except possibly in the most serious cases, such opinion would not make disobedience acceptable in many societies. What, however, if the consenter believed the orders to be or to require something immoral? Here, also, in various societies the matter would have to be thought quite serious in order to render disobedience acceptable, if it is acceptable. These questions will be discussed further in Chapter Thirteen, on civil disobedience and revolution. For the present, we may observe that consent as a legitimating device is neither so powerful nor yet so weak as has sometimes been supposed.

In consequence, however, its scope and impact, though of considerable significance, are not very clear. Consent to order-giving clearly involves some surrender of the idea that one might act always and only on whim or on one's private judgment in every situation. Indeed, precisely this (and not the coercive backing for order-giving) seems to be focused on by many anarchists' complaints about the state. The consensual giving up of acting always and only on one's private whim or judgment, however, has also been treated instead as no sacrifice whatever of one's personal autonomy precisely because the abandonment was consensual. This important topic was considered earlier in this book, and will again surface (in Chapter Ten: Representation).

(3) and (4). There are communal actions that are supposed to be legitimate only when collegiate (community) decisions have been made to support them and not merely a decision by some one individual. We will thus need rules or principles for transcribing myriads of individual decisions into collegiate decisions, and we will need an understanding of the relationship between individual and collegiate decisions sufficient to explain exactly what the individual has the power of disposition with respect to in relation to these collegiate decisions.

A rule of responsibility that most everyone would accept as sufficient, though many would not accept as necessary, is unanimity. *Consensus* has a cozier sound, though in the end *unanimity* and *consensus* mean pretty much the same thing. To some, however, the former suggests a well-developed franchise, whereas the latter suggests merely an undefined mass of "participants." Talk about a "rule of unanimity" is more widespread in political thought than talk of a "rule of consensus," though the latter has its proponents.

The rule of unanimity depends, of course, on what the decision is about. Rules for legitimating decisions range from the demand for unanimity, at one extreme, to the demand merely for plurality (not even majority, let alone such a thing as a "two-thirds majority") at the other. A rule of unanimity is a stringent requirement. In fact, it is regarded as too stringent to be practicable in any but the most vitally important collegiate decisions. Given probable differences of human opinion and human perception, a rule of unanimity might be impracticable unless the importance of reaching a single, collegiate decision is also understood.

Rules of unanimity have been criticized, not only because they are often thought impracticable, but because they give enormous power, veto power, to individuals, and thus bring about a form of limited minority rule. Minorities as small as "a minority of one" can, if the rule of unanimity is strictly enforced, block communal decision on anything to which the rule is applied—just by not agreeing to what might otherwise have been decided. Pluralities and even overwhelming majorities may thus be rendered helpless to act through the opposition of one lone person.

Thus, though a rule of unanimity has been widely thought to be sufficient, hardly any careful thinkers have been prepared to propose it as a requirement for much of anything. It does, however, raise questions about the limits of communal cooperation and congeniality. Anarchists tend to believe that these limits are very broad, though even they sometimes propose methods for dealing with the lack of unanimity that are difficult to distinguish from the uses of coercion that they are supposed to be protesting (see our earlier mentions of this point). Communities have sometimes (as in the case of medieval Dutch cities under siege) gone surprisingly far in imposing a rule of unanimity (among the city fathers).

Majority rule (whether the rule of bare or heavier majority) has the advantage of not permitting minority vetoes. Its disadvantage is that it requires extension of the ideas of self-limitation and self-rule. A dramatic illustration of the strain of this extension is found in an edition of Locke that I read years ago, in which, when talking about certain matters such as the taking of a person's property, Locke says that it cannot be taken "without his own consent—i.e., the consent of the majority." We are told by scholars of the period that "with his own consent" meant "with the consent of the majority." The identification here between the consent of an individual person and consent of the majority not only requires special argument but provides occasion for suspicion that something common though "funny" is going on. The special argument that has pushed or drawn so many political philosophers to identify the consent of an individual person with the consent of the majority certainly requires careful examination.

The distinction between bare majority rule and the rule of heavier majorities is commonly made, the latter being favored on especially important matters. Whether the importance of the matters justifies a demand for more than a bare majority because in such cases it is more morally acceptable or because it assures that whatever decision is made will have a broad base of community support is not clear. At any rate, the closer one comes to a demand for unanimity, the closer one is to minority veto power and the less extended is the argument required to identify the eventual decision made with self-limitation and self-rule.

In our earlier introduction to these four problem areas we distinguished agreements to form societies from agreements to adopt particular forms of government or constitution, and these in turn from agreements to choose authorities, and from agreements to adopt particular rules and orders. In discussions of the details of government operation, it is common to find a distinction as well between matters on which bare majorities are required and matters on which heavier majorities are required.

Useful distinctions can therefore be made between various versions of "social contract" theories—a form of theory roughly endemic to political philosophy. Raphael, for example, distinguishes a variety of such theories (which, by the way, he distinguishes from pure theories of consent—a distinction of his we have already examined). His categories of social contract theories are (1) theories of citizenship, where the agreement is between the individual person and the state or government (which latter, one should note, are quite different from each other for him); (2) theories of community, where the agreement is of each person with every other person to form a community—that is, to set up laws, and so on; and (3) theories of government, which are very much like theories of community but involve the second of two contracts often distinguished from each other: (a) an agreement to form a community and (b) an agreement to set up a government in that community, and intent to identify only the latter. This yields a large array of circumstances thought appropriate by philosophers to "contracting." As some of these may clearly coexist with the need for others, one can consider the desirability of asking for rules of unanimity in some and for rules of varying majorities in others.

The demand for pluralities, in contrast with demands for majorities, finds its rationale in rather special circumstances of life in political communities. As members of those communities affiliate with and distribute themselves among three or more factions on an issue, majorities become increasingly difficult to achieve. Reliance on pluralities rather than majorities or unanimity is a practicable response to the resultant problems. The major difficulty is that the "collegiate" decision of the community is less and less plausibly declared to be a "decision of the community." The number of persons straightforwardly declarable to be mandating communal spokes-persons can become smaller and smaller, and still remain a plurality. Thus, "the community" speaks quite possibly with the voice of fewer and fewer persons in the community. The majority of members may, in fact, disagree with what is said. Declaring a plurality to be the communal voice requires increasingly greater reliance on participation in the decision-making process.

We are now in a position to discuss more deeply the two questions posed at the beginning of the previous section of the chapter and answered there: that is, questions concerning the significance of consent and what may be demanded or permitted in its name. We have seen that at the bottom of many of the issues in this area is how one commits oneself to various courses of action. There are a number of ways of doing this apart from promising or contracting.

Some discussants of this issue in a different context—where issues of interpersonal relations are concerned rather than issues having more prominent political importance—state that committing oneself may be done by such things as "the giving of an impression," "not correcting a misapprehension," and "beginning a course of conduct on the basis of which someone else has taken action." One should note that the results might sometimes be better describable as *becoming committed* than *committing oneself*. The clinching circumstance in these cases may be failing to correct an impression that one has every reason to know that one has created. There may also be degrees of commitment that one will perceive as one works through cases going down to the case where a person recognizes that someone else is acting in reliance on one's doing something, though one hasn't given that person to understand anything at all.

The interesting difference here is between what one has knowingly done, and what one merely comes to realize about what people have gathered from what one has done. There is also some pressure on the claim of commitment. It may not be entirely appropriate to discuss this matter only in terms of the obligations one incurs. The issue may gradually become what kind of a person one is or shall choose to be, how "influenced" by and how perceiving we shall be about the situations and feelings of other persons, and the extent to which one will alter one's course of conduct in the view of such considerations. Here, one should also consider alternative courses of conduct—such things as warning, apologizing, and recompensing. The questions are not only whether but also how you will open or close your feelings to the other person's situation, and its connection, now and in the future, with your own conduct.

Such issues as these may very well lie behind discussions of "consent" in connection with our two initially posed questions. Consideration of them again will lead us to understand the depths of interpersonal relations and personal character lying underneath attempts to utilize and "legitimate" consent. The resulting interpretations of obligation-talk may very well be awkward but not outrageous.

Obligation-talk in connection with politics may appear to be more largely *ad hominem* than it may have formerly appeared to be. The decision to find and enforce "obligations" may also seem to be a basis for repression and the relatively crude rendering of perceptions and sensitivities—some of which may seem too sensitive for such treatment. One may become increasingly aware of how common views of sanctions and justice in politics would be too crude to do us good service in political life if they alone were relied upon. Fortunately, the realities of political life are more flexible than suggested.

In political contexts, for example, there are places where members of the political community (or even persons outside that community) have formed expectations about and have relied on or merely been susceptible to what has been done "in the name of" or "on behalf of" the community, whether intentionally or unintentionally. These places will test our perceptions not only of what we are, but of what we shall become. This important distinction of Dewey's (in *Human Nature and Conduct*) provides us with a more sensitive and hence more adequate base than is common when discussing, for example, when notice of "change of plans" is sufficient, and when compensation is required if plans are to be changed, and the like.

EIGHT

Constitutionalism, the Rule of Law, and Limited Government

John Locke said that one of the main advantages of living in a civil society (roughly what we have been calling a political community) is having known and settled laws to live by. Even if everybody were generally reasonable, the partiality of persons to their own special interests would create instability and uncertainty in the rules (and in their application) in accordance with which we are trying to live. The effects of the instability would ramify on persons and arrangements between persons. Many benefits of current arrangements could not be reaped because there would be insufficient security in the arrangements themselves. In contrast, a known, settled law not subject to the partialities of formulation, interpretation, and application by those subject to it would provide some security for undertaking arrangements such as we now make between ourselves.

A known, settled law to live by is not achieved merely by entering into communities possessing powerful and coherent schemes of authority. The schemes themselves may be operated in accordance with the whims and fancies of the persons operating them. In such cases there may be a known law, but it may not be sufficiently settled to provide a secure basis for the expectations that underlie arrangements of the sort we want. On the other hand, the law can be too settled in either its formulation or application. Law is merely a corrigible human artifact, and must not be so rigid as not to be somewhat adjustable to varying circumstances.

The philosophical concerns focused upon in the present chapter have arisen out of considerations such as these. Our problem is to explore the coherence and helpfulness of customary expressions of aspirations and ideals in this area. Efforts to reap the advantages of stability must accommodate needs for flexibility to meet suitably varying circumstances, and must also provide protection against arbitrary rule. Protections against arbitrariness in rule need not express a demand for perfect rule, but may simply reflect a desire for some protection against imperfect rule.

Rule that is in any way less than maximally beneficial, wise, reasonable, and the like, is surely best avoided. But we do not normally pitch our demands so high. We might promote perfect rule, but not expect thereby to prevent imperfect rule in all its guises. It is normally thought enough, and by no means easy, to establish effective limits on rule and thus to render it at least in some respects nonarbitrary.

Thomas Hobbes posed this problem as sharply as did anyone. If rulers (sovereigns) are to have authority and power to settle disputes among their subjects, no person or agency within the commonwealth can have the power or authority effectively to countermand the decisions of the sovereign. Any limits on the power or authority of the sovereign would involve a presumption otherwise; therefore, no such limits can exist.

Hobbes realized how open this leaves subjects to abuse by the exercise of sovereign authority and power, but believed less risk to be involved than would be if there were no final arbiter (that is, sovereign) to settle disputes among subjects in the commonwealth. According to Hobbes, without such an arbiter, peace within the commonwealth could not be reliably preserved.

Hobbes's views expose just one set of considerations supposed to make limitation of rule difficult or inappropriate, if not practicably impossible. They have, however, been the most persistently troubling, and mention of them alone will suffice for the present occasion. Principal headings under which the need for limitations on rule are discussed by political philosophers and political theorists generally are "constitutionalism," "the rule of law," and "limited government." We shall begin with a brief introductory discussion of each of these ideas.

CONSTITUTIONALISM

Constitutions, on the common understanding of Aristotle's view of them, are descriptions of the principal features of the political cultures of communities, especially the distribution of power among the governing persons or agencies. But even on this understanding there is something normative about them. Political cultures consist of the accepted practices in a community, and these practices embody expectations and even demands concerning how things are to be done in that community. Accepted practices, and hence constitutions, thus provide bases for criticism and bases for demands for special justification when things are not done in the established ways.

Of course, a political culture may be unstable or in transition, and thus not have much in the way of accepted practices. (Resulting problems with the identity and identification of the culture's "constitution" and parallel problems concerning its "legal system" will be introduced in Chapter Thirteen:

Civil Disobedience and Revolution.) The constitutions of such communities would not have enough in them to provide bases for judgments concerning politically right and wrong ways of doing things. These would, in the extreme cases, be cases where the normative aspect of a constitution disappeared.

If in "constitutionalism" one has or advocates a constitution on the foregoing "Aristotelian" understanding of "constitution," then every society or government would be a constitutionalism. Most commentators, however, agree that some governments are constitutionalisms and some are not. Either "constitutions" are not as Aristotle understood them or their relationship with "constitutionalism" is not what we hypothesized it is at the beginning of this paragraph.

Constitutionalism is perhaps the condition produced where the normative features of constitutions are most fully developed. That is, when there is a clearly identifiable ruler or government whose ways of doing things are subject to expectations of and demands (for example, of some form of what comes to be known as "due process") by the populace generally *and* these expectations and demands provide bases for possible criticism of and restraints on the way things are done.

There is an important distinction between criticism of and restraint on rulers and governments. A practical possibility of the latter is generally thought essential to fully developed cases of constitutionalism. If the political culture provides no mechanism for restraint, designations of the political life of that culture as "constitutional" would be at best controversial. There are, however, debates about what constitutes such a mechanism. Some commentators, for example, believe that limited government or even popular sovereignty are necessary to constitutionalism.

The restraint commonly thought to be characteristic of and essential to constitutionalism is where rulers and governments are restrained *by* law and govern *through* law. Traditionally, "the rule of law" was contrasted with "the rule of men" (though we now might want to change this to "the rule of persons").* The latter was supposed to consist in the arbitrary use of political power—arbitrary not in the sense of unreasonable, but in the sense of unrestrained.

Restraint perhaps does not itself require the existence of some other power, but may simply consist in the fact that the effective exercise of the ruler's power depends upon the regularity, recognition, and respect for procedures characteristic of law. As Nannerl Keohane describes the views of Claude de Seyssel, a commentator on French "absolute monarchy" of his time, "arbitrariness . . . is diminished, not by independent control from above or below, but by the institutional and legal instruments through which that authority itself is exercised."** It is, perhaps, like a bird feeling the resistance of the air through which it flies; air resistance enables it to fly, but is also something to which the bird must adjust.

The distinction between "the rule of law" and "the rule of men," insofar as it has a bearing here, has not always been understood only as a distinction

*These two slogans will be examined more fully in the next section.

**"Claude de Seyssel and 16th Century Constitutionalism in France," *Constitutionalism* Pennock and Chapman, eds. (New York: NYU Press, 1979), p. 76.

between restrained and arbitrary power-wielding. For purposes of constitutionalism, the "restraint" has had to be sanctioned by some power on earth—for example, popular opinion—and not merely, for example, by "reason." This, in turn, raises questions about the relationship between how a ruler or government is to be restrained and its ability to exercise discretion.

Consider the case commented on by Seyssel. Here, the arbitrariness eliminated by rule *through* law contrasted with restraint *by* law was thought at least to eliminate the discretion of rulers to do simply as they wish, and do so in ways involving more than merely an appeal to reason.* Our question must be, does the limitation of which she speaks limit the discretion of rulers to do as they want or think best?

In political cultures where rulers are thought to be servants of somebody—for example, of the people or of God—it has sometimes been thought necessary to assure that service by permitting the rulers little or no discretion. But will this latter limitation assure or only frustrate service? That is the question to be discussed next.

THE RULE OF LAW AND THE RULE OF MEN

It has often been said that if law is to be effective it must be administered by men (persons), and so all rule of law is rule of men (persons) anyway. This remark may make one wonder what there is to the distinction between "the rule of law" and the "rule of men."

It has also often, though not quite so often, been said by commentators that they do not care who *formulates* the law just so long as they can determine who *executes* or *administers* it. This may make one wonder of what importance the distinction is even if it can be sustained.

In view of the preceding discussion of Seyssel, one may think it also plausible to assert that most cases of rule by men will also be cases of rule by law. (Controversies about the nature and essence of law are dealt with in another book in this series, Martin Golding's *Philosophy of Law* [1975].)

To retrieve whatever sense remains in the contrast between these two slogans, the rule of law, if it is to receive the usual approbation, must not extinguish, though it may narrow, the extent to which rulers can do what they think best, and the rule of men cannot proceed without any administrative apparatus and must not proceed with unreasoned arbitrariness. Under these understandings, what importance can be attached to the slogans?

(1) By emphasizing or de-emphasizing the distinction between an office and the person holding that office, one slogan reduces and the other enlarges whatever view prevails in the political culture that political power and authority are personal. Each extreme of the contrasting views has some weaknesses and each has some strengths.

When the personal character of political power and authority are emphasized, we are reminded that fellow human beings, and not, or not merely,

*As Keohane notes, "His [Seyssel's] theory of decision-making recognizes that royal decisions are not simply formal moments of pure disposition of *volunté* but are shaped by advice and information and depend heavily on the quality of counselors of the king" (p. 27).

gods or impersonal forces are at work in our political system. Understanding the vulnerability of human nature may put us on guard concerning the various ways in which things may go wrong.

Contrariwise, making a sharp distinction between the powers, authorities, and statuses of offices and the identities of the persons holding them, we are enabled to see the powers and authorities as stemming from the occupancy of the office rather than from any personal attributes of the office-holder (though the occupancy of the office by a given person may stem in some way from personal attributes of that person). This view makes possible a distinction between what the office-holder does qua office-holder and what he or she does qua person, and thus helps to sustain a view of what the office-holder does as interpersonally neutral.

The advantages and disadvantages of one emphasis or the other may be exposed by an exploration of *ruler*. Rulers, as distinguished from mere participants in a government, are persons at the top or top reaches of a government. By extension, they are members of the social or economic classes from which rulers regularly come (should they regularly come from any particular one or several of these classes). By further extension, rulers are persons having great influence over rulers characterized in these other ways.

But difficulties sometimes occur in determining which persons *are* at the top or top reaches of government. For example, when there exist (a) separations of powers (judicial, legislative, and executive powers may be more or less clearly separated and held by different persons), (b) systems of checks and balances, and (c) indefiniteness in the boundaries of what constitutes a government, arguments are sometimes launched that one of these powers is superior to the others. But these arguments are hardly knock-down ones, for no office-holders may be able to propose or act without being liable to have their proposals vetoed or action blocked by someone else.

Sometimes such difficulties are met by extension of the notion of "ruler." But such extensions must be dubious. And it is not clear in certain countries whether the political parties, religious or economic sectors that dominate government should themselves be considered the government (or part of it). Likewise, in some democratic countries it is not clear whether the electorate should be considered a branch of the government (see Alexander Meikeljohn).

With respect to some governments, and in some contexts, there may not be any person or persons who therefore can comfortably be called *rulers*. Notice that this conclusion is true anyway. Despots can comfortably be called *rulers*, but presidents, premiers, and prime ministers are sometimes more comfortably called *leaders* or *heads of government* than rulers. Discomfort about calling them *rulers* arises from difficulties in determining who, if anyone, is really at the top of the political authority structure. This may be partly because of confusion about who is in authority—a confusion perhaps resolvable by asking who is in office, and, in any case, less troublesome if one remembers to apply the distinction between authority and power.

The difficulties, however, may be because no one is clearly at the top: perhaps there is a top office, but no one is presently filling that office; perhaps there is no office clearly at the top; perhaps there is a set of offices that could be characterized jointly as at the top. The occupants of the latter might occasionally, for some purposes, and to point up some contrasts, be characterized jointly as rulers. If there is difficulty in calling these persons *rulers*, then there is certainly difficulty in calling whatever they engender *rule of persons*. It instead seems to be a function of the structure of the legal and political apparatus.

Our account in an early chapter of rulers presents them as determining what, when, where, and how things are to be done in endeavors where systematic mutual reliance is useful and univocal directions are needed. Those determinations may be apportioned or shared by a number of people just so long as their activities are sufficiently coordinated to sustain the enterprise. Further, determination of the activities or kinds of activities in which the governments attempt systematic mutual reliance may be made by any of a number of possible decision procedures. Thus *rule of persons* emphasizes the contributions of individual rulers within the frameworks established by what could be identified as *rule of law*.

(2) The rule of law may narrow, though it does not eliminate entirely, personal discretion and judgment. The narrowing may not only be of what is done, but of how it is done. Contrariwise, the rule of persons will leave these factors comparatively untouched. Thus, the rule of law may sharply narrow, and the rule of persons comparatively enlarge, the areas in which political authority and power *can* be personal. There are at least two famous places in the history of political philosophy where important issues surrounding this question have been discussed. The first is in Aristotle's discussion of justice and, in particular, the relationship between justice and equity in the *Nichomachean Ethics*. The second is John Locke's discussion of the prerogative of the sovereign in his *Second Treatise of Government*.

Aristotle's discussion is too complex to discuss in detail here, but its gist is that the rule of law must be relieved by equity if complete justice is to be done, because law cannot take into account everything that needs to be taken into account in all cases. This view has provided subsequent commentators with reason to say that the rule of law must be relieved by the rule of men (persons).

Locke's most striking remark on prerogative was that good rulers can be a danger to their people. People will allow a good ruler abundant opportunity to use prerogative because the ruler is likely to use it wisely and well. This can be a danger in that it provides an unfortunate precedent when less-able or less-benign rulers come to power. The apogee of rulers of the sort that concerns Locke was possibly the guardians in Plato's *Republic*. These rulers, as wise and benign as careful selection and training could make them, were, within very broad limits, supposed to exercise *only* their discretion (roughly, Locke's "prerogative") about what would be best.

It is important to recognize that Locke characterized prerogative as a power to act not only for the public good where the law does not prescribe, but also even against the law. The addition carries his discussion far past any other of the mere incompleteness of the rule of law, and allies it with Aristotle's discussion of a more general deficiency of the rule of law. The assumption seems to be that both the law and the prerogative have common aims; they both aim at the common good. The puzzling thing is why, if the aim of prerogative is on occasions both appropriate to promote the public benefit and to be more accurate than the rule of law, prerogative is not utilized constantly.* Locke suggests that prerogative, being a danger to the people when exercised by a good ruler because it paves the way for exercises of it by bad rulers, is a helpful but nonetheless hazardous remedy to the insufficiencies of a generally desirable reliance upon the rule of law.

Ronald Dworkin's distinction between kinds of discretion (some of which are exercised in prerogative) alerts us to the importance of distinguishing between discretion granted by a rule or a scheme of rules, and discretion to alter, add to, or correct a scheme of rules. A rule may, for example, grant a judge authority to impose a sentence from one to twenty years and direct judges to use their discretion in determining how large a sentence between these limits to give convicted individuals. There is no idea here that judges might sentence someone against the rules, or that judges are correcting any insufficiency in the rules. These exercises of judicial discretion are expressly called for by the rules themselves. These are not, therefore, cases of the exercise of the discretion initially considered earlier, that is, prerogative. Prerogative is the exercise of discretion where the rules either prescribe nothing, or what they prescribe is deemed unsatisfactory. If discretion of the second sort is to be exercised, and not merely whim or caprice, a judgment is made that is neither granted nor guided by the rules (except possibly indirectly). What is supposed to guide such judgments is controversial.

At least three kinds of discretion can be discriminated. First, there is discretion granted by and exercised in accordance with rules (laws). Such discretion is generally limited to a clear range of possibilities, presumes adequate understanding of the rules granting it, and presumes that the discretionary judgment will be exercised in ways guided by some set of common aims, values, and beliefs shared with the authority granting the discretion. Second, there is discretion not expressly granted by or limited by the rules, to decide in situations not covered by the rules, and to decide contrary to the decision that might be dictated by the rules. Such discretion may be allowed when the rules are recognized to be deficient in leading to the aims and values they were acknowledged to be designed to further.

Aristotle's rather confusing remarks in Chapter V of the *Nichomachean Ethics* about the relationship between justice and equity constitute a historically highly influential argument that rules will inevitably be deficient in this respect. The deficiency, as well as the authorization to do something about it, must, however, not be too prominent or prevalent if members of the community are to continue to be described as generally proceeding in accord with a system of rules.

Third, there is the discretion or judgment exercised in determinations of how to understand and apply rules. This is not granted by rules, but is generally presumed by them. In many situations the need for such judgment will hardly be noticed. But it will appear prominently when the rules are not

---

*Plato (in *The Statesman* and later) and Aristotle suggest that it is because the users of prerogative will not be sufficiently wise and constant to do without the guidance and restraint of the laws.

thought clear or the applications of them for one reason or another seem dubious. To many, it may seem that, again, the exercise of this judgment presumes guidance by reference to common aims, values, and beliefs guiding the formulation or continued use of the rules. Controversy occurs, however, over whether and how such judgments should be explained or justified—for example, how statutes are to be understood or, in the common terminology, "interpreted."

LIMITED GOVERNMENT

It would not be surprising to learn that there is a lot of overlap between "constitutionalism" and "rule of law," and between each of those two and "limited government." But given the flexibility we have found in each of the former two, it would not be surprising either to find a lack of coincidence.

At least two important questions about constitutionalism and the rule of law press upon us from the earlier discussion. (1) If rulers and governments are to be limited, who or what is to provide the sanctions presumably needed to make the limits effective? (2) How are we to make the limits sufficiently firm so that we can find protection in them against arbitrariness and oppression, and yet sufficiently flexible to allow for wise and beneficial decisions in unusual circumstances?

With regard to the first question, Hobbes thought that reliance must be placed upon the ordinary course of nature. We have already seen his reasons for believing that no power on earth could limit the sovereign. The limits thus for him were "the laws of nature," and sovereigns who transgressed them would, at the very least, be less prosperous than they would otherwise be. Gross transgressions by them might even bring about a downfall, resulting in the sovereign's incapacity to protect citizens from one another and from external enemies, capacities (both of them) upon which Hobbes believed sovereignty ultimately rests. These consequences were presented also by Hobbes as God's sanctions against violations of the laws of nature. Contemporary commentators, however, frequently insist not only on an earthly power to do the sanctioning, but also that the sanctions be human artifacts and depend not merely on the intelligence or desires of the ruler.

The view of Seyssel, as presented by Keohane, gives the limits as unavoidably present in the combined machinery of human wills and cooperation needed to effect the sovereign's will. The reluctance of some commentators to accept this as an account of true constitutionalism stems in part from doubt about whether a true "artifact" is involved. Behind this demand for an artifact lies a Hobbesian view of human nature and human motivation, though Hobbes saw no consistent way to apply it to the sovereigns themselves.

The view is that limits on political power and authority will not be effectively observed unless there are sanctions resulting from human artifice. These sanctions need not, however, be imposed by law (unless *law* is broadly characterized to include by definition any sanction), and thus constitutionalism and the rule of law may part company, unless there is equivocation. For example, regicide and revolution have both been acknowledged to be qualified sanctions for constitutional limitations. On the other hand, Gordon Schochet says that before early modern Europe, when there was hardly true constitutionalism, "the legal ability of Governors to ignore constitutional standards was insurmountable . . ."*

This could mean any or all of several things. First, the governors had the legal power to act contrary to the standards. Next, if the governors acted contrary to the standards, they would not thereby be violating any legal obligation. (As Thomas Grey notes later in *Nomos* XX, [pp. 192–93], constitutions do embody extralegal norms, such as the norms of the British Constitution that Dicey called *conventions*. Actions by a governor contrary to these conventions might be regarded as gross violations of the constitution though, presumably, protests against them would have no legal standing. If the governors did not respect these conventions, and they were all that the constitution contained on the topic, the respects in which the constitution restrains the governors would be difficult to discover.)

But there is a third possible understanding of Schochet's remark, that no one has the legal power to proceed against sovereigns who act contrary to the constitutional standards. If the "legal" abilities of governors are determined by hard-nosed positivist views of what is "legal" (see Golding's volume in this series), these abilities may be thought to extend until someone else has the legal ability to stop them. On this account, neither governors nor anyone else will have legal abilities limited only by themselves. No matter what the relevant conventions are or what the empowering documents say, authority will be unlimited unless someone else has the capacity to limit it. This view of "legal ability," however, is not universally accepted.

Restraints on governors' legal abilities are not the only restraints on their acting contrary to constitutional standards, though they may be the sum and substance of the issue in stable communities. This is offset, however, by the idea that the reasonably stable communities are the only ones readily recognizable as constitutionalist. Further, if restraint is to be made central to constitutionalism, then the character of that restraint should be clear if the boundaries of *constitutionalism* are to be clear. Thinkers should also ask whether they wish the boundaries to be clear, why they wish them to be clear, and at what cost.

The second issue posed at the beginning of this section was how to make the limits sufficiently firm so that we can find protection in them against arbitrariness and oppression, yet sufficiently flexible to allow for wise and beneficial decisions in unusual circumstances. This combination should not be expected easy to find. Attempts to provide it both within the legal system in particular and the political system in general proceed along two lines: adjustment of the interplay between rule and discretion within the system as they standardly operate within the expectations, usages, and practices of the system; and provision for the revision of these expectations, usages, and practices.

These attempts appear most clearly within legal systems, where they have received much attention and are more clearly delineated than within political

---

*Nomos, XX, p. 2.

systems generally. Consider, for example, the interplay of rule and discretion (mentioned in Chapter Six) as one goes up and down the line of authorities acting in the name of the legal system in a criminal case. From the arresting officer through the parole officer there are interestingly different patterns of reliance on rule and discretion concerning different matters. It all fits together in an intricate, it is hoped, reasonable pattern for the distribution of power and responsibility.

It appears that no one has all the power or all the responsibility. (Thus President Truman was regarded as showing a piece of bravado when he exhibited on his desk a sign reading, "The Buck Stops Here.") The interplay within a particular legal or political culture may vary widely. Fine-scale examination of this in particular cases is an essential part of determining for that culture the interplay of, and proportion between, the rule of law and the rule of persons.

Likewise, for any legal system as well as for any political system generally, there will be opportunities within the system, at least broadly conceived, for alteration of its expectations, usages, and practices. For example, most agents of the legal system standardly have the capacity to repeal (often merely by implication) any directive they have themselves previously issued. There will, however, be aspects of the system that were not engendered by directives, some of which may be readily alterable, and some of which may not. Alteration of them may not amount to anything so simple as the issuance of a directive.

They may instead be given special importance, be specially "entrenched," so that a more elaborate or at least different procedure may be necessary to change them. Perhaps they will be so entrenched that nothing *within* the system can change them. They may even have constitutional importance, in which case we will have a part of a constitution or a constitution itself being what some commentators have called *rigid* rather than *nonrigid*, or even *flexible*. Again, this has bearing on the balance between the rule of law and the rule of persons.

NINE

Sovereignty

Traditionally, sovereigns, when they are not coins, are often monarchs. Some monarchs are called *sovereign* only by courtesy or tradition; they are sovereigns, though not sovereign. Besides monarchs, other things are sovereign: bodies (some legislatures, and the like), norms, states or countries, and remedies. This list is not intended to be exhaustive.

Things are sovereign often by virtue of possessing sovereignty. The correctness of understandings of sovereignty has been much disputed by philosophers. This chapter addresses that issue. We shall examine principally only the clearly political cases of sovereignty and sovereign things. That is, we shall overlook "sovereign remedies" and the like.

Sovereignty is traditionally, roughly speaking, either superiority-dominance or independence (see later in the chapter for a discussion of a rationale for the disjunction) relative to or within an order, arrangement, or aggregation. The order, arrangement, or aggregation may be purely formal and normative—as with a purely hypothetical order or partly actualized historical order long extinguished—or not either formal or (much) normative—as with spheres of influence or dominance in communities of a sort that might be studied by a historian or a sociologist—or some mixture of these.

The evidence and argument needed to support claims concerning who *has* sovereignty in a particular situation or whether there *is* a sovereign will fluctuate with differences in the character of the orders considered. They will range from exclusive concern for the stipulations and implications of formal systems to sociological and historical inquiries. Formidable difficulties are confronted when, as is often the case, these orders, and so on, are mixtures, and not pure cases, of our two extreme types.

We shall consider sovereignty, then, as a set of qualities possessed by some cases of political authority. Traditionally, the principal settings in which importance is attached to sovereignty are (a) the relations of political communities and their governments to other political communities and their governments, and (b) the relationships of some political communities to their own governments. Respecting the first, the key quality is independence; as to the second, the key quality is supremacy. Thus, there are two important aspects to sovereignty—the external, in which sovereignty customarily means independence of and lack of subordination to any other political community; and internal, in which it means undivided and unlimited power and authority (that is, supremacy) within the community. Some difficulty within political philosophy and political theory as well has resulted from failure to recognize important differences in these settings and to consider them separately.

INDEPENDENCE

Some political communities are straightforwardly parts of or politically and legally subordinate to other political communities. For example, American cities and counties are parts of or subordinate to other communities and goverments, such as the various American states. Consequently, one does not expect to hear talk about the sovereign city of X or the sovereign county of Y. The United States of America and Iceland, on the other hand, are known to international law as sovereign entities. They each may be members of various treaty alliances, or signatories of various fishing agreements, but these connections are thought to be expressions of, rather than infringements on, their sovereignty. These connections do not make them parts of or subordinate to the legal and political structures of any larger or distinct political communities.

There are difficult cases, of course, and one cannot always be clear with respect to confederacies or federations which communities are sovereign and which are not. For example, the government of the United States of America is supposed to be a federal government, and one hears still much talk about "the sovereign state of Nevada" or "the sovereign commonwealth of Massachusetts." The extents to which Nevada and Massachusetts are really sovereign political communities may not be perfectly clear. Theorists of federalism do not agree on how to analyze the phenomenon. And the effects of organizations such as the European Economic Community upon the sovereignty of its member "states" are debated.

At the bottom of the difficulties and disagreements is the difficulty of specifying precisely the nature and degree of independence required for sovereignty. This difficulty is not due to neglect. The importance of precise specification has long been recognized, and has been given much attention. The difficulty is due, rather, to the conditions created by the gradual emergence of an idea of sovereignty over many centuries in diverse cultures, sometimes loosely and sometimes tightly related to one another, and whose relations are resistant to standardization, of an exact idea of sovereignty. As with many other ideas in human experience, such conditions of emergence and growth have made us not always sure, in our attempted analyses of the idea, when we are clarifying an idea already there and when we are creating or stipulating something new.

Sometimes, as in the case of sovereignty, the idea comes to play an important role in the formulation of and the solution to practical problems of large scope and importance. When this occurs, the difficulty in distinguishing between clarification and stipulation becomes of practical importance. Vested interests of considerable magnitude are attached to just where the distinction is to be drawn.

Sovereign governments are not subordinate to and not parts, divisions, or branches of other governments. But precisely what is included by this exclusion? This is not merely a theoretical question. On its answer hang urgent practical questions concerning the constituent parts of leagues, treaty organizations, confederacies, and federations. When are the influences on and the obligations of the constituent governments sufficient to support the claim that these governments are subordinate to the governing body of the alliance (the agencies deciding and accepting responsibility for decisions in the name of the alliance), and when is the subordination sufficient to support a claim that the constituent governments cannot therefore be sovereign? The questions embedded in this complex question are much contended by political scientists.

The leading idea is that a sovereign government will be independent from other governments. What is not clear is precisely what kinds of influence or subordination are inconsistent with the independence required. Clearly, colonies, trust territories, and puppet governments are not independent in the requisite way. But even with puppet governments there are problems. Governments resist such a description of themselves, preferring, perhaps, to describe themselves as merely "very friendly" to the dominant government—the government of which they are presumably puppets. It is easier to recognize puppet governments within one's "enemy's" area of influence than one's own. For example, consider the governments chosen and installed in Korea, Manchuria, and Norway by Japan and Germany in the era of World War II. Compare them to some Central American governments. Imagine the debates between Americans and Soviets concerning certain governments in central Europe compared to some in Central America. Perhaps we now have (had) apparently clear cases of puppet governments (in the past) only because the influences wielded have been extinguished or no longer have the importance they once had.

It is not our purpose to pursue this topic further. Our purpose is merely to trace debates about sovereignty to such issues. Governments are subject to various kinds of influence and subordination. The influence and subordination may be formal and legal or they may not be so. Even if formal and legal, they may be insufficiently complete or pervasive to exclude the subordinate government from being considered a sovereign government. Even if neither formal nor legal, the influence may be so complete, as in some World War II cases, that there will be grave hesitation in calling the subdominant governments sovereign.

Perhaps in consequence of such complications the notion of sovereignty as a particular form of independence should be jettisoned. The question then is how well we will do without it, and how well we will do with what, if anything, takes its place. For the notion of sovereignty is deeply embedded in our perception of the political world and our formulations of its problems and victories.

SUPREMACY

Supremacy is the key notion instead when sovereignty is claimed to pertain to the relation of a government to the community governed. Supremacy may appear important also in the matters just discussed—as embodying an approach to the problems concerning the independence of governments. This, doubtless, is one reason why these two aspects of sovereignty have become on occasion so confused.

When a government is said to be sovereign relative to a given community, questions arise as to whether the persons who are members of that community look to or are controlled by any other potentially competing government or agency, and with respect to what matters the potential competition may occur. Students of the growth of the idea of sovereignty say that it was only gradually, as communities became something identifiably distinct from their governments, that this aspect of sovereignty came to the fore. Prior to the emergence of this idea in Western Europe, no community was distinguished over which the government could have supremacy. There were persons and agencies to be ruled, of course, but the community found its identity so thoroughly through the ruler and the apparatus of ruling that, apart from the persons and institutions to be ruled, there was nothing perceived separable over which to rule. As the community gradually became perceived to be distinct from its government, protocols became established for the governing relationships, which then became less personal and more formal.

Apart from the rightness or wrongness of any particular story of this historical development, what we now have is the idea that the sovereign (political) authority in any given community is supreme in and over that community. As is so often the case in philosophy, great pressure has been put upon the term *supreme*. In part, it gets cashed in in terms of relations to external influences and authorities. Because of this, many of the same issues are raised as are raised in discussions of independence. But additional issues are also raised, such as questions of subordination to or influence by forces more or less "internal to the community." This brings into view disputes about the identity of the "*real* government" of the community and also about how to weigh the competing claims, official and unofficial, on or about persons or agencies all claiming jurisdiction and possibly in competition with one another. For example, a church may claim supremacy in jurisdiction over all or perhaps only some matters of daily life. Or a comparatively small set of plutocrats or aristocrats may stand behind the government and influence profoundly its every move. In such cases, identifying the sovereign may not be something that one can do to everyone's satisfaction.

At this point, the notion of sovereignty can become very complicated as scholars attempt to negotiate such difficulties. For example, some scholars declare that sovereignty must be indivisible, apparently because a divisible sovereignty would increase the difficulties in identifying "sovereigns" in situations such as we have just sketched. For how is one to settle questions of supremacy among the parts of a divisible sovereign? Controversy has raged because sovereignty has been thought essential to fully developed political communities, and yet many apparently fully developed political communities seem to have no locatable sovereign.

Much has been made of this in connection with the United States of America, for example, and ingenious accounts of the sovereign there have been offered. Confederations, leagues, and various empires have offered other challenging cases to the thesis in question. Most often, perhaps, the thesis has been utilized as a ground for rejecting the idea that these political communities are fully developed. But some such communities have been very powerful and long-lasting, and thus the conclusions that they were in some sense not "fully developed" is itself controversial.

In view of the difficulties just sketched, one may reasonably wonder why intelligent people have gotten themselves into such a fix in the first place. The main pressures to which the concept of sovereignty as a whole has been a response are, I believe, (1) the growth of the idea that there are in the world a large and variable number of separate communities of persons "running," and perhaps having a right to run, their own affairs, and thus mutually placing some stake in identifying where one of them leaves off and another begins and thus in their capacity to pick out and identify independent communities; and (2) the idea, highly burdened with presumptions about human nature, that there must in every human community be a supreme authority, an authority to whom appeal may be made to settle any possible dispute whatever between the members of the community, and that without the existence of such an authority there would be no real end to the warlike conditions of a presumed state of nature. A priori arguments that sovereigns (in this internal view) are necessary to fully developed political communities are most often called "Hobbesian," after their most prominent propounder. The fundamental idea behind them is that there must be some final authority for settling all disputes, else a return to the state of nature—that is, a state of war—cannot reliably be avoided. This line of argument seems to overestimate the extent to which (a) agreement is necessary in order to avoid a state of war, and (b) prudence and the pressure of circumstances will lead people to reach agreement among themselves. (Concerning this last point, for example, members of the Netherlands Confederation, which had no single, undivided, central authority, seemed prudent enough to reach general agreement time after time in the face of initial disagreement.) Thus, high valuing of local control and independence and an intensely Hobbesian view of human nature operating in a "state of nature" appear to lie behind the importance we currently attach to the notion of sovereignty. If we were to abandon attaching importance to either of these ideas, we might very well lose altogether our practical interests in the idea of sovereignty. If we were to abandon our attachments to both of these ideals, it is extremely unlikely that there would remain any practical interest at all in the idea of sovereignty.

TEN

Representation

Though representation plays a role in art and elsewhere, this chapter will focus only on political representation. Despite our rich and fervent interest in political representation, and, indeed, perhaps even because of it, there is no agreed-upon and even reasonably precise understanding of what it is. In what follows, several models of "representation" will be examined. No case of political representation with which I am familiar is a pure case of any of these understandings, and no claim is made that this list is complete. Political representation seems to involve a rich mixture of these understandings in which sometimes one, sometimes another, model becomes preeminent. It seems to be reasonable, therefore, to aspire to understand political representation by tracing the most prominent of these elements in the mixture that one is likely to confront. This is what is provided by these models and it will help remind us of the elements underemphasized in any particular discussion of the topic.

The models are viewed here in isolation, each as though it occupied the field by itself. Much care will be needed in determining how they "fit" together or conflict. What one model justifies requiring, another model counts irrelevant. What one model finds problematic, another model finds not problematic. One model describes what is "here and now," and another model describes more, perhaps, what ought to be rather than what is.

Further exploration of the matter than is offered here might involve closer examination of the processes by which someone becomes a political representative. In addition, further exploration is needed than offered here of what makes various principles or standards of evaluation of the activities of political representatives appropriate. (No evaluation is offered of the models as compared to feasible alternatives.)

REPRESENTATION AS "ACTING FOR"

A common understanding of *represent* is where one person represents another by being authorized to act as a legal agent for the second. This is the understanding developed by Hobbes in his short but famous Chapter 16 of *Leviathan*, "Of Persons and Things Personated." It is the understanding that emerges when a salesperson represents a company, a lawyer a client, or a judge a ward of the court. Its scope varies and is generally stipulated at the onset of the relationship—sometimes only partially, as in the case of a salesperson, and sometimes totally or nearly so, as is commonly the case with judges and wards of courts. Authorization is for one person "to act for" another person or group of persons, but the expression in quotes lends itself to different understandings. The person authorized may act instead of, in the name of, on more or less detailed instructions from, or exercise his or her judgment on behalf of the authorizing person or persons.

If the instructions are very detailed—for instance, someone gives power of attorney to someone to sign a specific, known document for him or her on a specified date, or fellow planters deputize someone to go to the colonial capitol to hear an agreed-to, expected, and known imposition of taxes—the situation will be relatively simple, though there will nevertheless be rich and interesting possibilities in detailing the social practices involved and tracing the patterns of trust and reliance, obligation and responsibility, that are present. These are the clearest cases where person X, representing Y, acts "instead of" Y.

But if the instructions are less detailed—for instance, if the owner of a company designates someone to represent the company in negotiations on a labor contract between the company and its employees, or fellow planters designate someone to represent them to the colonial governor in presenting a grievance and pressing for a satisfactory remedy or recompense—the situation is more complicated. First, on this understanding of representation it is expected that the representative will act on behalf of—that is, further the interests of—the represented. But by whose lights? (The relevant actions of the representa*tive* must conceivably have been intended to benefit the represent*ed*, but the courts in the Anglo-American legal tradition have interpreted this requirement broadly.) Purposefully furthering someone else's interests when instructions are not detailed requires judgments about what is valuable, rankings of values, and beliefs about matters of fact, including beliefs about the consequences of doing this or that.

With what degree of independence should the representative make these judgments? Suppose that the representative's vision of the good life differs in a significant way from that of the represented—for instance, the representative attaches maximal importance to achieving and preserving an atmosphere of friendliness, whereas the represented attaches greatest importance to adherence to firm and demanding standards of honor and justice. If the representative is aware of this difference, how should he or she act so as "to further the interests of the represented"? Perhaps you will believe that the vision of the represented should carry the greatest weight here, but it is also quite possible that your judgment on the matter will be influenced by your evaluations of the conflicting visions in question. In adopting a position on the matter you should explore your reactions to a variety of such circumstances to be certain that the position you adopt is one to which you wish to attach general importance, irrespective of your views about the merits of the particular beliefs held by each.

Suppose, on the other hand, that the representative and the represented differ in their beliefs concerning the consequences of some proposed relevant course of action—for example the employer believes, as capitalists used to, that higher wages will reduce incentive for hard and efficient work; whereas the representative believes that nothing of the sort is the case and, furthermore, that failure to raise the wages that he or she regards as already perilously low will be highly destructive of worker morale and efficiency. What is it acceptable for the representative to do "to further the interests of the represented" in such a situation? Should he or she proceed on his or her own judgment of the consequences, or on the judgment of the represented, known to be different? What is it to represent the employer in such circumstances?

When the instructions to the representative cannot be or are not highly specific, a need appears more clearly and forcefully than before to distinguish between, roughly speaking (see the following two paragraphs), (1) cases where a single person or unified or formally deciding group of persons is being represented, and (2) those where an informal group or a group that is likely to contain some internal differences of opinion concerning matters of the sorts just discussed is being represented. When instructions are quite specific, there may be minority opinion, of course, but the representatives' courses of action may be fairly clear in consequence of a vote or eventual consensus concerning what they are to do. But representatives may have to act on issues where there has been no such firm guidance. They may have very good grounds for beliefs concerning how the issue *would* be resolved were it to appear before the group for formal decision, but it has not received unified or formal decision and the representatives' positions cannot be so well grounded as if it had. Here there is not merely the problem of how representatives are to represent minority opinions within the group, but also greater degree of uncertainty concerning what these minority opinions are and the representatives' mandate from the group.

Applying the general idea to representative democracy, this last complication is intensified manyfold by the absence most often of any "instructions" to the representative at all, or at least in any but the most general terms. Talk about the mandates given to elected candidates for office in representative democracy by their receiving more votes than their opponents can only be extremely dubious in view of the diversity of motives and intentions, hopes and understandings that people have when they vote for their representatives. Thus, such representatives and their critics cannot expect a great deal of guidance from the represented on how, in detail, to promote the interests of the represented.

They do, of course, have general knowledge of the values and beliefs of the people they represent, but, apart from the difficulties indicated earlier, including the problem of "representing" persons having minority beliefs (for the ideology of representative democracy is that these people too are represented), considerable "creativity" by representatives is unavoidably called for. Not only are the values and beliefs of the represented stated almost always in at least somewhat general terms, and are seldom stated formally by the represented as an organized body, but the ranking of the constituents of what they believe to be the good life is almost never stated, certainly never stated with any precision, and probably never even thoroughly thought through—certainly not by the whole body of persons being represented, and most probably not by many individual members of that body. In consequence, the specific instrumentation and execution of public goals by the representative must be "creative"—that is, not much mandated by his or her public.

As we move from cases, as here, in which one person represents one other person or unified or formally deciding group to cases in which one person represents an aggregate or group of persons or an organization not always deciding formally (or not unified), we move away from cases in which we may say straightforwardly and uncomplicatedly that the representative is acting "instead of" the represented. The idea embodying that phrase seems to be that the represented or their spokes-person might equally well have been there and doing what the representative is doing. But an ununified or not highly organized aggregate of persons cannot negotiate and sign agreements, and the like, unless it has a way to speak and act univocally.

As stated earlier (Chapter Four), a number of considerations such as the size of the aggregation, the previous and present relationships of its members to one another, and the relative simplicity or urgency of the problems to be confronted influence how this need can be met. Proceeding through consensus may not always or even often be possible. But if consensus is not in the cards, and even if the rule of consensus is feasible, there must be some way in which the persons before whom the aggregation is or would be represented can discover who speaks or acts for the aggregation. Unless it is so determined that any member of the aggregation would say or do exactly what any other member would say or do (there might be a rule within the aggregation for proceeding thusly), some person(s) would have to be designated to represent the aggregation.

Thus, the phenomenon of representation would be likely to surface even if the whole aggregation were present at the hearing or whatever. The idea that the representative acts where the aggregation being represented could have acted thus breaks down except in certain special cases. The idea of acting "in the name of" rather than the idea of acting "instead of" may thus generally make more sense. Acting "in the name of" must, however, be distinguished from pretending or purporting to act in the name of. The latter presumably would be acting without or beyond the bounds of authorization while purporting to act with and within the bounds of authorization.

Likewise, as one moves from the specific to the relatively nonspecific instructions, as most often in political cases, acting "in the name of" is a more fitting label for what is done than acting "instead of." The judgments involved may be intended to promote the interests of the represented, but we are unclear about whether they are supposed to be as close as possible to the judgments that the represented would have made. Insofar as we do not always require the latter, and are not often certain, given the kinds of judgments involved, how close the representative's judgments come to it, we would know ourselves to be correct to say only that the representative's judgments are "in the name of" the represented. This means that the judgments will obligate the represented just as they would have if the representative had made them him or herself.

The reason to occupy oneself with traversing this ground with such care is that there has been so much talk in the ideology of democracy concerning the way in which representatives must do exactly what they are told to do by the persons they represent; otherwise the latter will be "disenfranchised." Far from being the case, however, it appears that the whole idea that the representatives in a political context *can* be confined to doing exactly as they are told by the represented is a nonstarter, because circumstances do not often make it even possible. The ideology of democracy, which has sometimes tended to make representative democracy merely a convenient substitute for direct democracy involving few essentially new ideological considerations thus needs reworking, at least insofar as "to represent" is "to act for."

REPRESENTATION AS "STANDING FOR"

In the throes of expositing on a tactical situation, a person may say "let that eraser represent a tank." This use of *representation* or its cognates sometimes figures in politics, as in modern political life when we think of a member of a minority group who has been appointed to governmental office as a representative of that group. (There often is, but need not be, as with the model in the previous section, any similarity between the representative and the things or persons represented.) In a similar way to this, lions and eagles in heraldry represented courage and regality, and a representative's election may come to represent—that is, to symbolize—certain hopes or aspirations of those persons who elected him or her. In this way also, Hitler thought it was at least part of his role to represent the German people, as he claimed to symbolize or stand for, and even, he thought at times, to constitute the unity of the German nation and people.*

For another variation, suppose instead that the function of representatives is to receive information—to attend certain meetings, deliberations, announcements, and so on. Such persons may not conduct any business, and may not even have been directed by anyone to transmit whatever was observed or learned to those represented. Their function may be merely to be there, as a kind of witness. This set-up can be motivated by many concerns, such as to show that things are not going on "behind people's backs" in some hidden way; to avoid the impracticality of having everyone in attendance; or to expose some people who are not involved in the observed activities to the workings of things as a way of showing them how things are done (rather than

---

*Hitler's views on "representing" contain more than this. His views are laid out in the selection by Williamson in Pitkin [1969].

making them responsible for disseminating the information about what is done).*

REPRESENTATION AS "TYPICAL OF"

When a person is said to be representative of a certain kind of person or of persons holding a certain opinion, rather than being said to be a representative of them, this understanding of *representation* is emerging. In the political realm, a person may be chosen *as* a representative because he or she is thought to *be* representative of the group to be represented. Places are sometimes made for persons in representative assemblies on precisely such grounds, as when it is thought, for instance, that the assembly should have some blue-collar workers, some members of certain minorities, and so on.

The grounds for such an organization of representative assemblies are probably too rich to be caught by only one notion of representation. Nevertheless, this understanding of representation is felt most often when a representative assembly is criticized, for example, for having members so untypical of the population being represented. Untypicality, as we have already said, would not matter at all if representation were merely to stand for or to symbolize: there is no necessity for this latter kind of representing that the representative be similar in any respect to the represented. The connection between them is totally "artificial" and conventional. If representation were merely "to act for" or in the name of the person(s) represented, there would be no inescapable need to have the representative resemble the represented in any way. Arguments are launched that representatives act with greater understanding and effectiveness when they resemble in some ways those who are represented, but these arguments in any given case might fall far short of being conclusive or even highly persuasive. At any rate, there may be no good arguments to support without further ado that a representative assembly was defective insofar as its members were untypical of the population represented.

But if representatives are to be typical of the population they represent, in precisely what respects ought they to be typical? We could imagine circumstances in which it became a point of contention whether the representatives have the same hair color and physical proportions as the represented. But, by and large, the points of contention concern such things as religion, race, economic status, occupation, language, national heritage, and the like. Generally, when an assembly is said to be unrepresentative, the focus is upon some small set of these characteristics. But the focus is, often enough, unsteady or easily shifted. This understanding can be treacherous because of this fact.

Some writers, especially those attracted by the idea of proportional representation, believe that representative assemblies should be descriptively representative. That means that something about the members of these assemblies—for example, their feelings or opinions or social situations before they became representatives—should resemble something about the persons

---

*The points in this paragraph were made by Susan L. Feagin.

being represented. But philosophers know that the idea of resemblance is tricky. If no limits are to be placed on the qualities that are to provide a basis for resemblance or for difference, everything resembles (and is different from) everything else in infinitely many ways. For example, I resemble you in not being a piece of chalk. I differ from you in having a different name. My feelings differ from yours in being mine, while yours are yours. Thinking along such lines is not an exercise in futility, because it demonstrates our need to decide what is to be the basis for the judgment of similarity and difference in any given case. For, this determination *is* a matter of choice (though not necessarily arbitrary or unjustified choice), and not inevitable or unavoidable, something of considerable importance. We too often overlook the fact that it is a matter of choice. Thus, when we are told that a representative assembly is or fails to be representative enough because it contains or fails to contain the proportion reflecting the proportion in the population at large of working people to entrepreneurs, men to women, and so forth, we are apt to fail to inquire sufficiently sharply into why those characteristics have been chosen as the relevant ones to determine resemblance and difference. Age, handicaps, degree of overweightness, left- or right-handedness, and any of a number of other things might be chosen equally relevantly, given certain social or political circumstances. Our choices on these matters reflect our judgments concerning which characteristics of people are politically important at the time of the formation and activity of the representative assembly. Different political circumstances would make different characteristics important.

The idea of typicality can be problematic in another way. Perhaps one will be reduced on occasion to saying that a particular representative or candidate is "not untypical." (This understanding slips over into an understanding of to represent as "to stand for" and into an understanding of the just previous model, as we have seen.) It is, let us suppose, a working-class district and the candidate is a working-class person. But it is also a district badly split along religious lines between Catholic and Protestant, and the candidate is Catholic. Is the candidate typical or not? There is no saying, perhaps, but at least the candidate may not be untypical in the way that would clearly be the case if the candidate were Buddhist. In districts badly split along some grounds or other, there may be some grounds along which no candidate would be straightforwardly typical, and in that sense "representative."

There are two further things to notice about this understanding of *representative*. First, in some applications it is claimed to mean something slightly different, that is, "exemplary of." These applications are similar to "he is the flower of American manhood" or "she is the flower of American womanhood." But these applications are really only cases of the understanding we have been discussing. The difference (I think should be noted and thought about) is that a person is not said to be typical of, for example, either American manhood or American womanhood, but the best of each type. Second, being representative in this way does not, in itself, make a person a political representative, though it may provide grounds for doing so.

Lastly, there is an understanding of representation coming very close to the one presently under discussion but not quite the same. It is an understanding of representation as "to be a sample of" or "to be an example of." If a representative is thought to be a randomly chosen instance of the population being represented, then the representative may be thought of in part in this way. Random choice might be thought likely to turn up someone typical, in which case this understanding would be difficult to distinguish from the former understanding. Random selection might not, however, be thought to turn up someone typical of the population from which the selection is made, in which case this understanding *would* be distinguishable from the former one.

REPRESENTING PEOPLE BY "REPRESENTING THEIR INTERESTS"

The transition from representing interests to representing (the) persons (with those interests) is not without problems, unless the "interests" being represented are persons themselves, such as, for instance, banking interests sometimes are. Aside from that understanding of "interests," there are three further understandings we should note: (1) on the presumption of self-interestedness of a certain self-interested view of human nature, the characteristic concerns that members of a certain group or class would have if they wished to prosper and to avoid loss; (2) the interests, generally only a subclass of the former, that these people have a right to have; (3) the concerns these people have qua members of a group or class when they have mistaken beliefs about what would bring them prosperity and avoid loss. These three understandings are not the only possible understandings, but they will be enough for now.

What is it to "represent" interests on such understandings? Persons "representing" those interests can be relied upon to speak either on the behalf of these people or on what they believe to be their behalf whenever the occasion arises.

The way the people come to represent persons with such interests is by speaking on what they (and at least some large portion of the persons represented) believe to be on behalf of interests those people characteristically have. Thus a person may "represent" the banking interests, for example, by speaking on their behalf, or by believing oneself to do so, when the occasion arises.

Persons doing this job of "representing" do not need to be designated representatives by anyone. They may be, in a manner of speaking, self-chosen. They may thus have no official staus, though they may come to be relied upon by the persons whom they are representing or by others.

REPRESENTATION AND SELF-LIMITATION

Being elected by a majority of those represented (instead of, for example, being appointed) gives a plausibility to the claim that whatever results is a piece of "self-imposition" or "self-limitation." This becomes important when characterizing the relationship between voting and self-limitation.

Typical cases of self-limitation are promising and contracting. Perhaps voting for a representative is itself another model of self-limitation, having its own grounds of legitimation. What these grounds might be is open to speculation.

On the contrary, if voting is relied upon as analogous to these former clear cases of self-limitation in being sufficiently like them in the relevant respects, we would also then have grounds for saying it is a case of self-limitation. Of course, as with all analogies, there will be some differences. The decision will have to be made on the basis of whether, in light of those differences, the similarities are significant enough. There will always be points of difference about which to complain, and thus debate will probably be endless.

With voting, even those who vote with the majority cannot be guaranteed to have chosen the winning candidate, for reasons we have already seen. The position of those who do not vote with the majority is even more problematic. Have they "elected" the majority candidate even though they did not vote for him or her, just because they took part in the election? What of those who didn't even take part in the election?

PREFERRING, VOTING, AND CHOOSING

Some "representatives" are appointed, some are more or less self-appointed, and some are elected. Since the last is made so important in democratic theory, it will be focused on here.

Scholars have studied elections, turning up much of interest. One of the preoccupations has been with aggregation devices (for example, various methods of voting and counting votes). I shall not discuss or challenge their conclusions, but am concerned rather with what they happen to choose as the chief examples of what they are aggregating. The easy transitions they seem to make between preferring, voting, and choosing should be challenged. (The relevance apparently attached to their results is subverted by the attenuation of the key terms needed to protect "formal results.")

The transitions seem to make it "natural" to make preferring, voting, and choosing pieces of consent. We examined consent in Chapter Six, and found reason there to distinguish "consent" as a psychological condition from "consent" as a social act. No such distinction is drawn in the literature. Concerning "consent" as a social act, there is no problem about the identification of consent with, for instance, voting; voting is a form of it. But there is a problem with the identification of voting (or of the others) with "consent" as a psychological condition. The connection between them is at best contingent, though important. (This whole matter is not discussed as thoroughly as it might be in this book, though it should be thoroughly discussed eventually.) Thus, one of the concerns will here be to show the lack of necessary connection between voting, and the like, and consent as a psychological condition.

My questions about what is aggregated (preferring, voting, and choosing) will show that they should in their full-bodied forms be distinguished from one another, and the questions will, not incidentally, shed light on their individual rationality or lack thereof.

First, a remark about rationality is in order. The alternative to rationality is not necessarily irrationality. There is a "thick" notion of rationality in which rationality is the contradictory of irrationality. But there is also a "thin" notion of rationality in which it is only the contrary of irrationality. There is a third category between the designations possible, known as the "nonrational." Much depends on which understanding of rationality we are using. Not much is risked when the "thick" understanding of rationality is being used, but quite a bit may be risked when the "thin" understanding is being used (a perhaps quite mistaken model is offered as what various activities are or even should be), and the chances of equivocation between the two understandings is ever present.

We may ask whether preferring (or the others) can be viewed as (a) an activity rather than as something that merely happens to whomever or whatever it does happen, (b) having an intended goal that is often achieved, and (c) having an intended goal that is at least not of net harm to the person or principles of the actor.*

(a) With respect to preferring, the answer to the first question is "probably not always," and the answer to the other two questions is at least indefinite. Choosing and voting may be clearly activities, but concerning the denial that preferring is probably always an activity, if we say of someone that she is preferring X to Y, we may imagine that she is doing something, pointing to or starting toward something, or perhaps merely doing these things "mentally" (whatever that would be). But we may find ourselves able to say without obvious change of meaning that she prefers X to Y where we and she would find that this preferring is something she discovers about herself, rather than something she does.**

Of course, one may be trained to prefer rightly (for instance, beneficially), but if, as is often the case, such training is absent or incompletely effective, preferrings cannot be explained as due to past actions that might be rational. One may instead believe that the relevant preferrings can be considered rational in case the resulting preferences are beneficial to the actor in some way perceivable by an observer. But there would be no more reason to regard the latter as rational than to regard an eye as rational because it was beneficial to the person in whom it was found. This view is then unfortunate because it has led us to overemphasize vastly the extent to which our preferrings and our preferences are voluntary and controlled, and to underemphasize the extent to which they may simply happen to us or present themselves to us. Proportionately to the extent to which those are the case, we may talk about our preferrings and preferences being beneficial or not, but we will be making no clear sense if we also say of them without careful elucidation that they are rational.

Turning to condition (b), the answer to which, in the case of preferrings, is at best indefinite, supposing that our preferrings are rational will also involve us in making presumptions that they have often achieved intended goals. One may believe that this requirement is too strong, and that it is necessary merely

---

*I owe the way this last point is put to Susan L. Feagin.

**If this preferring is an activity at all, it is more like ordinary finding than like choosing, and the sense in which it can be rational must be quite different from the sense in which choosing can be rational.

to require some presumption or other of benefit. But, as our question and Hobbes suggest, if a person were to do something ignorantly or clumsily that had a fortuitous and highly unlikely outcome for him or her, we would not, without further presumption, say that the activity was rational. The further, and highly questionable, assumption may be that there is something operating here like an inarticulate and inarticulatable "wisdom of the race." But this simply introduces the required presumption about intention without seeming (to oneself at least) to be doing so.

Concerning condition (c), the answer to which, in the case of preferring, is also (clearly) indefinite, the preferring cannot ordinarily be perceived a net harm to the person or principles of the preferer if it is to be recognized as rational. This is a source of our difficulty in regarding suicide as rational. We regard self-inflicted death as a great net harm. Debates rage concerning whether there are greater harms than self-inflicted death, and whether therefore there may be circumstances in which suicide is or could be rational. A preferring is not considered fully rational unless it is perceived to be of the most net benefit to the person or principles of the preferer of the alternatives he or she is considering, except when quirks of personal character are counted heavily and, even then, the preferring cannot be perceived to be the most harmful of the alternatives considered by the preferer.

In sum, in order for preferrings to be considered rational, they must be activities, they must have commonly achieved purposes, and these purposes cannot be perceived of net harm to the person or principles of the preferer. Perhaps we have some rational preferences. But if the preceding analysis is correct, I leave to your careful consideration and discovery how much of significance about human preferrings is omitted if only they are considered. In particular, you might consider the linking of preferring with choosing and with voting, and consider not only how much is omitted about the way people do function (there is no real argument in this connection about that), but how much is omitted of what we appreciate about the way people function. This is ground one must treat cautiously, because the past excesses of romanticism and irrationalism have given departures from rationality a bad record. And defenses of rationality can have amazing breadth and resilience. Lastly, we have by no means offered an attack on the desirability of rational preferrings, supposing that we can do them. The principal idea that we have sought to put forward is that depiction of acceptable features of life (including political life) solely in terms of rational preferrings will miss much of importance and value.

In contrast to preferring, voting is clearly an activity, and choosing is much more clearly an activity than is preferring. As activities, choosing and voting, insofar as they are considered rational, are purposive and have purposes perceivable at least as not of net harm to the person or principles of the actors. As we have noticed, preferrings, choosings, and votings that are not rational are not thereby irrational. They may be simply nonrational. Some of our activities and, in the end, some of our most valued activities are too spontaneous, too casual, too inexplicable to ourselves and to others to count straightforwardly as purposive.

The truth of such a claim might be admitted more readily in the case of preferring and choosing than in the case of voting. Political philosophers, at least, tend to take voting very seriously. Not that they believe that everyone who votes takes it seriously. But voting seems to political philosophers to have such serious consequences that it should, they believe, be taken seriously. The interesting question here is whether taking voting seriously requires that it be fully purposive. If voting *is* closely related to preferring, and even those preferrings that are clearly activities (if any) are sometimes too spontaneous, too casual, and so on, to count fully as purposive; and if these and other nonpurposive preferrings give some valued zest and flavor to our lives, then the preferrings to which the theorists have so closely related their analyses of voting must be a special class in order for us to insist that voting should only and always be purposive. I do not presently wish to deny that they should generally be; I wish merely to provoke some thinking about the matter. What are we doing when we vote? (The claim that we are choosing something of consequence to us will be examined shortly.) Without some presumptions concerning the function or purpose of voting, and some presumptions concerning the benefits to voters of voting, the insistence upon and the significance of the claim that voting should be rational will be difficult to understand.

If choosing is considered only insofar as it is clearly an activity, it is still interestingly different from voting. The respect in which voting for something is choosing something must be very extended. What would most commonly be said is that voting is participating in choosing something. Participating in the choice of something is not straightforwardly choosing it. Voting is generally a collegiate procedure. One generally votes "jointly" with another person or persons. Participating thus in making a choice is not simply making a choice. More is generally going on. One chooses, of course, how to vote—whether, for example, to vote yes or no. But one does not, in voting, thereby choose the thing voted for—except in our extended sense. Try to think of other activities where the fact that the activity is being done jointly significantly alters what would be done if one were to try doing it alone. It is logically possible that one of us alone would be designated to choose the next President of the United States. But there is no practical political possibility of this. Therefore, we must at best "choose" the president jointly. There is a logical possibility that we could, alone and unaided by machinery, lift heavy logs and boulders. But we lack the strength. Therefore, we must join with others if we are to lift such items unaided by machinery.

The parallel lacks subtlety, but even this crude comparison provides a starting point for understanding how voting for something differs from choosing it. As we observed before in discussing systematic mutual reliance, it is reasonable for us to behave differently when we are depending upon others from the way we would behave if we were attempting to do something alone. We attend to different matters. When rolling a log down to the riverbank, we apply all the pressure at one end, knowing that someone else will apply pressure at the other end. Perhaps our behavior when voting and choosing reasonably differs similarly. Are there clearly no circumstances in which this is so?

The discussion in the preceding paragraph is conducted on the assumption that both the choosing and the voting will be purposive and collegiate. I have argued earlier that purposiveness is necessary for rationality. (Because irrationality is the contrary and not the contradictory of rationality, purposiveness is not necessary to avoid irrationality. But our current understanding of rationality is so diffuse and emotionally loaded that were I to claim that voting perhaps need not be rational, my claim would find little chance of acceptance. But, claiming, as I have, merely that perhaps voting need not be purposive, my claim will not be dismissed so precipitously.) I have presently no great confidence that voting need not be purposive. Why, then, am I belaboring the point? I am belaboring it because doing so may lead you to consider carefully some aspects of human life quite possibly too little integrated by political philosophers into accounts of our political life.

If nothing is foreseeably lost or gained in or by an activity, that activity may, as we have seen, be neither unreasonable nor irrational, and likewise neither reasonable nor rational (except in the weak sense of "not irrational" and "not unreasonable"). If there are difficulties with this, it is probably because so many of us have learned to be wary in making judgments about what count as costs or benefits for different people. We have even learned to be wary on occasion about what count as costs or benefits in our own cases. It is not only that we cannot see so unmistakably as we would like the consequences of what we do. It is that sometimes we are in doubt about whether to count a certain consequence as a cost or a benefit. Such doubts make some of us prefer to err on the side of judging activities to be reasonable or rational. Still, we do not do this without supposing that there *are* determinable foreseeable benefits and costs of the activities. That is why, both with respect to others and with respect to ourselves, we tend to give wide scope to our attribution of rationality to preferrings, choosings, and votings. When one adds to the operation of these considerations the somewhat different consideration that *rational,* as we have seen, sometimes means no more than "not irrational," attributions of rationality become very wide indeed. On the superwide understanding of *rationality,* not much is risked or prejudiced by saying that preferrings, choosings, and votings are rational. On the other hand, if one utilizes the much narrower understanding of *rational,* quite a bit is risked (with respect to the correctness of the claim) and quite a bit is prejudiced.

Concerning the difference between preferring and choosing, on the understanding on which choosing is clearly an activity, and whether or not preferring is or is not considered a (perhaps inner) activity, preferring and choosing are differentiated by the acceptability of our sometimes claiming that we have chosen something other than what we "would have preferred." This shows that when we are being asked to choose, we understand ourselves not to be asked what we prefer. We understand that considerations of duty, obligation, and the like, may lead us deliberately to choose something other than what we do prefer (the claim that we did not choose "what we would have preferred" merely remarks on our understanding that we were asked to choose, and not to say merely what we prefer). Choosing, in contrast to preferring, thus is more clearly an activity (perhaps this is why Aristotle thought of choice as possible with respect only to nonultimate ends), and, perhaps, has something more in it of the judgmental than does preferring, which puts us closer to a feeling-response to the things being considered. There is nothing excluding a feeling-response to the one and a judgmental reaction to the other; the association of judgment with choosing, and of feeling-response with preferring, are merely somewhat favored by our normal treatments of the two.

Voting is more nearly like choosing than like preferring in this respect. We have noted already, however, how it in turn is unlike choosing. However, to say that it is in the foregoing respect more like choosing than like preferring is, in saying that it is more likely to be a matter of judgment, saying that it is more likely to be done *with* a certain intention or range of intentions—that is, purposively. But this is no more to say that voting is done irrationally when done without some specific intention than it would be to say that choosing is done irrationally when it is done without some specific intention. Choosing is sometimes a feeling-response (as often when choosing a flavor of ice cream), and none the worse for that. Indeed, it is the essence of some choice situations that choosing be without a specific intention, but be merely a feeling-response. As we have said, only our solemn attitude toward politics, and the apparent importance of voting, appear to prevent us from admitting the same thing about voting. Voting and choosing are different, however, as our discussion has suggested. The matter should be considered carefully. There are situations in which the essence of the situation is to make choices that are feeling-responses. Are there political situations in which the essence of the situation is to vote expressing or in accordance with a feeling-response? Your answer will depend upon what you think people ought to be, or might reasonably (that is, not unreasonably) be up to when they vote. Voting can, for example, reasonably be considered a ceremonial as well as an instrumental act, and its instrumentality may be very widely conceived.

The limitedness of our prevailing conceptions of the instrumentality of voting is perhaps revealed by the connection commonly made in our political culture between voting by the governed and consent of the governed. Voting, it is said, is or implies consent. The idea is that the voter is at least tacitly consenting to subjection to the winning candidate or the successful referendum, and so on. But if, as we have seen earlier, consent is viewed as a psychological state rather than a social act, there is no good reason to think that voting and consent are so related. A voter may be focused merely upon making a show, provoking a response from some person(s), rendering the results of the election unacceptable and thus throwing the election or even the election process into disrepute, and so forth. We might not like such aims and might even think them rather nasty. But they are aims that people might have and might consider reasonable. A voter with them is hardly "consenting" (understood as a psychological state) to subjection to the winning candidate or the successful referendum. The instrumentalities to which voting lends itself may, as this discussion has shown, range widely and even wildly. Remembering especially that voting is not simply choosing what is voted for, can we say confidently that there will never be situations in which voting as feeling-response is reasonable?

ELEVEN

Subjects, Citizens, and Aliens

Governments do not claim dominion over every person on or off the face of the earth. Nor are persons said to owe loyalty, and the like, to every government, even to every just or beneficial government. The present section of this book considers some of the problems arising when one attempts to understand and justify the extents and limits of the aggregations of persons over whom governments conventionally claim dominion.

Some human beings place themselves within the ambit of particular political communities. Some of them do it with a view to permanence—as with immigrants. In the earlier days of the United States of America and of Australia, these countries were populated largely by these means (and by transportation). Others form a political community around them, as with the Plymouth settlers. Yet others have a political community thrust upon them, as through conquest and transportation. Most human beings, however, on reaching consciousness of their surroundings find themselves within the ambit of some political community or other, where they remain. According to many political philosophers, these differences in the way in which people come to be within the ambit of political communities do not all ultimately make a difference in their responsibilities or obligations to the governments of the community in question or to or from neighbors in that community. Nevertheless, we normally mark a number of different statuses of people within political communities, and it will be important for us, before discussing responsibilities and obligations to government, and so forth, briefly to explore some differences in status.

SUBJECTS

To say that people are subjects of particular rulers or subject to them or to governments of particular political communities is to suggest that these people have been subjugated by or have submitted to these rulers or governments. Whether subjugation and submission can provide adequate grounds for the common claims to loyalty and allegiance, as well as to obedience (all three claims are made of citizens too), depends upon what can be such grounds and also upon what practices, attitudes, and sensitivities are or ought to be involved in the particular case.

Subjugation and submission could be said to be one event seen from two different perspectives: first, from the perspective of the superior power, and second, from that of the subordinate power. (You will notice that changing the voice of each of the two terms produces an opposite effect.) Politically, the model or mark of this so-called event in many places is the kneeling of the subordinate before the superior and the swearing by the former of an oath of fealty to the latter. Thus, the model of the event is a formal, ritual act. It is an act of the rough sort that in most any community the world over is utilized as a means of acquiring claim rights over another or assuming obligations toward another. Of course, the subjugation does not, realistically speaking, always accompany the submission. People may engage in an act of submission who have been docile since birth and of whom it would be quite misleading to say that anyone had ever subjugated them. Also, people may be subjects of a given ruler and expected to give allegiance and loyalty to that ruler well before swearing fealty if, indeed, they ever do the latter.

Notice, however, that the claim in question is to loyalty and allegiance, not or not merely to obedience to rulers or governments. Loyalty and allegiance might be thought to be attitudes confirmed by obedient behavior. But is generally or even universally obedient behavior a sufficient condition of loyalty and allegiance? Loyalty and allegiance seem to a certain measure to involve feelings as well as behavior. Can subjugation and submission, even when accompanied by the provision of subsequent protection by the subjugating rulers or governments of those peoples submitting to them, give rise to either obligations to obey or have those feelings? As we can imagine from our discussion in previous chapters, the complexities of such a question are great.

Subjects of rulers or governments are commonly said, of course, to have a claim to protection therefrom. (The point is Hobbesian.) Recognition of such a claim by a ruler or government would be a highly relevant fact about any particular case. If such a claim were acknowledged and effectuation of it pursued respecting subjects engaged in commercial activities or traveling abroad and with respect to protection of subjects on the domestic front from one another as well as from external enemies, there could be some basis here for talk about reciprocity and some places for talk about loyalty and allegiance. If, on the other hand, subjects had no such claim or no claims whatever upon rulers and governments for any service whatever, legitimation of claims to obedience or to the loyalty or allegiance of subjects to the ruler or government might be difficult to come by.

People who are held to owe loyalty or allegiance to a ruler or a government may simply be people who are held responsible to that ruler or government for beneficent conformity to orders or commands issued by the ruler or the ruler's deputies and rules, principles, and standards promulgated by the government. Whether the ruler or the government can hold the people responsible fairly and unobjectionably for such conformity is another question. If rulers and governments demand such conformity as manifestation of the allegiance and loyalty said to be owed to them, and back up this demand by the imposition of a liability to punishment or penalty for failure to conform, then we may have reached near to the justificatory foundations of that coercion-backed authority commonly said to be characteristic of political community. As we have said, the demand by rulers and governments for obedience, allegiance, and loyalty of their subjects and citizens is supposed to be correlated in some way with an obligation on the part of the subjects and citizens to that obedience, loyalty, and allegiance.

We shall speak later in this chapter of the status of persons who are neither subjects nor citizens. We notice now only that the demand is supposed to be legitimate and the correlative obligation genuine because the people to whom they pertain have the status of subjects (or citizens, or the like). The compliance of everyone may be demanded to criminal laws concerning control of theft and violence. But some laws—for example, those concerning political participation, taxation, and military service—may be applied differentially to citizens or subjects on the one hand and noncitizen-nonsubjects (or visitors and permanent residents) on the other hand. The situation in each case is alleged to follow from the status.

CITIZENS

A discussion of the principles of good citizenship would consider the ways in which being a good citizen might conceivably differ from the ways in which one would be a good person, a topic of interest at least since the time of Aristotle, who, realizing that good citizenship was relative to the constitution of the state and that the constitutions of various states differed and therefore that good citizenship would differ among the various states in ways in which being a good person would perhaps not differ, distinguished them. Thus, in some states a prime virtue of citizenship might be obedience, wheras in other states the prime virtue might be independence. But our interest here is in the reasons for and the consequences of making a person a citizen, and not in what makes a good citizen. What are the principles in accord with which persons are sorted into citizens and noncitizens? First, consider what that status is and how it compares with the status of subjects.

Is every subject a citizen? Clearly not. There are ancient empires testifying, it seems, that not every subject is a citizen. Is every citizen a subject? Many people would deny this, though others seem to use the terms interchangeably. Either people use the language inaccurately, or they have many different agendas when they speak, not all of which are well marked (and some of which may be hidden, some multiple).

There is a rationale for what we find. It is that insofar as power is personifiable (as in a king, someone who could impose burdens), persons are regarded as subjects. The crucial question is: to what authority are they subject? In contrast, the crucial question with respect to a citizen is: of what group or association is this person a member? Which group's rules and restrictions does the person assume responsibility for fulfilling? (The fulfillment of this condition merely contributes to the person's being a citizen. It is not a necessary condition.) According as one or the other question makes predominant sense, the interest is expressed in the appropriate term. Beyond specific interests, custom takes over. Sometimes, interest is so clear or exclusive that only one term appears. Sometimes, transition is so common, or the facts support either use, that either term may appear.

In sum, and more accurately, the terms are matters primarily of what one chooses to emphasize (which may find support in what is close to what *seems* correct, which may, in turn, find support in what is close to what *is* correct). This explains their flexibility and availability.

Some facts support one term; some facts support the other (and some either). What facts support *citizen?* Whatever supports the notion that the responsibilities (whatever they are) and the legal rights and privileges (if any are present other than by largess) have been assumed rather than imposed—anything, that is, that presents an independent source of action in a community, rather than a passive receiver.

For example, the wanted image finds support in the status (not through largess) of a person as an independent, self-starting litigant in court. Therefore, the status of "plaintiff" in civil suit is something that citizens are generally expected to have available. It also finds support in the privileges of inheritance and property possession.

In contrast, the common situation of subjects and visitors is that, while they may be granted rights by the legal system in question, they need not be granted any rights whatever. The rights are a sort of gift that may be withdrawn at pleasure. These persons may even only have duties, a situation perhaps rather difficult to imagine in modern political communities, but not at all difficult to imagine in earlier ones.

Citizen does not carry any suggestion of a history of submission or subjugation. Acquisitions of the status "citizen" may have such a history, but there is no suggestion conveyed by the term that they have it.

There is often, and the suggestion is powerfully though not inevitably made, the idea conveyed that the people who are citizens have privileges and powers of participation in the political affairs of the community in question. The so-called "voting rights" or privileges thus often possessed are really Hohfeldian "powers," being "rights" (loosely called) to change (some of) one's own legal relations or those of others. (This remains true even though Hohfeldian analysis, though generally very good with private law, has notorious difficulties with public law—for example, what legal relations are changed and whose they are [for instance, a voting clerk's] is not always clear without discussion.) These privileges and powers may be minimal—as, for example, to have one's representatives told by the king in person what levies are to be imposed—or more substantial—as, for example, voting.

There is evidence that the facts of citizenship have changed through time, and consequently that the supporting data have ultimately changed. For example, commentators on modern society lament the loss of acceptance of responsibility by parents for their children. The large-scale communities of modern mass societies are most often held to blame. What is not so often noticed is the changing status of citizenship through the centuries and the effects thereof upon the problem. Adequate notice has probably been given to the dropping of property requirements and the altering of literacy requirements in establishing the status of citizenship. Some notice has also been given to the extension of citizenship status to females and the occasional lowering of the minimum age requirements. But citizenship also was gained by an increasing number of other persons within households. Early on in many societies, only heads of households or even only heads of families were accorded citizenship status. For example, in ancient Rome, only the heads of households were citizens. Being citizens, they were expected to participate actively in the decision making for the whole community. (Any supposition that in later times, however, this was the expectation accompanying citizenship would be wide of the mark.) An important consequence was that the state dealt only with the heads of households or of families and these in turn dealt with the members and servants thereof. Few residues of this former condition remain. (One should note that, however, in prerevolutionary France, persons under twenty-five could be imprisoned on their fathers' orders.) An echo of this condition was found until quite recently in the relationships of students to school officials.* As state willingness to intervene in relationships between students and school officials has grown, the responsibility of school officials for the conduct of students has lessened. This may be said to be a "natural" consequence of the assumption of increased responsibility by the state. Similarly, the state has accepted a little further back in our history responsibility for intervening in relationships between heads of households and families with their household and family members and servants. The household and family heads have accepted less "moral" responsibility as they have been provided less complete legal responsibility.

This development was not continuous, but in a further development, in revolutionary and prerevolutionary France a *citoyen* was often thought to be a person who, because without special privileges, was a part of the common order of the nation. Persons with special privileges (members of the estates) were deemed to have interests in conflict with the general interest, and thus could not (in the theory) vote in the name of the people. In this context, "privilege" was deemed in conflict with and inconsistent with natural equality (not absolute equality). Natural equality (presumptively possessed by *citoyens*) was thought to demand that every member of the same species had the same rights. (Sense can be made of this requirement, given our evidence concerning how it was understood at the time, only if we distinguish between primary and consequent rights. Suppose that the demand was applied only to the

*Compare also, until recently, the absence of legislative attention to child abuse and wife abuse.

former, and suppose that consequent rights are to be understood as the ones accruing to a person out of exercise of that person's primary rights.)

As well, in prerevolutionary France the rights so contrasted with privilege and reference to which played such a role in the characterization of natural equality were legal (not political). The aspiration was not for equal distributions of political authority, but for equal distributions of legal rights to do what one wished with one's property and not receive any special protection or exemption from the operation of the law. The abolition of privilege is to be connected with such a characterization of *citoyen*. As we have seen, that abolition was thought to create a direct relationship between the citizen and the state rather than allowing the citizen to be related to the state, as before, by intermediary bodies (the corporations). This directness of the relationship was a crucial part of the *citoyen* conception of citizenship. Note that this conception is thus confined to legal and not to political rights except insofar as it underwrites the legitimacy of the citizens' claim to vote "in the name of the people."

The policies under which citizen status is granted to various persons have differed of course from state to state and time to time. In some places blood relationship to persons who are already citizens is either necessary or sufficient. In other places, this is not the case but there are, as in the United States of America, what we call *naturalization* procedures for becoming a citizen. Sometimes, birth in the country granting citizenship is sufficient. In other countries (and times) it is not. Persons departing from within the geographical borders of the state in question do not customarily thereby lose their citizenship. Thus, there are many citizens "abroad."

ALIENS AND OTHERS

Alien is often a technical designation for a foreigner. But in recent times, it has acquired other uses, as in "alien creatures from another planet." This suggests that the creatures under discussion are not only without affiliation to our own political communities, and not only likely to be very different from us, but creatures with whom we have had very little or no experience and of whom we are consequently likely to have little or no understanding. In its use in such expressions, *alien* suggests the latter point far more than either of the first two, if, indeed, it suggests the first two at all.

We might expect that the more traditional uses of *alien* in connection with the affiliations, obligations, privileges, and so forth, of political communities has at least traces of suggestions that aliens are persons with whom we have had little experience and may be expected to have little understanding. These suggestions have been attached to and enriched a technical understanding of "aliens" as persons who at least do not owe allegiance and loyalty to one's own political community and perhaps even owe them to another identifiable political community.

There are, however, uses of *alien* to apply to persons having the same political allegiances as oneself. When applied to members of the same political community, *alien* rests upon divisions within the political community—

between races, for example—and emphasizes, on the part of at least one of the groups in question, the importance of the lack of experience and lack of sympathy or understanding between the groups.

Subjects include persons who may not be citizens, such as aliens. That is to say, the government in question may claim authority over persons who are citizens and authority as well over other persons, perhaps those resident either permanently or temporarily in a geographical area over which it claims jurisdiction. These latter persons might legitimately be called merely subjects.

Just as there may be persons readily recognizable as alien rulers in newly conquered countries, so there may also be persons readily recognizable by the rulers as "alien subjects." This might be so, at least, in cases in which the conquered territory had previous status as a "country." For example, in England shortly after A.D. 1066, the Normans were readily recognizable as alien rulers and the Saxons readily recognizable as alien subjects to those rulers. But as time goes on after a conquest, the clarity of the distinction between alien and nonalien gets muddied. The persons formerly identified as alien subjects and the persons formerly identified as alien rulers do not yet quite, perhaps, regard themselves as compatriots, but they may have too much in common in the way of political or religious cultures to continue to see one another as "alien." There may be little or no sharing of privileges and benefits. But, still, the judgment by either group that the other group was alien might seem too extreme. Thus, while no longer having "alien subjects," the rulers might hold in subjection persons not appropriately regarded as citizens.

Even in Latin America, where native populations not previously organized into well-recognized political communities were subjected to political rule by foreign invaders, there have been long periods during which the categorization of persons into citizens and aliens would have failed to capture a substantial portion of the persons habitually residing in those communities. In the early days of the United States of America, the slaves and the Indians would likewise not have been captured. In medieval Europe, serfdom presented similar problems, and in some modern societies felons and mental incompetents would likewise present cases not fitting easily somewhere into a distinction between citizens and aliens.

Without carrying the discussion further, one might find it justifiable to suppose that classifications of permanent residents of political communities might have to be considerably more complex than such a two-part classification. The distinctions may well be consequential for discussions of the grounds for and morality of demands issued in the name of various political communities for obedience, disobedience, and so forth.

WHAT A DIFFERENCE A STATE MAKES . . .

It is commonly acknowledged that the advent of a state makes, or at least often makes, a difference in the obligations of persons merely subject to the laws, and the responsibilities and powers of persons who act as agents of the state. When persons are aliens or visitors they will commonly owe support and compliance also to the rules, regulations, and regime of some other government. What to do when there are conflicts between the rules and regulations of the governments involved may become a complicated matter, with respect to the dictates of both prudence and political morality. Different political communities make different claims upon persons within and outside of their territorial borders. Citizens, visitors, and permanently resident aliens comprise the most commonly recognized categories among which distinctions are made, but the distinctions do not have the same ramifications in the case of every political community making them. More subtle examination of the common situation shows that the advent of states most often enlarges the powers of persons who are merely citizens as well as of persons acting in the name of the state.

Membership in those political communities called *states* is merely a special case of membership in communities. Membership in any community whatever may well be expected to have some effect upon the moral obligations of the person who becomes a member. As we have previously characterized communities, they involve at least some mutuality of interests and responses, a mutuality extending over some indefinite but respectable length of time. This recognition may be expected to create a network of expectations and reliances, a network characteristic of the sort of relationships among persons commonly acknowledged to provide sufficient bases for claims of moral obligation.

It is important to observe that the identity and character of everyone's moral obligations are most likely profoundly influenced by their community memberships and relations. Further, because people play varying roles in varying communities, the networks of expectations and reliances in which they are involved may thereby be profoundly influenced. Their obligations, responsibilities, and powers may thus be—to some extent, at least—dependent upon these roles. Of course, persons occupying a given role may occupy various other roles, and the other roles might differ from case to case as occupants of the initially considered role change. Thus, not every occupant of a given role will have exactly the same obligations, responsibilities, and powers. Nevertheless, insofar as occupation of that role in particular is concerned, there will be a traceable similarity of pattern in the influence of the occupation of the role upon the occupant's moral position.

In working out the specifics of the claims made here, one should examine cases drawn from a variety of categories of moral relations that agents of the state may have. While acting in the name of the state, they may have morally significant relations with other agents of the state, persons who are merely subjects or citizens in the state, persons who are acting in the name of other states, and persons who are subjects or citizens in those states. The claim has often been made that persons acting in the name of states, when dealing with persons acting in the names of other states, are not subject to the "laws of ordinary morality." The foundation of this claim is that these persons may, while occupying these roles, rightly do things that other persons could not rightly do. The question to be raised for consideration here is whether, if this last allegation were true, it would follow that the persons in question were not subject to "the laws of ordinary morality."

The discussion in the preceding paragraph suggests that such a conclusion would not follow. "The laws of ordinary morality" deal with the way differences in our communal roles affect our moral responsibilities, obligations, and powers. Once this is recognized, one should be led to consider whether the cases of persons acting in the name of states are merely particular cases of a very general phenomenon. We may hear *merely* in order to emphasize the suggestion that there is nothing special about these cases.

NATION-STATES, CITIZENS, NONCITIZENS (INCLUDING REFUGEES), AND A SENSE OF COMMUNITY

Nation-states commonly claim authority over given geographic areas. Every person within those geographic areas is normally subjected to at least some aspects of state authority. But, of the persons so subject, some are citizens and some are not. The distinction between citizen and noncitizen, for example, is an important one, well worth separate study. The categories of noncitizen "subjects" to some authority of the state are many and various. They include tourists, students, documented workers who are in the country only temporarily, immigrants, permanent resident aliens, subject native peoples, refugees, and undocumented workers. The last two categories have received considerable attention in recent times, and this attention reveals another facet of problems connected with the nation-state besides the traditionally recognized ones associated with where the boundaries of nation-states are to be placed relative to the existence or nonexistence of entities plausibly described on cultural grounds as nations. Our understanding of the particularity of the tradition of the nation-state will be increased if we try carefully to understand the political, ethical, and conceptual problems associated with the notions of refugee and undocumented worker.

The offering of at least temporary and perhaps permanent residence to political refugees has strained the good offices of many states in modern times. These are mostly political refugees. But in the nineteenth century there were several notorious migrations of masses of people who could have been called economic refugees. We might usefully consider what makes a person recognizable as either a political or an economic refugee. Refugees are persons who are seeking sanctuary or refuge from forces endangering them. The idea of seeking shelter and safety from such forces is uppermost in the concept.* One may be a refugee from a storm or from law-enforcement pursuit. One may also be a refugee from economic and political forces endangering one. But most everyone may be considered at least somewhat at risk because of perfectly normal economic and political forces. What conception of these

---

*My characterization of "refugee" departs from current UN protocol in that the latter requires that the refugees be unable or unwilling to return to either their country of nationality or their country of original residence because of persecution. I do not wish utterly to reject this definition without consideration, but dealing with it would raise issues I cannot consider in this book.

forces must we have in order to regard them as something from which some persons may take refuge?

These and natural forces may be considered something from which one may seek refuge if they are seen as endangering the person seeking refuge. They may be so seen when the person seeking refuge is in some clear way defenseless or undefended against them, and their effects upon that person will be deleterious. Normal persons normally have defense against or are defended against normal natural forces and normal political and economic forces, or so we often think. Sometimes, however, these forces are overwhelming relative to the resources of the person they endanger.

The crossing of national boundaries suggested by the way in which this problem has been posed to us presumably counts as a taking of refuge because the crossing of the boundary, whatever boundary it may be, marks the end of the operation of the endangering forces, whatever they were. At least, this is the hope of the refugee. On this understanding, refugees from religious and/or racial persecution are also possible.

The notion of undocumented workers is related to a practice of modern nation-states that might conceivably be otherwise than as it is. It is the practice of requiring foreign workers of any description to register with the government. Such registration is often required because it is recognized by the registering country that such workers may profoundly influence the economic life of the country to which they come and work. Registration provides both a possibility of control over how many of them arrive and some possibility of tracing their influence upon the economy or some particular segment of the economy of the host country.

Undocumented workers can often be regarded as refugees. But they most often need not be so regarded and there need not be any basis for so regarding them. They need not be fleeing forces that endanger them but merely seeking better opportunities than they had in their initial country of residence. Likewise refugees may or may not be undocumented workers. They may be fully registered upon arrival in the host country, or they may not be employed at all (as with political refugees who carry with them considerable wealth). Thus the two categories require separate examination, and significantly different problems may appear in connection with each.

Especially in connection with refugees of all sorts, and thus with undocumented workers who are also refugees, but also in connection with the remaining undocumented workers, serious issues are raised about the moral acceptability of the influence of "national" (for instance, state) boundaries on the creation and nature of these problems. Is it morally acceptable that national boundaries have such profound influences? Of course, if there were no national boundaries having political effects, these problems would not even be statable. The question might in part be about whether there should be any politically important national boundaries, and might in part be about whether national boundaries should have the particular effects that they commonly have in modern political life.

Despite difficulties in determining precisely where national boundaries should be placed, questions might be raised about whether there should be any national boundaries at all. Causal accounts of how present boundaries came to be as they are would include a mix of considerations. As one writer observes, the sources for a true causal account "are doubtless lost in the mists of antiquity." Conquests and whatever resources went into bringing about effective government doubtless played major roles. The mere history of these and other circumstances must have played a role also in building the inertia that commonly supports effective government. Distributions of languages, racial stocks, cultural and economic considerations also must have played a role as well as the purely political considerations. Also, natural boundaries such as rivers and mountain ranges must have had an effect. In short, at issue was whatever, given the technological resources of the time, played a role in enhancing or limiting the communication, whether benign or malignant, among various people. Constant advances in the technology of these matters must have played a major role in alterations of the boundaries. The leading question about a world without boundaries must be whether considerations such as these would or would not limit a range of effective governance geographically. Of course, such a matter would be relative to the intensity of the governance expected. And given the cultural histories of various locations in the world from time to time, more or less intense governance might be expected. Here, the ingenuity of leaders would make a difference. Large empires of the past have succeeded or failed in part because the ingenuity of leaders was or was not up to getting for the given geographical areas the intensity of government required or expected. A sense of community also might be expected to contribute to the capacity of leaders to effect their common governance.

So much for explanation. Concerning justification, much of the same ground must be covered though from a different perspective, and the sense of community will be important.

A shared sense of community with the rulers or with one another is neither a necessary nor a sufficient condition of effective common rule of people. Colonial governments have shown often enough that it is not a necessary condition; the successful redrawing of national boundaries at various points in history has shown that it is not a sufficient condition (for example, the division of Korea in the 1950s). But a sense of community, whatever it is based on, contributes to the acquiescence to rule that provides a foundation for effective governance. Effective governance in its absence must be explained by reference to such things as overwhelming force.

What is a sense of community? Josiah Royce characterizes it as a belief that many events important in the lives of another person are also important in one's own, and the reverse. This may have a geographic extent or a temporal extent or both. The belief need not be founded on any opinion concerning the causal connection between the events. It need merely be present for whatever reason, including highly ideological reasons. Thus, whether one develops a sense of community relative to certain other specific people has little to do with the facts of one's relationship with those people. It has to do, rather, with the way that one believes or feels about the relationships.

The question to be raised here is not whether a sense of community *ought* to be shared by this or that group of people, but whether it *is* so shared. Thus, attractive humanitarian ideals of a universally shared sense of community among humans are not directly relevant. The presence or absence in a given population of a shared sense of community is one of the facts with which persons who consider whether there should be national boundaries and precisely where they should be must deal. Given the presence or absence of a certain sense of community, national boundaries here or there would or would not be justified.

These considerations do not include something also important: family reunion. Nor do they include, with respect to problems associated with undocumented workers, explicit consideration of the competition that these workers give to citizen workers. Citizen workers in much of the modern world have a choice between work at the offered wage and accepting welfare. Undocumented workers do not ordinarily have the latter option and are therefore subject to the attractions of the offered wages, which may be very low, in ways that citizen workers are not. Also, citizen workers make the employers liable for insurance program payments and so on, whereas undocumented workers most often do not find employers who feel compelled to make these payments on their behalf. Thus, the employers find undocumented workers often an attractive prospect, when the prospect of employing these workers is compared to the prospect of employing citizen workers. Curiously, however, the citizen workers most affected are of the same ethnic groups as the undocumented workers. Because this is the case, they see enforcement of the law against the undocumented workers as a threat to themselves, opening up prospects of harassment and mistreatment generally. The citizen workers are thus generally against active and vigorous enforcement of the law against undocumented workers. They see themselves as losing too much in the way of personal security and civil rights thereby.

The foreign-policy implications of treatments of undocumented workers and treatments of refugees should also be considered. An alteration of a national policy concerning either of these could drive the country of origin or of eventual residence of these persons either to the right or to the left. The implications for the domestic policy of the sending or the ultimate receiving nation should also be considered when dealing with these problems.

MULTI-NATIONAL CORPORATIONS, SOVEREIGNTY, AND CITIZENSHIP

Nothing is unique or unprecedented about the impact of multi-national corporations upon sovereignty or upon citizenship. Nevertheless, the number of multi-national corporations and the sizes of some of them (with annual budgets larger than the annual budgets of some nations) has made their impact noteworthy.

National sovereignty is characterized as national autonomy of some sort (though the precise nature of that autonomy is controversial), and national citizenship, involving, as it does, distributions of special privileges and obligations, is not generally possessed by an individual in more than one nation, though cases of double and perhaps even more multi-citizenships do occur. Multi-national corporations have sometimes seemed to interfere with the "true" sovereignty of nations in which they have conducted their activities, and questions have been asked about whether their top management in this or that nation, who may be citizens in the nations in which they work, have the loyalties appropriate to citizenship in that nation.

Pursuit of these issues offers opportunity to continue our pursuit of precisely what is involved in national sovereignty and in national citizenship. Why should the activities and interests of multi-national corporations give rise to these issues?

Are multi-national corporations identical to international corporations? I should suppose that international corporations might be ones merely that engage in marketing activities in more than one nation. In contrast, multi-national corporations might be corporations engaging in production or service activities as well as marketing activities in more than one nation. Other things being equal, the latter corporations might be considered to have more potential for impact on the economy and politics of the nations in which these activities are conducted. In any case, it is the impact of the corporations upon the political and economic life of the nations in which they conduct their activities that is one of the focuses of attention. That impact is considered sometimes to be so large and potentially important to the nation concerned, that it is considered to impair the political autonomy of that nation, where the autonomy provided grounds for speaking of that nation as sovereign. The other focus of attention is the impact of the corporation's investments, command of resources, or markets in a given nation upon the corporation's welfare and hence, naturally enough, its policies in the other nations in which it conducts activities. This latter impact contributes to the suspicion that the corporation's top management, even if its members are citizens of the nation in which they work, will probably, as we have seen, not have loyalties appropriate to citizens of that nation, and thus constitute an alien force within that nation.

Again, such suspicions, and the like, are not unique to the case of multi-national corporations, nor are they unprecedented. One or more of them have appeared before in connection with other phenomena.

TWELVE

Obedience to Law and Political Obligation

As is well known by now, obedience is not the only conformity issue raised in or by the laws.* For example, empowerments and privileges constantly raise the questions of whether behavior has conformed to them, yet there is no (legal) demand that behavior conform.** Empowerments and privileges are there to be used (and may considerably enlarge one's capacities) if one wants them; thus, no normal question of obedience is raised in connection with them. It is part of the flexibility of a normal legal system.

But issues of obedience have fascinated political philosophers. The question is why. Perhaps it has been because of mistaken doctrines of the past; for instance, Austin's view that every law has a sanction. Perhaps it is because of mistaken doctrines of the present; for example, that rights universally have correlative duties and thus that all the relevant issues may be discussed in terms of duties. Perhaps it is that coercion appears most clearly in connection with obedience, and coercion, as has been seen, has most often been thought characteristic of political (legal) systems.

OBEDIENCE TO LAW

Governments and legal systems gain what effectiveness they have through a variety of means. Such emphasis has been given to their coercive backing, however, that this has figured most prominently in discussions of why govern-

---

*Insofar as compliance to a proviso of a law is unconditionally demanded (commanded) of all or some of us, either expressly or impliedly, the law is obeyable. The law is unconditional except perhaps for designation of the type of person or behavior covered.

**Or one might say that the demand, if there *is* something to be counted a demand, is conditional upon the option of the ones whose persons or behaviors are covered. That is, the only legal consequence of failure to comply as described is that the actors' actions will have no legal effects.

168

ments and legal systems are effective. But this cannot be the only legitimate consideration, even with respect to demands alone. Depending upon the enforcement technology that one plausibly allows oneself to imagine in place, depending upon the sacrifices the enforcers are willing to make for the sake of fulfilling demands made upon them personally by what is needed for effective enforcement of whatever they devise, and depending upon the need for enforcement, more or less effective cooperation is required from at least most probably a considerable few and perhaps very many other persons. This cooperation, as Plato pointed out (and not at a decisively early period in this account with respect to technology), cannot be coerced, at least in any simple way, without depending upon always at least some preponderant proportion of the coercive personnel to enforce dictates against the remainder. One thus needs generally to ask, with respect to some preponderant proportion of the enforcing group, how their uncoerced cooperation is to be gained in enforcement endeavors. Historians of politics have pointed out that simple inertia is a prominent factor in obedience to political dictates. But inertia figures in connection with going concerns, and one must consider how even the temporary cooperation that got the concern started was gained. Rewards of various tangible and intangible sorts may motivate reasoned obedience out of the consideration of personal benefit. And, of course, such rewards can figure prominently in gaining the cooperation of not merely the enforcers of one's dictates but some of the persons to whom the dictates are addressed. But rewards cannot plausibly generally be offered where political obedience is demanded. It is true, exceptionally, some rewards (and accompanying punishments) may be "natural" and not need accompanying enforcement. Perhaps, as Hobbes saw, certain rewards and punishments will be brought about without monitoring by enforcers; for example, ones that may be treated as the natural consequences of one's acts in certain situations (perhaps situations contrived by the rulers). For instance, if one who is not overwhelmingly the strongest in a group acts brutally toward other members of the group, he or she may expect to be visited by retaliations that are unwanted by him or her, and the consequences of which would be regarded by that individual as unacceptable. Likewise, depending upon the dictates in question, the effects of conformity may bring about happy consequences for the conformer—as, for example, if the dictates were to require behavior that is kindly and friendly in appearance; other persons may respond to such behavior so favorably and beneficially to the actor that these responses will in themselves constitute "rewards" for such behavior.

Still, it is generally anticipated that there will be occasions on which behavior is required that will not have such "natural" rewards or the neglect of which will not have such "natural" punishments. The question then appears: how does one gain conformity on such occasions, where perhaps the actor in question must not only fail to gain any rewards or avoid any punishments for the action in question, but must actually undergo some sacrifice in conforming?

If a large portion of the persons whose conformity to political dictates is required can be convinced that they have a (moral) *obligation* to conform to those dictates, then effectiveness will not depend so heavily upon the monitoring (let alone coercion) that would be required at least somewhere for reliance solely upon a system of rewards and punishments. Some of the people some of the time will conform in such cases, and the efficacy of the system of governmental or legal coordination would be thereby strengthened. Some commentators have made vast claims for the connection between a belief in political obligation and efficacy, saying that the acceptability of government and laws to a populace is necessary for the efficacy of these devices (which may very well be true), and supposing that this acceptance may have as a necessary condition the general belief that the laws impose (moral) obligation, but even if this last claim is inflated, the contribution of this belief to efficacy is probably substantial enough to be of some importance.* The acquiescence of populations to systems of law and of government probably has very many aspects.**

THE OBLIGATION TO OBEY THE LAW

Aside from a belief that there is an obligation, is there one? This question requires speculation because there are many somewhat plausible possibilities. The law is said to impose a duty or an obligation.† To remind us that this is a duty or obligation imposed by law, we often call it a *legal duty* or *legal obliga-*

*The presence of a belief in a (moral) obligation is neither necessary to produce obedience nor a sufficient condition of obedience. That it is not necessary to produce obedience has been obvious to commentators for a long time; for example, consider James Bryce's previously alluded-to essay on obedience. As a historian, Bryce notes it more probable that obedience to law through the ages has been secured primarily through the operation of human inertia, rather than through either the operation of fear or of reason commonly cited. In any case, belief in the presence of a (moral) obligation to obey has doubtless secured obedience in some cases down through history, but, in vastly more cases, obedience has been secured in other ways. Concerning the sufficiency of the belief in the existence of an obligation to obey the law given the possible presence of a belief in conflicting obligations (and thus of obligations that might conflict with the obligation to obey the law) and given the possible presence of belief in outweighing moral considerations other than merely the presence or absence of beliefs in obligations (see the next section), such as the presence of conflicts with moral aspirations or ideals, the presence of a belief in an obligation to obey the law cannot safely be considered to settle in and of itself even all significant moral issues concerning obedience.

**The acquiescence we are considering is read in the conformity to governments and legal systems that results from belief that the dictates of these systems impose upon us an obligation of conformity. Perhaps this conformity is brought about by belief that obligation was imposed by some prior acquiescence. But the conformity cannot be read as in itself the acquiescence that legitimates, because it is possibly coerced. Prior conformity is eligible to count as acquiescence of a sort that legitimizes rule and results arguably in an acquisition of an obligation to obey. Whether such an obligation is acquired depends upon the reason for the acquiescence. If the acquiescence is out of fear, results from trickery, is, speaking practically, unavoidable, or the person conforming does not know that he or she is conforming, then the conformity cannot be reasonably taken as a sign of acquiescence at all or of acquiescence of the sort that legitimates, and so on. But in any case the acquiescence must be prior to that demanded in the instant case. The temporal spread of *prior* may vary from case to case, for the cases where conformity is being demanded may be ones that have quite a temporal spread, and however wide the time for that is, the conformity that is taken as having been ground for acquisition of an obligation must be prior to that.

†No distinction need be drawn between duty and obligation in this context, though there are contexts in which a distinction should be drawn.

tion. We sometimes, however, forget this simple reason for doing so, and wonder if anything else is afoot. We wonder, in particular, whether the modifier *legal* can be dropped altogether (are our legal duties also "duties" *simpliciter?*) or replaced by some other modifier (for example, are all our legal obligations moral ones?).* The inquiry into them is one of rather large scope, and only in rather special circumstances could there be any serious question about whether there was a legal obligation to do as the government or the laws demand. And, of course, the words we use (or don't use) make a difference in what we think.

These questions have another point. They can help us clarify the relationship of our duties/obligations to one another. Few questions in political science get discussed more thoroughly. We are subject, each of us, to various systems of authority, most of which impose some duties/obligations of obedience upon us. Are these duties/obligations neatly coordinate or not? We justifiably feel the need to know.

There are obligations that a person may feel he or she has, or that a group of persons may feel each of them has, but the nonfulfillment of which is not regarded by some other person as a good reason for criticizing those who think themselves under these obligations. The actors and the critics differ as to what the obligations of the actors are; and either may be right. But consider a special case, the case where the actor, although feeling that he or she has certain obligations, does not expect to be criticized directly by other people for failing to keep these obligations, and, indeed, has no view that they ought to so criticize the individual.

Some of what persons may regard as their social, business, or civic obligations may be of this sort; they feel called upon to do certain things and to refrain from doing others solely because of a conception of themselves as, for instance, social leaders, business-people, or persons with civic pride. Others would not say of them, unless the situation were quite exceptional indeed, that they ought to recognize and fulfill these obligations. (Unless the commentators were thinking of the person's own psychological welfare, and if the latter were their reason, then they would not hold that one ought to fulfill one's obligations, but rather that one ought to fulfill what one believes to be one's obligations). Obligations, the nonfulfillment of which is thought by persons to provide good reason for self-criticism, but which neither those persons nor anybody else regards as good reason for criticism by others, are not presently of interest.

Regardless of whether these are parasitical upon, or metaphorical extensions of, obligations the nonfulfillment of which someone regards as good reason for anyone to criticize one who has not fulfilled them, they are of no interest here, because only the latter allow for the kind of criticism that gives a point to discussions of political obligation.

There are also obligations that others may feel a person, or each member of a group, has, even though the person in question doesn't feel so oneself. He or she may not feel an obligation to treat one's own parents respectfully, or

---

*As commentators generally point out, the obligations they are after are not legal ones, and thus, given their generality, are most probably moral ones. These are (most generally) called *political obligations.*

may not feel an obligation to avoid stepping on the cracks in the sidewalk, and others may feel that such an individual has these obligations.

Narrowly conceived, as we have suggested, political obligation has been thought of as an obligation that everybody has to obey the law. This view is plausible because it is thought that what we are obligated to do, we are in some way required to do, and perhaps vice versa, and law is generally thought to be the principal mode in which political requirements are expressed. If there are political requirements beyond legal requirements, however, then these requirements also should be included in the intended scope of political obligation, and, *ex hypothesi*, will not be legal. The boundaries and limits of what is to count as law are, however, sufficiently controversial so that this point can get tangled in dispute. Some disputants will say that if something is political and is required, then there is good reason to think the requirement a legal one; other disputants will say that if something is not legal, then it is not really required. The disputants agree that political requirements must be legal, but disagree on whether this alleged truth can be used as grounds for holding that something must be legal or instead holding that something cannot be required. Others disagree with both of them. This available flexibility of approach reveals, among other things, that the notion of what is politically required may be as controversial as the notion of what is law.

We must ask further about the thoughts at the basis of these positions. Obligations and requirements can both stem from the application of rules to particular circumstances. But there can be requirements without corresponding obligations. A person can be required to do something when given no prudent alternative to do otherwise. But being given no prudent alternative to do otherwise appears to have nothing whatever to do with whether the person has or has not an obligation to do the thing in question. On the other hand, can a person have an obligation to do something without at the same time being required to do it? Certainly, a person may be obligated to do something while still having an opportunity prudently to do otherwise. If the presence or absence of the latter opportunity is considered relevant to the question of whether a person is required to do something, then being obligated may have very little to do with being required, at least on this understanding of being required. But there are other understandings, for example, "having no honorable alternative to do otherwise." This understanding may have considerably more to do with being obligated. Thus, whether one can be obligated without being required depends in important part upon one's understanding of the philosophically treacherous notion of "being required."

Another facet of the possibly difficult relations between the two ideas, and one not unrelated to the features just noted between the two, is our greater willingness to say that a person is required than to say that the person is obligated. For reasons at least of the divergence just noted in the preceding paragraph, we generally hold that a person's obligations are less extensive than the requirements to which the person is subjected.

Perhaps "one is obligated to obey the law" means only that disobeying the law would be wrong, and one has an obligation to avoid the wrong. Given this obligation, no special grounds would be needed for why it is wrong. It could be any ground or combination thereof. No special ground would be needed.

But can one correctly say that one has an obligation to avoid the wrong, and that disobeying the law would *always* be wrong? One quick way with the larger claim is to note that it leaves us with no account whatsoever of civil disobedience or of revolution (unless obligations can be outweighed, for instance, by other obligations). The claim would have to be examined carefully, and must be considered dubious until that is done. Until that is done, and done successfully, the idea must be considered not satisfactorily explored.

The moral reason of citizens to obey the law, and so forth, may also be thought to depend upon the content of the law alone (though, as A. John Simmons notes, this doesn't [a] explain why laws of even faultless content need not be obeyed by persons not within the jurisdiction of those laws, and [b] allow for the fact that citizens may on occasion have good moral reason to obey laws with faulty or bad content). Moral reason to obey the law may be thought, too, to originate in part in the authority of the lawgivers. That authority, as we have noticed, has often been seen, rightly or wrongly, to function to establish a right in the lawgiver to impose coercion-backed rules upon citizens.

Further items needing consideration on the general topic of an obligation to obey the law are the following: (1) Are there distinctions useful here between obligations, duties, and responsibilities? (2) If there are obligations, what are the obligations to do, to feel or believe, or to be? John Rawls says, "to support and comply with the relevant institutions." How much, in particular, is conveyed by *support*? (3) Commentators these days generally agree that the presence of an obligation to do something constitutes a strong but not conclusive reason for doing the thing in question. There might be other, conflicting obligations, and there might be conflicting moral considerations of other sorts. The strength of a reason for doing something provided by the presence of an obligation to do it is agreed to surmount at least the strength of conflicting whims and desires. Commentators do not, however, commonly discuss what other considerations might be outweighed by an obligation to do something. This omission is understandable because obligations themselves may have varying strengths. Nevertheless, there would be some interest in considering the possibilities here, not only with respect to personal desires— for example, the desire to favor one's relatives—but also with respect to (a) familial obligations and duties one has relative to private associations of which one may be a member or even an officer, and (b) dimensions of what might be called *political morality*. Examples from the latter might come from aspirations to ideals of citizenship considered too demanding and possibly even too remote to be subject to the expectations of common performance of the sort associated ordinarily with the imposition of obligations. We cannot be so sure beforehand that political morality is sufficiently coherent with morality generally or internally to remove all possibilities of conflict between such aspirations and commonly imposed obligations.

Given the lack of moral conclusiveness of consideration of merely the presence or absence of obligation to support and comply with the dictates of this or that government, the moral issues connected with support and compliance cannot be considered comprehensively solely by consideration of the presence or absence of obligation thereto. The moral standings of a person vis-à-vis

governments claiming dominion over that person will be considered comprehensively only when a broader range of moral considerations is canvased.
Such broader consideration will be invited, perhaps, when we ask, not, "What
are the political obligations of the person in question?" but, rather, "What
would make it right or wrong for the person upon whom the claims to dominion are made to support or fail to support, to comply with or fail to comply
with, the orders of the government in question?" and "What would make
those orders and orderings right or wrong?"

Obligation may instead have been discussed by the theorists on a curious
assumption—that the coercion characteristic of politics could only be justified
if obedience to the law (where obedience is called for) were a duty. The possibility has been overlooked that it need not be a duty (with a corresponding
right of punishment) but nevertheless all right (no offense).

The question of whether it can be all right (the ethical propriety of "all
right" has been argued by William Hay) for the enforcers of the law to enforce it against others when the others have no duty to obey it is worth asking.
The answer is, "of course"; we have a model ready at hand of what things
could be like. It is the model of a legitimate competitive situation. There are a
good many of these, to judge by our recreative sports, our recreative games,
and our lives. In these cases, what the enforcers are doing is thought all right
though the persons against whom the law is enforced have no duty to obey
because the two camps are in a competitive situation on the matter. What
makes a competitive situation acceptable is complex. It will not be gone into
here, especially in connection with the law.*

EFFECTIVENESS AND VALIDITY

Although the matter is controversial (concerning both this and the point to be
made next; see Fuller and Dworkin, and reviews thereof), I know of no theoretic or even practical requirement that enforcing the law, if done by a properly authorized person, must be not morally wrong in order for the law to be
valid (though it still could be morally wrong).** Perhaps one could understand Carl Friedrich to be arguing against commentators who believe that
there is such a requirement when he argues (in *Authority and Tradition*) that
authority and legitimacy are not connected (this should be distinguished from
the earlier argument herein connecting authority and legitimacy or purported legitimacy). But what about the idea that there is a theoretic or practical requirement that enforcement of the law by a properly authorized person
be *thought* not morally wrong? There is no requirement short of supposing a
connection (on which we have remarked earlier in this book) between validity

and effectiveness. A certain degree of effectiveness may be needed for validity, and a certain degree of obedience for effectiveness. Are there any necessary conditions of a sufficient degree of obedience (whatever is sufficient)? In particular, must what is proper (legally proper) be not thought (or not generally thought) morally wrong?

It would be plausible to assert that the bulk of the citizens must believe that enforcement of the law must not be morally wrong. It would be safer to say, however, that the bulk of the citizens must not believe that such enforcement is morally wrong. The latter leaves open, as the former does not, that the bulk of the citizens have no thought whatever on the subject. Perhaps we would be best off to leave this question to the social scientists. As we have seen, Lord Bryce, after all, named the most prominent cause of obedience to be inertia. Other than the common working of inertia, however, there is no reason to believe that there *is* a widespread obligation to obey the law or that enforcement of the law is, on other grounds, not morally wrong.

Would enforcers of the law purport legitimacy for their activities if they didn't at least sincerely believe that the latter had a trace of actual legitimacy? It depends on whether there are limits on the effrontery of some people (the enforcers) or on the gullibility of others (the bulk of the public). Again, it seems a question for social scientists.

It should be emphasized that I am not examining here "One ought to obey the law," or even the claim that some governments provide bases for arguing that citizens have political obligations. Those claims may be right or wrong for all that is said here in particular.

THIRTEEN

Civil Disobedience and Revolution

Civil disobedience and revolution are two of a number of often politically significant, roughly called "acts of resistance" that commentators have distinguished. Among the other types are coups d'état, riots, rebellions, and civil wars. This situation presents a number of interesting different borderlines for examination, including between these acts themselves and between these and other acts with which they may be confused. We will examine only two of those borderlines. The features customarily attributed to civil disobedience are explained best, perhaps, as features distinguishing it, on the one hand, from ordinary law violation and, on the other hand, from revolution. The border between civil disobedience and ordinary law violation will not, however, be explored on the side of ordinary law violation, except for one class of interesting cases. In contrast, the border between civil disobedience and revolution will be explored on both sides.

CONCERNING THE CONTRAST BETWEEN CIVIL DISOBEDIENCE AND ORDINARY LAW VIOLATION

These points should be made:

1. The following limitations are customarily placed on law violation that is to count as civil disobedience: (a) The violation must be overt, and there must be no effort to escape detection. Thus, civil disobedience is distinguished from much ordinary illegality, and the distinction supports the idea that civil disobedience is, indeed, "civil." It is here "civil" in both the sense that it is polite ("tame," "safe") (some persons object to the whole idea of "civil disobedience" on this ground) and the sense that it is an act on the public, civic stage.

(b) There is no resistance to arrest or punishment, as would commonly be the case with ordinary crime. The lack of resistance to arrest and punishment supports again the "civility" of civil disobedience in both senses. (c) There are, perhaps, also restrictions on the manner of disobedience (that increase its "civility," at least in the first sense).

In the same spirit, there can be restrictions also on the law disobeyed. Many commentators have denied that the disobedience could involve any violent activity. But this restriction is likely to create some difficulties about what is to count as violence—for example, how intimidating can a peaceful demonstration become before it involves reliance upon violence? And is the pouring of blood on draft records violence? (d) Civil disobedience is law violation limited to the following intentions: (1) incidental to acting in accord with conscience in doing what one feels one must do or avoid doing what one feels one must not do, (2) to vindicate (to affirm, insist upon, or obtain judicial judgment on) what one believes to be one's legal, and possibly even one's political or moral rights, (3) incidental or instrumental to doing (1), (2), or bringing public attention to governmental action, policy, or behavior that one believed to be unwise, immoral, or illegal. Personal gain, avoidance of detection or punishment, and the like—all of which are commonly attributed intentions of ordinary crime—are excluded. (More support to "civil," at least in the second sense, is provided by the requirement that disobedience may have a political point.) (e) M. K. Gandhi would also include the requirements that very few engage in civil disobedience, and that those engaging in it not accept the benefits of the laws or institutional systems being protested.

2. Civil disobedience is often conscience-guided. But commentators are chary of advising that persons simply disobey the law whenever they believe that doing so is right. Many commentators insist that persons take special care and special pains to assure themselves that their views are correct before they disobey the law. Curiously, no special pains-taking is advised for persons about to obey the law because they believe that doing so is right. And the imposition of penalties in the two cases is also asymmetrical. These asymmetries are revealing, and should be carefully explored.

3. The law disobeyed in civil disobedience is not always necessarily the law being protested. The disobedience may be only instrumental to the protest. This is likely, of course, only when the civil disobedience is a form of protest. As we have seen, it is not always so. Sometimes civil disobedience is a conscientious avoidance of an act required by law or legal order, or conscientious performance of an act prohibited. An element of "protest" may be present, but the primary focus is upon the supposed immorality that the law requires. Examples would be refusing compulsory service in the military forces, and the like. The element of protest becomes the primary focus when a law violated is clearly not the law objected to, as is often the case with laws prohibiting unlawful assemblies, or unlicensed parades. Often enough, unlawful assemblies or unlicensed parades have been held in order to publicize objections to quite unrelated segregation laws or tax laws, and the like. When the importance of various kinds of costs to civil disobedience is being assessed, this difference between law violations may very well become important.

4. In its exclusion of resistance to arrest and punishment, common civil disobedience provokes serious questions in some minds concerning whether it should be punished. Seemingly, to some commentators on the topic, to say that the disobedience is justified or to say that it is acceptable is to say that it need not and possibly should not be punished. But neither of these conclusions follows. And even if persons were not to be punished, the legal disposition of their cases would not yet be utterly clear. For example, should they be acquitted or given suspended sentences, and should they be paroled? The ordinary punishment for the crime in question could be imposed in order to insure that persons with other motives than the ones we have discussed do not try to travel under this banner. Possibly, the ordinary punishment could be lightened, or even increased. There are plausible alternatives, and some may seem to fit the circumstances of the case more fully than others.

5. Activities of legal or political agents or agencies that are equally illegal may nevertheless differ respecting what may justifiably be disobeyed. Illegal orders or commands by law-enforcement officials on the spot of a potential civil disturbance are most commonly excepted from disobedience. It is commonly said that one should obey these commands and launch an appeal later. The extent to which this is true may vary with the circumstances. The idea that disobedience would not be justifiable in some such cases is not based upon consideration of personal risk, but rather on consideration of the social risk of civil disturbance. This, then, is a distinction between illegal acts of officials that, of course, ought not to be imposed but ought to be obeyed if imposed, and illegal acts of officials that both ought not to be imposed and ought not to be obeyed if imposed. Aquinas similarly distinguishes between directives violating divine law, which persons had a duty to disobey, and directives violating natural law, which persons had a right to disobey, unless disobedience would produce "scandal and disturbance."

Violation might be attended by certain risks to one's safety or fortune, and the legal system might exacerbate or mitigate these risks. And in either case, there may be alternatives of varying promise to law violation. Obedience to an illegal command or conformity to an unconstitutional statute, followed by complaint to persons in a position to do something effective about what they hear, may be best. It depends upon the circumstances, how serious they are, whether they are isolated or part of a recurring pattern, whether there are persons by whom one can be heard who are in a position to do something about what they hear and willing to do it.

Discussants of civil disobedience often assert that resort to it is justifiable only after every legal means of reform has been tried. There is no need to be dogmatic about this, but, in view of the personal risks of civil disobedience, it must count for most persons as rather low on their agenda of things to be attempted. Civil disobedience is also alleged to have social risks. In cases where the legality of what is being imposed is being tested, the social risks of disobedience may be no clearer or more dramatic than the social risks of obedience. Estimates of the likelihood of various risks, personal or social, are not for philosophers per se to make. But assessments of the relative importance of various kinds of risks are commonly offered by philosophers. Before we discuss them, however, we must understand more fully what civil disobedience *is*.

CIVIL DISOBEDIENCE AND ONE CASE OF ORDINARY LAW VIOLATION

The clearest cases of civil disobedience are normally thought to occur when the law violated is clearly valid, constitutional, or whatever, but is objected to for some other reason. These are cases where the disobedience is clearly disobedience to a law or directive having no defect in its title to lawfulness. Where there is a defect or purported defect, and this is part of the invoked reason for violation, there is always at least a color of reason for saying that the apparent violation was not actually a violation or, at any rate, not a violation of any valid law or directive. Some writers might find sufficient reason here to group together any cases of law violation intended to test the legal or political acceptability of legislation or administrative directives, and to separate them off from other law violations. But political tests will too often, in Western political tradition at least, slide into tests of the moral acceptability or the wisdom in the view of a populace of the items in question. Unless firm boundaries can be established between (a) legal and political tests, or political tests of the sorts often grouped with legal tests, and (b) core cases of civil disobedience in connection with law violation of legislation or administrative direction (when they are clearly both legally and politically valid—whatever this notion may involve), discussions of civil disobedience may have to shift uncomfortably among them all.

There is then another distinction not supported squarely by any commonly attributed features, between civil disobedience and law violation, that is intended to provide legal or political tests of the validity, constitutionality, or general acceptability to the populace of the law in question. Some writers on these subjects do not separate out this latter kind of law violation from core cases of civil disobedience, and treat it, at best, as a particular sort of civil disobedience. This treatment, however, results in labeling, as civil disobedients, persons seeking court tests of various legislations who certainly have never thought themselves so, nor have they been thought of in this way by anybody else. Not that so thinking of them wouldn't be useful, but it might require recasting our attitudes toward civil disobedience more completely than has yet been acceded.

In the proceedings of many such court tests, many commentators have found no hard and fast distinction between legal and political tests. Perhaps, however, the use of some such distinction would help us here. The idea that one might launch a *political* test of the validity, constitutionality, or acceptability of some piece of legislation, is the aspect of such cases that is most closely adjacent to the core cases of what is commonly regarded to be civil disobedience. If one is attempting to launch merely a *court* or *legal* test of a piece of legislation or an administrative action, with a clear intention to abide by official determinations after feasible appeals, perhaps this process has been sufficiently customary, well worn, and familiar to raise none of the tension associated with core cases of civil disobedience. It is so much a piece with our political and legal traditions, in any case, that the procedure is considered part of the settled practice to which persons living within the ambit of the system may occasionally have to resort. The moves made are standard; and this is of

critical importance. In contrast, efforts to launch a political test of the acceptability of some piece of legislation or administrative action through law disobedience are not so standardized and accepted. They do not fit so comfortably
within the normal operation of the system.

CIVIL DISOBEDIENCE AND REVOLUTION

Some political philosophers have perceived clear and important differences
between civil disobedience and revolution. Others, apparently, have not. Often it is not easy to tell whether the latter have ignored the distinction, not
perceived it, not perceived one or the other of the phenomena, not thought
one or the other worthy of discussion, or have thought them similar or fundamentally similar enough so that both could safely be discussed under one or
the other heading alone (sometimes "civil disobedience" and sometimes "revolution").

As we have said, some of the subtle and more difficult problems about civil
disobedience concern whether obedience should be given or withheld when
the validity of the law-making or of the purportedly authorized orders or
commands is dubious (perhaps by apparently being *ultra vires*), and when the
law-makers have lost their title, or at best have a dubious title, to obedience (as
in many revolutionary situations in which government power has been seriously eroded). Concerning the first, suppose that illegal censorship or con-
scription laws have been enacted. Concerning the second, suppose that orders
or commands are being delivered by the declared winner of a provably fraudulent election for sheriff.

The intention of revolution is normally much broader than the intention of
civil disobedience. The latter can indeed be quite narrow. Revolution may intend something so broad as the overthrow of an entire political or legal or
social system, or something so narrow as the replacement of one government
by another by nonconstitutional means (though the borderline between revolutions and coups must be observed here). Civil disobedience, on the other
hand, intends no such overthrow, and, most often, no such replacement, but
rather has objectives ranging from something so broad as the revocation of a
governmental or social policy, to something so narrow as avoidance of an act
contrary to the dictates of one's conscience (with no suggestion whatever that
avoidance of the act in question might be contrary also to anyone else's conscience). The differences in intention between revolution and civil disobedience are thus substantial enough to be extremely significant to citizens in general and to supporters of the existing scheme or order in particular. Civil
disobedience, by intention at least, is much less threatening to the latter. And,
as we shall see, the differences in the intentions provide a framework for understanding why there are significant differences between the activities of revolution and civil disobedience; for example, that civil disobedience is overt
and involves no resistance to detection, arrest, or punishment. Revolutionary
activity, on the other hand, may very well be covert, involve serious efforts to
escape detection, and involve serious and often violent efforts to escape arrest
and punishment.

As the difference in scope of intentions between revolution and civil disobedience remarked upon suggests, the justification of revolutionary activity is likely to require more weight than the justification of civil disobedience. There is no universally correct claim to be made about this, perhaps; unusual circumstances may always be imagined. But, commonly, the risks of social costs will be higher in the case of revolutionary activity than in the case of civil disobedience. We are therefore reasonable to require a higher justification threshold for the former than for the latter. This difference in justification threshold is reflected in what are likely to be determinants of one's personal choices of one activity or the other in a particular circumstance. For example, the degree to which the evils that are to be resisted or corrected are (or are thought to be) systemic to the political or legal system in question favors (or is thought to favor) revolutionary activity; the degree to which they are (or are thought to be) less systemic favors (or is thought to favor) civil disobedience.

Concerning justifiable revolution, there are two further issues of special interest to political philosophers: (1) what considerations operate as good reasons for revolution, and (2) under what conditions the good reasons become sufficient reasons. This distinction between good reasons and sufficient ones directs our attention first to (1) whether revolutionary activity might effectively be directed primarily against mischiefs occasioned by a government, and (2) whether there is at least a chance of correcting or mitigating the mischiefs, or at least of bettering the situation by the revolutionary activity contemplated.

Another element of the sharp distinction to be made between civil disobedience and revolution is that the former does not involve violence and the latter may. But alongside civil disobedience and revolution, other forms of resistive action may be arrayed. While abstention from violence is not agreed upon by everyone as a necessary condition of civil disobedience, and difficulties may arise about what is to count as violence, as we have seen, the occurrence of intended violence in connection with purported civil disobedience may be counted upon to raise questions and debates about whether the purported civil disobedience is actual civil disobedience. No such questions are raised about the intended occurrence of violence in connection with any of the other forms of resistive action, though some of the forms may or may not actually involve violence (for example, coups d'état may or may not involve violence). Among resistive actions possibly involving intended violence, the distinction between revolution and the others generally rests upon the greater degrees to which revolutions are organized, deliberate, and aspire to large-scale changes in the authority and constitutional structures or the economic or social structures of the societies in which they occur. There are interesting and perhaps important differences between these various forms of resistance, but the distinctions between them are not always depicted by scholars in the same ways, and the two forms of resistive action on which we have focused here provide us with quite enough to discuss for the present.

The collection offered here of certain actions as "resistive" is overly broad unless further qualified. One should say something like, "resistive through measures involving at least incidental law violation." The attention given to this classification of resistive acts or even an unqualified classification of such acts should not be taken to suggest that the acts in either case are extraordinary or even antipolitical. Such acts may be part and parcel of political life in many countries, and at least not highly unusual in others. Our narrower classification is of some interest to us because some political philosophers and many members of our political culture have regarded such acts as in some way antipolitical, as destructive or disruptive of political culture. This is understandable, given presentations of political culture, including the presentation offered here, emphasizing stability and security. When seen to be methods of answering to our interest in stability and security, political culture may be thought inherently hostile to the threats to order apparently embodied in resistive acts of especially our more narrowly characterized and qualified sort. But this is by no means clearly the case. As Von Clausewicz said of war, it is merely another instrument of politics. Likewise, resistive acts involving law violation may very well be seen, even in cultures not inclined to see them so, as instruments for the conduct of politics. Political events are moved forward and changes of political importance may be made by such means. Depending upon one's views of human nature and human societies, resort to such means may be seen as entirely to be expected and even unavoidable.

FOURTEEN

Political Life
and Human Life

Does political life "fit" human life? Some commentators argue that it does not. This chapter will consider two of those arguments: about the development of humans into beings worthy of respect and about the development of relations among humans into intimate ones.

Both are in part matters of aspiration. Humans worthy of respect may turn out to be very special sorts of things and humans possibly may but need not develop into them. Likewise, relations among humans may, but—unless matters of ultimate gratification are being considered—need not, become intimate.

POLITICAL LIFE AND PEOPLE

Political life here means life as normally lived in a political community, such as that delineated in Chapter One and detailed in the rest of the book. Most commentators probably agree that political and human life worthy of respect are compatible. But some do not. And some believe that the two lives are not only compatible, but that political life will produce the life of a praiseworthy (in at least some respects) human. (Jean-Jacques Rousseau and Emma Goldman, the two figures on whom we focus in this section, said that of a man, though Goldman gives it less emphasis of position in her passages than it is given in Rousseau's passage. In this nonsexist age—aspirationally speaking—one ought to be able to convert it, which move might gain their positions new adherents.)*

*Neither Rousseau nor the anarchists say what it takes to make a human worthy of respect explicitly, but in my opinion there is no serious question that this is what they mean to offer. I shall not argue the point here.

The anarchists represent an extreme. They believe that the lives are not compatible. (Nonanarchists, such as J. S. Mill and Alexander von Humboldt, sometimes echo their views.) An especially full anarchist commentator on the relevant point is Emma Goldman. Some of the character traits and social conditions she mentions as making humans worthy of respect are: "free initiative, originality," "the freest possible expression of all the latent powers of the individual," "free[dom] to choose the mode of work, the conditions of work, and the freedom to work," "to [have] the making of a table . . . the result of inspiration, of intense longing, and deep interest in work as a creative force," and "spontaneity and free opportunity" (pp. 40, 43).

Whichever of these expressions one chooses to concentrate on, it is clear that she is talking about all of the quality in question—100 percent (other commentators have noticed the "all-or-nothing" quality of much anarchism).

One wants to ask the following:

1. Why all of it? Wouldn't less do? Generally people speak of personality and character traits as though they were not necessarily expressed *always* but only most of the time, though they are still one's character traits. This is true even when the reason for not expressing them reflects (at least somewhat) upon character. Perhaps Goldman and others are afraid of getting on a "slippery slope," so that one won't be able to stop until one reaches tyranny and oppression at the bottom, and fear that the bottom may not be very far. Perhaps all this is so, but the points need to be argued.

2. If this (the possibility of less than 100 percent of conforming behavior for a given character attribution) is so, then there is room for some exercise of authority. There will be room for *some* nonexcluded reasons for behaving or not behaving in a certain way against which countervailing reasons from authority can operate (see the discussion of Raz in Chapter Five).

3. As the discussion of authority in Chapter Five shows, if the restrictions on character (such as the laws, orders) are correctly claimed to be pieces of self-limitation, then they will be unobjectionable on the grounds being considered there. We have not, of course, probed the point as far as can be probed here, but at least it is a plausible and promising point. (There may, so far as the argument in this book has gone, be other sources as well of authority and legitimacy. But self-limitation has been suggested to be a source.)

Apparently, contrary to the position of Goldman and the other anarchists (*contrary* means that they cannot both be true) is that of Rousseau, who holds not only that the life of a man worthy of respect (in at least some ways) is compatible with political life, but that the latter produces the former.

In Chapter 8 of *The Social Contract* ("The Civil State"), Rousseau says:

The passage from the state of nature to the civil state produces in man a very remarkable change, by substituting in his conduct justice for instinct, and by giving actions the moral quality that they previously lacked. It is only when the voice of duty succeeds physical impulse, and law succeeds appetite, that man, who till then had regarded only himself, sees that he is obliged to act on other principles and to consult his reason before listening to his inclinations. Although, in this state, he is deprived of many advantages that he derives from nature, he acquires equally great ones in return; his faculties are exercised and developed; his ideas are expanded; his feelings are ennobled; his whole soul is exalted to such a degree that, if the causes of this new condition did not degrade him below that from which he emerged, he ought to bless without ceasing the happy moment that released him from it forever, and transformed him from a stupid and ignorant animal into an intelligent being and a man (p. 18).

There is little matching with Goldman. What matching there is, is of ideals, not of (translated) language. One may try to find more. For example, one may try to read Rousseau's well-known views on freedom expressed elsewhere into the present passage from him. But this will only provoke endless controversy about whether Rousseau and Goldman mean the same thing by *freedom*.

Thus, there is probably a difference of ideals as well as of how ideals are to be achieved. Anarchists may, of course, believe they are to be achieved only if people are left free of government interference and coercion. Rousseau may believe they are to be achieved if people are freed of instinct, physical impulse, appetite, regard only for oneself, and inclination. But it appears also that at least two different models are in part presented here concerning what it is to be a human worthy of respect. This only raises an issue for discussion concerning what it *is* to be a human worthy of respect. As with Goldman, one must ask whether, in the case of these behaviors and character traits presented as ideals by Rousseau, "a miss is as good as a mile," or whether they are subject to significant variations in degree or quality that, in turn, produce differences in how they are to be evaluated.

Even if there is no significant difference (of ideals) between the lists of the anarchists and that of Rousseau, despite the lack of match between the lists in language, nevertheless there are, on each writer's own account, multiple items on each list; and this is a matter of additional importance. If each list has a number of items, then the items may or may not be achieved in the same way. One wants to be careful that the differing items on each list, as well as the items on the differing lists, do not have differing causal conditions, and hence different achievement conditions.

PERFECTION OF PEOPLE VERSUS PERFECTION OF SOCIETIES

Commentators largely agree that the point of societies is the perfection of people or the perfection of something about them (for instance, their virtue, their happiness, or their development). Disagreement is found, however, on whether societies must be perfect before people, or whatever it is about them that we want to perfect, can be perfect. On behalf of the claim that perfect societies are needed for perfect people, we hear such things as "No man is an island." On behalf of the opposite thesis we hear such remarks as "I am not my brother's keeper." Disagreement on the matter is partly due to disagreement about what are effective means for achieving this or that goal. For example, if the goal is perfect happiness, can that be achieved for each individual without achieving it also for all individuals in the society in question or for at least most of them?

Disagreement about the dependence of the perfection of one of these things upon the other is doubtless sustained by differing views of what those perfections consist of. For example, if the happiness of people egoistically conceived is what one has in mind, then this happiness might not depend upon a perfection of the society in which that individual is to be found. On the other hand, if the perfection that one has in mind is the perfection of various virtues of individuals and these are thought to include benevolence of various sorts, then this perfection will not be well developed and perfected until society is so organized that this perfection can be expressed.

In the third quarter of the nineteenth century, this was a matter much debated between Mill and Carlyle and their associates. Other issues were entangled in this debate; for example, laissez-faire individualism versus authoritarian elitism. Central issues were whether societies could provide a fitting or helpful context for the perfection of whatever virtues or happinesses at which disadvantaged people should or did aim, and whether these virtues and happinesses could be effected in a society that is not controlled by individuals more than merely generally well intentioned and well informed.

PUBLIC AND PRIVATE

It is sometimes said that politics has no legitimate business with what is correctly designated private. Some of the things that can be designated public or private are behaviors and activities, interests and businesses, goods, virtues, aspirations, goals, and ideals. It is worth noting that, depending upon what is regarded as a background condition for the distinction, the rationale for the distinction and the place it is drawn may vary. For example, if the morality of public officials is regarded as a background condition for the distinction, rather than one of the consequences of where the distinction is drawn, then the morality of public officials in some so-called "Third World nations" compared to the morality of public officials in the so-called "Western world" will have interesting consequences for the distinction between public and private virtue. The distinction may be more difficult to draw as it relates to the former communities than with respect to the latter. In the latter, public officials performing public acts are not supposed to show the private virtue of loyalty to relatives and friends. Indeed, they may be accused of favoritism, partiality, and corruption if they do so. On the other hand, public officials in some Third World countries are in their public lives supposed to show favoritism and partiality to relatives and friends. Profound differences in cultural histories and practices may make each of these responses more or less understandable. But the fact remains that in some Third World countries this basis for a distinction between public and private virtue may not be available at all, or, if available, may be present only as a not-fully-assimilated Western import.

It is generally thought a defining characteristic of totalitarian community that every area of life is public, where *public* is plausibly defined as an area of life that is not or ought not to be closed to government scrutiny, rightly sacrosanct from governmental regulation, or irrelevant to governmental operation (the negative of a string of disjuncts). It is plausibly, though not indisputably, assumed that in this case the correlative term *private* (whether or not anything is covered by that term) is the contradictory—that is, a simple disjunction true if one or more of its disjuncts is true (and nontotalitarianism holds that some areas of life are in principle "private"). Provided that at least one of the disjuncts of this latter proposition is true, no difference is made to the truth of the string by which or how many of the disjuncts are true. Different commentators, or the same commentator at different times, think of a different disjunct(s) at different times and forget, overlook, or underemphasize the remainder. The "public" is sometimes then considered to be whatever is left over after the disjunct(s) that one has in mind has (have) been sliced out of the pie of human life.

On other occasions, however, the "public" is characterized positively as whatever is or can rightly be observed by the government or noninvitees, subject to governmental regulation, or considered relevant to governmental business or operation. These disjuncts, in turn, produce their own sources of confusion or misunderstanding. In cases of this second general approach, the "private" is characterized as whatever remains after the disjuncts that one has in mind for "public" and "political" have been sliced out.

One finds in political philosophy, in one of the most extensive and obvious overlaps with public discourse generally, discussions of whether this particular pie is to be sliced at all, and, if so, precisely where. The matter is, probably quite correctly, considered to be of considerable importance to the characters and potentialities of political communities and of the lives led within them. Not only are discussions of the matter carried on in discussions of the economic lives of human beings, their relevance to political community, and the consequences of the latter upon the former, but such discussions are also to be found in connection with scrutinies of the mutual• impacts of political communities and personal moral development (for example, "public virtue" versus "private virtue"), and upon the possibility and possible political regulation of intimate relationships among people (as we shall see).

NTIMACY AND POLITICAL LIFE

On the present account, the machinery characteristic of political life—rules, regulations, orders, commands, and the accompanying principles and standards—make their appearance and find their use when wordless mutual understanding is insufficient to sustain Systematic Mutual Reliance, either because the tasks at hand are too new or too complicated, or the people involved are too unfamiliar with one another, unrelated to one another, or culturally diverse. But we have not yet considered what happens when the characteristic machinery of political life intrudes upon the relationships of people who *are* capable of proceeding rather far into schemes of Systematic Mutual Reliance through wordless mutual understanding alone. And we have not yet considered the likely importance to political life of relationships among people not so goal-oriented as suggested by schemes of SMR. In particular, relationships to which such schemes or the machinery to which they give rise may be quite dissonant with, may involve intimacy. (No more precise term than *dissonant* would give satisfactory and reasonably concise coverage to the allegations that could be made here.)

Aspects of the general topic of intimacy and political life have not been much written on, although at least one article has been written, and the author suggests in his footnotes that some other authors have written relevant remarks.*

Simple friendship, marriage in some cultures, and family life in some cultures are ready examples of the probability of intimacy. Though, curiously, families generally are considered principal examples of social organizations making large contributions to Systematic Mutual Reliance, nevertheless, families in some cultures are found to be major sites of the birth and development of those intimate relations among persons with which political life can be thought to be dissonant. Friendship and marriage in some cultures are major sites also of such relations.

The reactions of political philosophers to these ideas and possibilities could be diverse. Before discussing what these reactions could be, however, we need to consider carefully what intimate relations are supposed to be.

The discussion of *intimacy* and its cognate expressions by political and social philosophers interested in this problem area has made the expression into something of a technical term. In our more general culture, the term *intimacy* and its cognate expressions concern largely though not exclusively the sexual. But discussions by political or social philosophers fail to make that point explicitly. The term may not have been completely desexualized, but no longer refers in such a clear and primary way to various aspects of sexual phenomena. It seems rather to refer primarily to certain aspects of the feelings currently commonly surrounding idealizations of various close relationships among people of which some sexual relations are only one instance. Thus, overtly asexual relationships among friends and among parents to their children are considered representative examples of the way in which people can be intimately related to one another. The treatment, though it elevates to importance aspects of *intimacy* undeniably part of the ordinary understanding of that expression, neglects, though it does not exclude, the sexual aspect of "intimacy" to which prominence is given in wider contexts.

These other aspects of intimacy and intimate relations are partly expectable outgrowths of, and partly constituent of, "close" relations among people. They are expectable outgrowths of such relations when the relations are benign and when *close* is understood geographically. They are constituent of such relations when the relations are benign and "close" is nongeographical, as when people are said to be intimates when, geographically speaking, they are widely distant from one another. A great deal of romanticism and idealization may be found in opinions of what such "close" relations amount to. Some of this can be jettisoned if we reflect briefly upon what is to be expected of people who are said to be intimate business associates. We might expect them, first of all, not to have many business secrets from one another. Accompanying this expectation, we might expect each of them to have rendered

---

*Intimacy, though not expressly (neither the term nor its cognates are mentioned; they are rarely used), and not per se (but in two of its principal settings), may be said to be a topic of Michael Walzer's chapter titled, "Kinship and Love" in his recent book, *Spheres of Justice*. His main interest there, as elsewhere in the book, is in how specific goods and goodies may be justly distributed. As ought to be acknowledged, that is not here among my topics.

himself or herself highly exposed or vulnerable to attack or injury by the other. Psychologically speaking, such exposure and vulnerability may have enormous consequences, especially as they continue without harm to the participants. The feelings and behaviors characteristic of (asexual) intimacy consist very largely of social and psychological aspects of this exposure and reactions to its nonharmful continuance. The nonharmful continuance of such exposure may be fostered by and itself foster attitudes and behaviors of affection, cooperativeness, trust, and, to plug the discussion into a bit of philosophical history, treating people as ends in themselves rather than merely as means.

People who are intimate business associates may be engaged intently in goal-oriented enterprises. Their relationships to one another may contain very little of some of the elements of the earlier characterization of intimacy. That is why contemplation of such relationships in business is useful to combat idealizations of intimacy. When one proceeds to consider relationships in some cultures between spouses or between parents and infants, elements of the characterization that are rare in cases of intimate business associates may be found in greater abundance. So there may be generally some correlation between some of the feelings, attitudes, and behaviors expectably accompanying intimacy and the absence of narrowly focused attention given in the relating activities to goal-directed enterprises.

This begins to raise some of the concerns occupying thinkers who believe or suspect that intimacy is dissonant with many of the normal accompaniments of political life. In particular, if political life is thought of along the lines I have been exploring in this book, and thus is seen as possibly largely "goal-directed" (as growing out of Systematic Mutual Reliance and the requirements thereof in certain circumstances), it may legitimately be thought to be dissonant with intimacy. The question may then be posed whether, when hopes for Systematic Mutual Reliance and the fruits thereof are afoot, intimacy may be endangered even when wordless mutual understanding, and so on, do seem to be feasible. If the accoutrements of political life can coexist happily with intimacy between people either in the same areas of life (such as in the provision of essential services or goods) or in different areas of life (as in friendships unregulated by the state), and we acknowledge that intimate relations constitute an important facet of satisfying and well-developed human life, then there may seem to be no urgency to careful consideration of the way in which political life may by itself fall short of constituting a fully developed and satisfying human life. But if the accoutrements of political life to which we have called attention endanger important elements of intimacy, either through regulation and oversight of relations that might otherwise be richly endowed with elements of intimacy or merely coexist with them, then careful consideration of the limitations of political life would be called for.

This, of course, is not to deny that intimate relations may themselves be fostered and developed in the context of political life. For example, public officials may become intimates. Their intimacy may explain much of what they do even *as* officials. If such associations, perhaps friendships, are possible, then the alleged dissonance between intimacy and political life must be examined closely. What need to be noted are the bases of the intimacy and the extent to which the appurtenances and requirements of political life may impinge upon those bases. For example, the demands made upon people as officials may provide the backbone of their intimacy, as would be the case if the fulfillment of their official obligations brought them constantly into association and gave them reason both to admire and to depend upon one another. On the other hand, fulfillment of the obligations of their offices might sometimes bring their inclinations and interests into conflict, as when faithful fulfillment of one official's obligations leads an individual to do something strongly contrary to the interests of another. (This, of course, could occur respecting conflicting obligations and interests of one official alone.)

The possibility of dissonance between political life and intimacy depends upon the possibility of conflict between the proprieties of political life and the proprieties of intimacy. The behaviors, feelings, and attitudes thought properly expressed in orders, commands, and regulations of political life and properly expressed in responses to those orders, and so on, may conflict with the behaviors, attitudes, and feelings thought appropriate to intimacy. The proprieties in expressions of and responses to the political life of a particular political culture depend upon the culture and may vary with variations in cultures. For example, the dramatic difference in some Western political cultures between public responsibility and private inclination is, as we have seen, not found in every political culture. In fact, even with respect to Western political cultures, the difference was less dramatic in the distant past than it presently is, and less dramatic, according to some commentators, in Mediterranean political cultures of the present and immediate past than in Nordic cultures in the same time frame. In any case, however, the orders, commands, rules, and regulations we have cited as characteristic of political culture per se will be such that proper response to them—that is, obedience and conformity—requires behaviors and fosters attitudes and feelings inhospitable to what are thought to be the proprieties of intimacy. In general, intimacy calls for and promotes behaviors, attitudes, and feelings stemming from and expressive of large areas of unspoken mutual understanding, and more or less spontaneous mutual sympathy and empathy. Indeed, intimacy proceeds largely in terms of such responses, being capable of surviving some but not a great many of those other responses.

Still, the dissonance may depend upon the origins of the regulations in question and upon the ways in which they impinge upon or regulate the intimacy. If regulations, and orders and commands perhaps issued in pursuance of conformity to them, originate from within the circle of intimacy, perhaps by mutual agreement of its members, then they may function to reinforce the intimacy rather than just to be dissonant with it. If, on the other hand, the regulations, orders, and commands have sources quite outside the circle of intimacy, then, unless the intimacy was formed in full consciousness of these phenomena as its background conditions, their effects upon the circle of intimacy will quite probably be regarded as intrusive and disruptive.

Though orders and commands seem hostile to intimacy, inequalities seem no bar per se to intimacy. The inequalities may be inequalities of almost anything. At any rate, one of the commonly cited loci of intimacy—the relationships between parents and their infants—suggests this. These family relationships are cited as test cases of the way in which political regulation of intimate relations—for instance, regulations enforcing minimum standards of care of infants and education of the young—can intrude upon and distort intimate relations. There may be some psychological and even sociological truth to such allegations, but they probably should not be accepted without careful critical scrutiny. A great deal depends, I should think, upon how far behavior meeting the minimum standards is from customary practices in the community, and upon how the standards are enforced when they are enforced. Such variety is possible here that it seems hardly likely that any very specific and unqualified remarks will be generally true.

The exposure and trust characteristic of intimacy are understandable when seen against the background of a presumption of mutual devotion. Even if the intimacy is not goal-directed, it might appear to be insanely reckless, given that it involves more or less approximation to extremes of exposure and trust, if there were no or little reason to believe that mutual devotion were not also present. The psychological and sociological conditions for the growth and development of devotion are themselves perhaps somewhat promoted by experiences, fortunate and without disaster, of at least degrees of mutual exposure and reliance. The dynamics of mutual exposure, trust, and devotion will reveal a great deal about the importance in human life of intimacies such as those found in some marriages, parenting, and friendships. The persistence with which human beings seek and invite such relationships, and may find their lives lacking when such relationships are absent, suggests that if persistent aspects of political life interfere with such formations, then the forms of political life may be not only seriously deficient but also counterproductive in at least some respects. The persistent suspicion that there is as least some truth in such an account may go a long way toward explaining some persistent hostility toward the appurtenances of political life.

Devotion, perhaps, is the element of intimacy most contributive to intimacy's exclusivity. There is something monomaniacal about devotion. Devotion cannot be spread too thin without evisceration, though a person can be devoted to a multiplicity of things, such as family, friends, and work. But, to say that an individual is devoted to such a multiplicity is to say that the individual is concerned with the members of that multiplicity and is not concerned very much with anything outside the circle. A good example of this is Charlotte's speech to Elizabeth in *Pride and Prejudice* upon hearing the news of Charlotte's impending marriage to Mr. Collins.* Charlotte tells Elizabeth that, of course, their intimacy must come to an end. Fidelity to her impending intimacy with Mr. Collins demands an end to her previous intimacy with Elizabeth. Why should this be the case? Her intimacy with Elizabeth includes a sharing of secrets and innermost reactions. Her impending intimacy with Mr. Collins must constitute an area opaque to such sharing with Elizabeth. There must therefore be an area of central importance to Charlotte, in which secrets and innermost reactions are no longer shared. Such sharing would be a betrayal of the intimacy she expects now to share with Mr. Collins.

There are, however, intimate relationships that apparently are founded on

*This and the preceding point in this paragraph were suggested by Susan Feagin.

recognized limitations. For example, intimate business associates need share only their business lives. The presumption is that their business lives will be naturally and more or less clearly compartmentalized from their family lives, and so on. Comparable circumstances of other sorts may also exist. Friendship, however, is more encompassing.

Privacy, autonomy, and responsibility could sometimes be said to characterize the contexts of intimate relationships. Perhaps this attribution could be because the full proprieties of intimate relationships could be thought not capable of operating in contexts without these characteristics. The exposure of normal adults in most cultures to uninvited others (as is widely, though not universally, agreed to be characteristic of governmental observation and investigation) produced by lack of privacy is likely to inhibit full absorption in the relationship;* reduction of autonomy generally and understandably reduces responsibility; reduction of responsibility, in turn, reduces justification for the intense feelings of exposure and trust characteristic of well-functioning intimate relationships. Therefore, political regulation of various aspects of intimate relationships, in reducing their privacy and autonomy, would tend to destroy fundamentally important features of the contexts in which these relationships can be developed.

*Some commentators appear not to agree that government need always be significantly "other."

BIBLIOGRAPHY

General Works in Political Philosophy

ARISTOTLE, *The Politics*, in *The Complete Works of Aristotle*, ed. and trans. Jonathan Barnes. Princeton, NJ: Princeton University Press, 1984.

HOBBES, THOMAS, *The Leviathan*. Michael Oakeshott, ed., Oxford: Basil Blackwell, 1960.

MILL, JOHN STUART, "ON LIBERTY," in *Collected Works of John Stuart Mill*, J. M. Robson, ed., vol. 18. Toronto: University of Toronto Press, 1977.

MILL, JOHN STUART, "UTILITARIANISM," in *Collected Works of John Stuart Mill*, J. M. Robson, ed., vol. 10. Toronto: University of Toronto Press, 1969.

PLATO, *The Republic, The Laws*, and *The Statesman*, in *Plato: The Collected Dialogues*, Edith Hamilton and Huntington Cairns, eds. Princeton, NJ: Princeton University Press, 1961.

Preface

FEINBERG, JOEL, *Social Philosophy*. Englewood Cliffs, NJ: Prentice-Hall, 1973.

MACCALLUM, GERALD C., JR., "NEGATIVE AND POSITIVE FREEDOM," *The Philosophical Review* 76, (1967).

Introduction

COBBAN, ALFRED, *The Nation State and National Self-Determination*, rev. ed. London: Collins, 1969.

OPPENHEIMER, FRANZ, *The State*, trans. John Gutterman. New York: Vanguard Press, 1926.

PENNOCK, J. ROLAND, *Democratic Political Theory*. Princeton, NJ: Princeton University Press, 1979.

PIEPER, JOSEPH, *Leisure, The Basis of Culture*, trans. Alexander Dru. New York: The New American Library, 1963.

VON CLAUSEWICZ, KARL, *On War*, ed. and trans. Michael Howard and Peter Paret. Princeton, NJ: Princeton University Press, 1976.

WALTER, E. V., *Terror and Resistance*. New York: Oxford University Press, 1969.

Chapter One

BEITZ, CHARLES, *Political Theory and International Relations*. Princeton, NJ: Princeton University Press, 1979.

BENTHAM, JEREMY, *Introduction to the Principles of Morals and Legislation*. New York: Hafner Publishing Co., 1948.

HART, H. L. A., *The Concept of Law*. Oxford: Clarendon Press, 1961.

HOCART, ARTHUR MAURICE, *Kings and Councillors*. Chicago: University of Chicago Press, 1970.

SANDEL, MICHAEL J., *Liberalism and the Limits of Justice*. Cambridge: Cambridge University Press, 1982.

Chapter Two

BARRY, BRIAN, *Political Argument*. New York: Humanities Press, 1965.

DEWEY, JOHN, *Human Nature and Conduct*. New York: Henry Holt and Company, 1922, repr. The Modern Library, 1930.

HART, H. L. A., *The Concept of Law*. Oxford: Clarendon Press, 1961.

LUKES, STEVEN, *Individualism*. New York: Harper & Row, 1973.

LYND, ROBERT S., *Knowledge for What?* Princeton, NJ: Princeton University Press, 1939.

Chapter Three

BENDIX, REINHARD, *Kings or People*. Berkeley, CA: University of California Press, 1978.

DIGGS, B. J., ed., *The State, Justice, and the Common Good*. Glenview, IL: Scott, Foresman, 1974.

FAIN, HASKELL, "THE IDEA OF THE STATE," *Nous* 6 (1972).

HEGEL, G. W. F., *Philosophy of Right*, trans. with notes by T. M. Knox. Oxford: Clarendon Press, 1962.

KANT, IMMANUEL, *The Metaphysical Elements of Justice*. Indianapolis, IN: Bobbs-Merrill Library of Liberal Arts, 1965.

SABINE, GEORGE H., "STATE," in *Encyclopedia of the Social Sciences*, Edwin R. A. Seligman, ed., vol XIV. New York: Macmillan, 1934.

WILLOUGHBY, WESTEL, *An Examination of the Nature of the State*. New York: Macmillan, 1896.

Chapter Four

ACTON, JOHN E. E. D. (LORD ACTON), *History of Freedom and Other Essays*. London: Macmillan & Co., 1922.

Beitz, Charles, *Political Theory and International Relations*. Princeton, NJ: Princeton University Press, 1979.

Cobban, Alfred, *The Nation State and National Self-Determination*, rev. ed. London: Collins, 1969.

Fallers, Lloyd A., *The Social Anthropology of the Nation-State*. Chicago: Aldine Publishing Co., 1974.

Fain, Haskell, "The Idea of the State," *Nous* 6 (1972).

The Formation of National States in Western Europe, Charles Tilly, ed. Princeton, NJ: Princeton University Press, 1975.

Gellner, Ernest, *Nations and Nationalism*. Oxford: Blackwell, 1983.

Minogue, K. R., *Nationalism*. Baltimore, MD: Penguin Books, 1970.

Renan, Ernest, *Discours Et Conferences*. Paris: Calman-Levy, 1887.

Sidgwick, Henry, *Methods of Ethics*, 7th ed. London: Macmillan & Co., 1907.

Chapter Five

Davis, Solomon R., *The Federal Principle*. Berkeley: University of California Press, 1978.

Sharkansky, Ira, *Whither the State?* Chatham, NJ: Chatham House Publishers, 1979.

Sidgwick, Henry, *Elements of Politics*, 2nd ed., rev. London: Macmillan and Co., 1897.

Simon, Yves, *The Philosophy of Democratic Government*. Chicago: University of Chicago Press, 1951.

Chapter Six

deGrazia, Sebastian, "What Authority is *Not*," *The American Political Science Review* 53 (1959).

Dworkin, Ronald, "On Not Prosecuting Civil Disobedience," *The New York Review of Books* 10, no. 5 (June 6, 1968).

Hart, H. L. A., *The Concept of Law*. Oxford: Clarendon Press, 1961.

Hohfeld, Wesley N., *Fundamental Legal Conceptions as Applied in Judicial Reasoning*. New Haven, CT: Yale University Press, 1919; repr. Westport, CN: Greenwood Press, 1978.

Lee, Dorothy, *Freedom and Culture*. Englewood Cliffs, NJ: Prentice-Hall, 1963.

MacCallum, Gerald C., Jr., "Competition and Moral Philosophy," unpublished paper.

Pound, Roscoe, *The Spirit of the Common Law*. Boston: Marshall Jones Co., 1921.

Raz, Joseph, *The Authority of Law*. New York: Oxford University Press, 1979.

Simon, Yves, *The Philosophy of Democratic Government*. Berkeley, CA: University of California Press, 1951.

Young, Gary, "On Authority," *Canadian Journal of Philosophy* 3, (1974).

Wasserstrom, Richard, "The Obligation to Obey the Law," *UCLA Law Review* 10 (1963).

WOLFF, ROBERT PAUL, *In Defense of Anarchism.* New York: Harper & Row, 1970.

WILLIAMS, GLANVILLE, "The Concept of Liberty," *Columbia Law Review* 45 (1945).

Chapter Seven

BENDIX, REINHARD, *Kings or People.* Berkeley, CA: University of California Press, 1978.

DEWEY, JOHN, *Human Nature and Conduct.* New York: Henry Holt, 1922, repr. The Modern Library, 1930.

DICEY, ALBERT V., *Introduction to the Study of the Law of the Constitution,* 10th ed. New York: St. Martin's Press, 1961.

FEINBERG, JOEL, *Social Philosophy.* Englewood Cliffs, NJ: Prentice-Hall, 1973.

HART, H. L. A., "Are There Any Natural Rights?" *The Philosophical Review* 64 (1955).

RAPHAEL, D. D., *Political Theory and the Rights of Man.* Bloomington, IN: Indiana University Press, 1967.

SIMMONS, A. JOHN, *Moral Principles and Political Obligations.* Princeton, NJ: Princeton University Press, 1979.

Chapter Eight

DWORKIN, RONALD, "Judicial Discretion," *Journal of Philosophy* 60 (1963).

GOLDING, MARTIN, *Philosophy of Law.* Englewood Cliffs, NJ: Prentice-Hall, 1975.

GREY, THOMAS C., "Constitutionalism: An Analytic Framework," in *Constitutionalism,* J. Roland Pennock and John Chapman, eds. New York: New York University Press, 1979.

KEOHANE, NANNERL O., "Claude de Seyssel and Sixteenth-Century Constitutionalism in France," in *Constitutionalism,* J. Roland Pennock and John Chapman, eds. New York: New York University Press, 1979.

LOCKE, JOHN, *Second Treatise of Government,* in *Two Treatises of Government,* intro. and notes by Peter Laslett, rev. ed., New York: The New American Library, 1960.

MARSHALL, GEOFFREY, *Constitutional Theory.* Oxford: Clarendon Press, 1971.

MEIKLEJOHN, ALEXANDER, *Political Freedom: The Constitutional Powers of the People.* New York: Harper, 1960.

SCHOCHET, GORDON J., "Constitutionalism, Liberalism, and the Study of Politics," in *Constitutionalism,* J. Roland Pennock and John Chapman, eds. New York: New York University Press, 1979.

Chapter Nine

HENSLEY, O. H., *Sovereignty.* New York: Basic Books, 1966.

Chapter Ten

ARROW, KENNETH J., *Social Choice and Individual Values,* 2nd ed. New York: John Wiley & Sons, 1951.

KAMMEN, MICHAEL, *Deputyes & Libertyes*. New York: Alfred A. Knopf, 1969.
PITKIN, HANNAH, *The Concept of Representation*. Berkeley, CA: University of California Press, 1967.
PITKIN, HANNAH, *Representation*. New York: Atherton Press, 1969.
TUSSMAN, JOEL, *Obligation and the Body Politic*. New York: Oxford University Press, 1960.

Chapter Eleven

BENDIX, REINHARD, *Kings or People*. Berkeley, CA: University of California Press, 1978.
KEELY, CHARLES B., *U.S. Immigration: A Policy Analysis*. New York: The Population Council, 1979.
ROYCE, JOSIAH, *The Problem of Christianity*, lectures 9 and 10, vol. ii. New York: Macmillan & Co., 1913; repr. in *The Philosophy of Josiah Royce*, Ohn K. Roth, ed. New York: Thomas Y. Crowell Co., 1971.

Chapter Twelve

AQUINAS, THOMAS, *Summa Theologica*, in *The Basic Writings of St. Thomas Aquinas*. New York: Random House, 1945.
BRYCE, JAMES, "Obedience," in *Studies in History and Jurisprudence*, James Bryce, ed., vol. ii. New York: Oxford University Press, 1901.
DWORKIN, RONALD, *Taking Rights Seriously*. Cambridge, MA: Harvard University Press, 1977.
FRIEDRICH, CARL J., *Tradition and Authority*. New York: Praeger, 1972.
FULLER, LON, *The Morality of Law*, rev. ed. New Haven: Yale University Press, 1977.
LYONS, DAVID, "Moral Aspects of Legal Theory," in *Midwest Studies in Philosophy*, vol. 3: Studies in Ethical Theory, Peter A. French, Theodore E. Uehling, Jr., and Howard Wettstein, eds. Minneapolis: University of Minnesota Press, 1982.
MACCALLUM, GERALD C., JR., "Competition and Moral Philosophy," unpublished paper.
RAWLS, JOHN, *A Theory of Justice*. Cambridge, MA: Harvard University Press, 1971.
SIMMONS, JOHN A., *Moral Principles and Political Obligation*. Princeton, NJ: Princeton University Press, 1979.

Chapter Thirteen

AQUINAS, THOMAS, *Summa Theologica*, part 2, vol. II., in *The Basic Writings of Saint Thomas Aquinas*. New York: Random House, 1945.
DWORKIN, RONALD, "On Not Prosecuting Civil Disobedience," *The New York Review of Books* 10, no. 5 (June 6, 1968).
GANDHI, M. K., *Non-Violent Resistance (Satyagraha)*. New York: Schoken Books, 1951.

Chapter Fourteen

GOLDMAN, EMMA, "Anarchism: What It Really Stands For," in *Anarchism*, Robert Hoffman, ed. New York: Atherton Press, 1970.

VON HUMBOLDT, WILHELM, *The Limits of State Action*, ed., introduction, and notes by J. W. Burrow. Cambridge: Cambridge University Press, 1969.

PACKE, MICHAEL ST. JOHN, *The Life of John Stuart Mill*. New York: Macmillan, 1954.

ROUSSEAU, JEAN-JACQUES, *The Social Contract*, rev. trans., ed. and commentary by Charles M. Sherover. New York: New American Library, 1974.

SCHOEMAN, FERDINAND, "Rights of Children, Rights of Parents, and the Moral Basis of the Family," *Ethics* 91 (1980).

WALZER, MICHAEL, *Spheres of Justice*. New York: Basic Books, 1983.